SERVICE
THE PATH TO JUSTICE

Calvin Redekop
&
Terry Beitzel

Suite 300 - 990 Fort St
Victoria, BC, V8V 3K2
Canada

www.friesenpress.com

Copyright © 2019 by Calvin Redekop and Terry Beitzel
First Edition — 2019

All rights reserved.

No part of this publication may be reproduced in any form, or by any means, electronic or mechanical, including photocopying, recording, or any information browsing, storage, or retrieval system, without permission in writing from FriesenPress.

The photo on the front is the copywrite of Terry and Myra Beitzel.

ISBN
978-1-5255-3584-0 (Hardcover)
978-1-5255-3585-7 (Paperback)
978-1-5255-3586-4 (eBook)

1. RELIGION, CHRISTIAN LIFE, SOCIAL ISSUES

Distributed to the trade by The Ingram Book Company

TABLE OF CONTENTS

v   Dedication

ix   Preface

1   Introduction

Section I. The Concept of Doing Good and Service

7   Chapter 1. The Problem and Promise of Loving Your Neighbor

33   Chapter 2. The Concept of Prosocial Service

51   Chapter 3. Perspectives on Service and Justice

73   Chapter 4. Science and Prosocial Forces

Section II. Radical Reformation Participation in Service

95   Chapter 5. Mennonite World-Wide Service to the Neighbor

113   Chapter 6. Quaker Multi-Faceted Service to the World.

125   Chapter 7. Church of the Brethren Serving Human Need

Section III. The Radical Reformation Ethic of Service

139   Chapter 8. The Ethic of Serving Others

169   Chapter 9. The Radical Reformation Understanding of Serving as the Path to Justice

191   Appendix 1: Reflections on Volunteering in Vietnam, Earl Martin.

195   Appendix 2: A Critique of Effective Voluntary Justice, Urbane Peachey

201   Appendix 3: A Brief Review of Service Organizations in the Twentieth Century.

203   Endnotes

DEDICATION

This book is dedicated to the thousands of young people from all parts of the globe who enthusiastically served in voluntary-service work camps, beginning after World War II in Europe and other parts of the world, as members of a wide variety of religious and secular groups and organizations, including the Quakers (Society of Friends), Church of the Brethren, and the Mennonite Church. These three religious groups are widely and collectively known as the Peace Churches, constituents of the Radical Reformation (earlier and also known as "Anabaptists"). These young people, growing into their teens during World War II (1939-1945), were desperately looking for some way to help assure that the world was not coming to an end, that the diabolical forces of extreme nationalism and genocidal ideologies were not the only option, and that the future was not totally hopeless and meaningless. This depressing condition was especially pertinent to Europe's millions of young people. The lay members of the Peace Churches and especially the youth wanted to actively participate in addressing social problems, especially the destruction of war violence.

It was this voluntary-service movement and experience that helped many find meaning and hope for the future. Many of these volunteers are now in their seventies. No doubt, they would agree that the altruistic, prosocial life stance expressed in their voluntary-service experience has contributed, even if in small ways, to the relative peace now existing in the world. [1]

The voluntary-service phenomenon described in this book is designed to inform those who have never participated in voluntary service, giving them some perspective on pro-social service and the contribution it makes to the human saga. They will probably agree that to participate in any form of voluntary service, whether motivated by Christian beliefs or humanist ethical commitments, provides one of the most accessible and tangible opportunities for loving thy neighbor and thus contributing to a just (and hence peaceful) world.

We would also like to dedicate this book to our parents, children and future generations.

All those who are born of God, who are, according to the Scriptures, called into one body and love in Christ Jesus, are prepared by such love to serve their neighbors, not only with money and goods, but also after the example of their Lord and Head, Jesus Christ, in an evangelical manner, with life and blood. They show mercy and love, as much as they can. No one among them is allowed to beg. They entertain those in distress. They take the stranger into their houses. They comfort the afflicted; assist the needy; clothe the naked; feed the hungry; do not turn their face from the poor. [2]

—Menno Simons

It being our principle to feed the hungry and to give the thirsty drink, we have dedicated ourselves to serve all men in everything that can be helpful to the preservation of men's lives, [but] we find no freedom in giving, or doing or assisting in anything by which men's lives are destroyed or hurt. [3]

—Benjamin Hershey

PREFACE

This book's title, *Service, the Path to Justice*, immediately intrigues and invites contemplation as to what, exactly, it intends to convey. This is because "service" and "justice" each beg for expansion and interpretation.

The word "service" works its way into many conversations. In the public arena, service can unite and occasion bipartisan actions that create agencies to encourage projects that reach into the troubled places of society with a goal toward introducing change. Such change, when initiated for altruistic or other reasons, is sometimes connected to the idea of the common good; that is to say, its benefits are intended to extend to the wider society. Of course, what is considered to be "good" can vary among various individuals and communities.

The idea of service is also re-emerging in faith-oriented institutions. It often appears trendy or even cutting edge as the newest move to reform the gospel. Perhaps the greatest catalyst behind the resurging interest in service is a sense that a commitment to peace and justice demands that we reclaim this focus. Some of the most fervent advocates for reclamation are those who fall into the "Millennial" demographic group. As they try to find their place in the world, perhaps more than others, they sense the inequities and injustices to which many of the rest of us have been anesthetized and which seem to hinder their own efforts to mature and succeed. All too often, established faith communities and orthodox answers fail to address their questions. As they see the world they are inheriting, and work to find meaning within it, many of them turn to service as a way of seeking answers and pursuing their own spiritual inclinations.

In reality, service arising from convictions of faith is hardly a new idea. What is often forgotten is that both "ministry" and "service" are good translations of the Greek word *diakonía*. Churches and seminaries frequently speak of ministry, but perhaps less often of service. If what is recognized, valued, and emphasized as ministry lacks visible connection to service, it may be an indictment of how far removed faith communities have drifted from a credible vision of ministry. We suggest "ministry" and "service" are interchangeable in most contexts.

Service, the Path to Justice recounts the commitment to service that is a strong part of the history, identity, and work of those denominations designated (in this book) as the Peace Churches (among other names). Their motives are rooted in faith commitments rather than in altruism, and service is for the sake of the gospel rather than the common good (though one can hope those are not mutually exclusive). We refer to this as prosocial attitudes and behavior based in the ethical teachings of the Peace Churches.

The articulation of motives for service will not be identical among these groups, but one can expect some points of connection. First, service will be motivated by the image of God that is operative within their tradition. A vision of God that requires an ethic of love can be sufficient to launch the drive to service. Second, threads of the biblical witness that rate servanthood highly contribute to this vision of Christianity as well. For instance, Isaiah describes an image of a servant found faithful through suffering. Jesus' posture as a servant is evident not only in his suffering and sacrifice but also in his choices to show compassion, care for the marginalized, and offer healing. As the path of faithfulness is described for those who would undertake the journey, those who want to be great, to be first, or to enjoy a portion of the spoils are considered "less than" or "last" and should be poured out.

The path to faithfulness provides another way to understand this commitment to service. The language of "calling", by which is meant a sense of summons or a nudge from the divine, is not infrequent as a foundational description of the importance of service. "Discipleship" as an obedient response to the power of God, through Christ in their lives, is another lens through which service may be observed and understood by some in these traditions. "Witness", in the sense that service is a practical, living testimony to faith convictions held by the one offering service, is another good descriptor of the path to faithfulness.

There is at least one other characteristic that unites those who serve, whether or not they are religiously grounded: a hope for change. Service is offered with more than a desire to alleviate present need. It is also embraced because those who serve cling tenaciously to the hope that conditions can change. More than merely feeding the hungry, servants hope that hunger itself will be eradicated. More than merely witnessing the end of violence, servants hope that peace shall prevail.

In this historical moment, the traditional model for "Church" has lost its appeal to many. Its standard of truth goes unacknowledged by a growing portion of the population. A similar statement can be made with regard to many of the values and practices that reinforce the status quo within society in general. The surging interest in service may provide a fresh opportunity for the Church's reengagement with its desired audience, as it reestablishes relevancy and builds bridges into the communities where it is called to minister. Though the motivations for service may differ, because it is a compatible idea for many non-religious groups, service may well provide opportunities for partnerships and extending the credibility of the Church as well. This book makes the case for service as religious practice, as an extension of the gospel, *and* as a commitment to the common good.

Jay Marshall
Dean, Earlham School of Religion
Richmond, IN.

INTRODUCTION

Will humans and human society survive? Will they nurture future generations? How? The following weaves back and forth between two related and complementary theses. One is the service motif and the second is the gap between prosocial and antisocial forces. We suggest that ongoing human existence is a question—a question best addressed by the prosocial act of service, which promotes procedural and distributive justice. Embedded in this argument is the contention that injustice threatens human existence and that serving others is one way of reversing or preventing the harms of injustice and providing necessary procedural and distributive justice modifications.

On April 5, 2009, the *Washington Post* columnist David Broder noted: "When Congress comes back from its two-week recess, members of both parties will be invited to the White House to celebrate what is, in today's context, almost a miracle: the signing of the "Serve America Act." [4] It was the result of a singular bi-partisan force. Congress had "decided to marry the expansion of traditional voluntary, part-time community service, endorsed by generations of Republicans, with increases in government-subsidized full-time service programs devised by Democratic presidents, beginning with the Peace Corps."The symbolism of this act is vast. With the adoption of the idea of "service for the benefit of all", partisan conflict and political ideologies melt away. Who does not want to be credited with promoting the welfare of everyone? And how better to achieve it than through serving in a voluntary and humanitarian way that heals rather than hurts and leaves only winners, and no losers?

Broder continues, "Often, passage of a bill leaves the winning side exhausted and the losers bitter. Working together on this bill [however] left most

Republicans and Democrats feeling good about themselves." When drafting a bill makes the parties involved feel rewarded, it must say something about the bill itself—and it will be best expressed in the actual service, which will be performed as the bill is implemented.

There is hardly a more pertinent way of introducing a tome on "serving your neighbor" than to see its relevance in the immediate situation. If all politics is local, so it is with service. The concept of service is found in all cultures and societies. This volume moves beyond the conventional understanding of service, which though universally used, limits the practical and ethical content of the concept. A more sophisticated understanding of service is central to our analysis. As it will be explained below, the noun "service" is so flexible that it can refer to anything from the work provided by slaves to enacting and celebrating the Eucharist. But it will need to be modified to refer to the many deeper ways of doing good to and for others, interwoven with the concept of service (this is also true of the word "justice").

Human intentions and relationships use the word "service" to span the spectrum from slavery to psychological and sociological manipulation, and even to love that is freely given. These imply an inner dynamic or motive for doing good for others, namely love for the other person, or "charity" as Thomas Aquinas defines it. But there are also the external social/cultural traditions and rules that make the word "service" ambiguous and complex. How is voluntary "service" different from all the other uses of the word? What are the differences between voluntary (humanitarian) and involuntary service, such as induction into the military "service" and the killing that is lauded therein. For example, "He was killed in the service" is usually not representative of service that is completely voluntary nor fully humanitarian in its purposes and outcomes.

This issue is universal and timeless in scope and therefore begs further study. It demands first an understanding of the role of service in human history. This book attempts to make a contribution to this task, from the Radical Reformation understanding of history, arguing that it has universal implications and utility. This frame of reference includes a number of denominations, such as the Church of the Brethren, Society of Friends

(Quakers), Mennonites (Anabaptists), some Baptist groups, and evangelical groups that identify in various degrees with this orientation.[5]

Service, the Path to Justice is interdisciplinary, using theology, ethics, social, and natural sciences to deal with a centrally important factor in human society, namely survival by the promotion of individual and social wellbeing, or said another way, by the promotion of greater justice. We propose that the concept of love and its expression through (voluntary) service provides the crucial requirement to increasing and furthering justice, especially the procedural and distributive forms of justice. We propose that the idea of loving your neighbor through service has been critical in human history because of its intended and unintended consequences. Justice is the only way local and global harmony and peace can ever overcome the deeply and historically engrained institutions of self-interest and corruption. We analyze the data on the emergence of voluntary service in the Radical Reformation, which (along with other religious denominations) are demonstrating a practical means for closing the gap between the hopes and the realities that are plaguing society today. Briefly, service as the path to justice is loving the neighbor by emphasizing service and emphasizing procedural and distributive justice.

Section 1 is divided into four chapters. Chapter 1 surveys the way service has functioned in a larger historical perspective. Its first chapter presents the *dynamics* that cause the gap between loving your neighbor (doing good and pro-social behavior) and its opposite: harming or rejecting your neighbor (anti-social behavior); Chapter 2 describes how this problem has been evolving, especially in the United States and the West. Chapter 3 presents the thesis: Loving your neighbor through voluntary service is the most effective and accessible solution to the problem of antisocial behavior where other methods have failed. Chapter 4 presents some scientific understanding of the ethical duty to love, which we propose is evolving as the solution.

Section 2 presents case studies of the love ethic in the Radical Reformation community. Chapters 5-7 describe briefly the Church of the Brethren, Quakers, and Mennonites "loving their neighbor" based on their vast voluntary service records and accomplishments. This record has been effective and pervasive far beyond the size and resources in promoting the love of neighbor, focused on procedural and distributive justice. We propose this record has been gaining increasing credibility on the global scene.

Section 3, including chapters 8-9, analyses how loving your neighbor, expressed by service, is forcing the Radical Reformation/Anabaptists to forsake dualistic two-worldly kingdom theology and to accepting involvement in and responsibility for the world, *without losing its servant stance* (i.e. voluntary service is the only way to break the cycle of violence, which is needed to achieve justice). This process is placing strains on the cohesion of the Radical Reformation/Anabaptist membership, but the direction of the evolution is clear and urgent.

We propose that loving your neighbor through service is the simplest procedure to achieve justice in both specific situations and generally. We hope to convince the reader that this is the way to accelerate the (generally assumed) evolving tendency toward the love ethic. We conclude by recognizing that there is no ready answer to the prosocial and antisocial gap in human history but propose that the paradigm discussed in this book seems to be gaining power and we invite the reader to continue the quest.

SECTION I.
The Concept of Doing Good and Service

CHAPTER 1.
The Problem and Promise of Loving Your Neighbor

> *Wonder at perplexity provokes thought, for 'all human beings by nature desire understanding.' Philosophy, born of wonder, seeks ultimately to know the nature and being of things, as well as the reasons for causes why things are the way they are."*
>
> —*Leon R Kass* [6]

At the core of the human story is the paradoxical relationship between empathy and entropy, which Jeremy Rifkin recently described as the "unfolding of the great drama that is at the center of the human journey—the evolution of empathic expression and the dark shadow of entropic debt that is its nemesis."[7] This concern has been echoed by many scholars who wonder about the growing crisis between civility and incivility,[8] altruistic and selfish behaviors,[9] and cooperation and noncooperation[10] that may threaten future human civilization. Will humans and human society survive? Will they nurture future generations? How?

Most social philosophers and ethicists accept the conclusion that human survival hangs on a slender thread, because the tendencies for the good are *almost* overwhelmed by the tendencies for dissolution.[11] We have the means to destroy ourselves, several times over, and make Earth uninhabitable for humans; we also have the means to promote justice and wellbeing.

Humans and human societies can survive and can nurture future generations, but it is not inevitable that they will. The terms we have chosen to juxtapose are prosocial (helping others and doing good) and antisocial behaviors and attitudes. What does it mean to do good to others? The following chapters of *Service, the Path to Justice* explores this mystery in greater detail, especially by following the story of how active, nonviolent members of the Radical Reformation, or what others call Anabaptism,[12] developed voluntary service as an alternative set of questions, praxis, and institutions with an emphasis on procedural and distributive justice. To our understanding of service, we should add the notion of voluntary service and develop what we mean by "voluntary" as we proceed.

Does "service" answer a specific set of questions or propose a solution to forces that threaten civilization? We suggest that it does both. We do not claim to provide the final solution but hope to suggest an area for others to explore further, both in the reality of daily life and in the search of truth. For example, M. K. Gandhi's grand "experiment with truth" and nonviolence was first informed by service to others, because "God could be realized only through service" for others. Gandhi continued: "All other pleasures and possessions pale into nothingness before service which is rendered in a spirit of joy."[13] Here, we will begin to explain service as the path to justice by focusing on the love of your neighbor. We also employ the term path to underscore that justice is a journey and often times we need to reevaluate and reconstruct by what we actually mean by justice.

The Talmud includes the story of a nonbeliever who told a Hebrew scholar that he would become a Jew if the rabbi could teach him the whole Torah while he balanced on one leg. Hillel's response: "What is hateful to yourself, do not to your fellow man. This is the whole of the Torah and the remainder is but commentary. Go. Learn it."[14] This volume examines one way in which religion can encourage doing good (service), although we are not explicitly apologists for religion and recognize that this form of serving justice can exist in many secular, institutional, and personal forms. Chapters five through seven provide descriptive case studies of the Radical Reformation organizations and the response of the members of the organizations in rejecting violence, and through service and possible risk to themselves, promoting the cause of peace and justice. The beginning and remaining chapters locate this story in more conceptual language and scholarship. Your *neighbor* is both problem and promise in serving as the path to justice and therein promoting human wellbeing.

"Prosocial behavior" (or voluntary behavior intended to serve and benefit another) is social action for the good of other people. [15] Doing good for one another is one of the foundation principles of social relations. It invites reciprocity. As many social theorists have taught us, society is built to a large extent on the reciprocity norm: I do something for you and you do something for me. For many, this expectation may be the most important reason to develop and maintain long-term social relationships. We know this social principle is important; when someone does something for us, we feel gratitude, which is both pleasurable and involves a sense of obligation to return the favor. In much the same way, we can have pleasure from doing something good for others.

The following illuminates this point: John was committed to a mental institution at the age of 19.[16] After a long period, involving John taking responsibility for his part in managing his own mental health, John is now one of the leaders in the peer-support movement in the United States. John once commented that, when he feels like he cannot manage his own mental-health issues, his first task is to find someone else to help! Voluntary service for the good of another has the reciprocal effect of helping John. [17] The irony is that, when John is most vulnerable and in need, his solution is to find someone else to help! Another point John often makes is that justice is not something we are automatically given but rather something that we must create in our prosocial interactions with other people—thus, service as the path to justice.

As the story above illustrates, however, not all prosocial behavior is predicated explicitly upon reciprocity calculus. [18] In fact, many traditions (especially religious traditions) accept the economics of reciprocity only as a *minimum* in human affairs. [19] For example, the positive interpretation of the *Golden Rule* to "do unto others" is an injunction to go beyond the reciprocity norm. [20] The strength of the reciprocity norm is that it brings attention to the idea of "neighbor".

Every society has the orphan, the poor, the homeless, the economically or emotionally or mentally disabled, and disenfranchised families and groups. What should be done? These injuries, throughout history, result from random negligence, the exploitation and degradation of persons and people through indirect or direct violence, and from antisocial practices that have become institutionalized within human social structures. *Direct violence* includes the obvious institutions of slavery and war. The documentation of this reality is as near as the morning newspaper.[21] *Indirect violence*, on the other hand, exists as racist and discrimination policies, gender inequalities in employment and wages, and environmental degradation caused by industrial pollutants, etc. Will the free market, other economic or political ideology, science and technology, the United Nations, or even the integration of global religions [22] ultimately bring wellbeing to humanity and the earth? Do we need more resources allocated for military and security expenditures?[23] What is to be done?

Who is responsible to what for whom? The phrase "justice is served" typically refers to the quantity and quality of punishment being delivered to someone who committed an infraction or has created an injustice, which is the retributive or corrective model of justice. However, as will become evident, serving your neighbor does not imply this same understanding of what is meant or involved in actions that promote more justice. We argue below that the full meaning of justice is not captured by the punitive, corrective, and *retributive* justice model stated above, and that service is an integral principle for promoting justice, provides a useful guide for reflection, and is a guide for action. Serving as the path to justice is about doing good for others. Therefore, service is much more closely aligned to distributive and procedural forms of justice. Briefly, *distributive* justice focuses on allocation of the costs and benefits of living in social groups and *procedural* justice concerns who is making decisions and how decisions are made. Serving, as the path to justice, is to focus on distributive and procedural justice.

One example of serving as the path to justice comes from a true story about a nineteenth-century Amish-Mennonite farmer living with his family in Western Maryland. Benedict Miller understood service as the path to justice. Some of his methods for doing this were creative. The story of Benedict

SECTION I. THE CONCEPT OF DOING GOOD AND SERVICE

and the corn thief has been handed down through seven generations of the Miller family:

> Benedict had a corn crib in his spring house loft with a ladder stairway leading to it. One day he began to notice that corn was missing. Day after day, things grew worse, and finally Benedict decided to set a trap for the thief. One morning while the Miller family was eating breakfast, they heard a shout from the direction of the corn crib. Hurrying to investigate, Benedict saw a man at the entrance to the crib. "Good morning," called Benedict, "do you need help?" "Yes," replied the man, "could you loose me from this trap?" "Oh, are you trapped?" asked Benedict innocently. Benedict informed the trespasser that he would let him go on one condition, that the man would share breakfast with Benedict's family.

At the breakfast table, the family talked about all kinds of things, all things that is, except, the missing corn. When the guest finally left, after a hearty breakfast, he and Benedict were friends. No corn went missing after that time. The Ohio version of this story, stemming from Benedict's son, adds that Benedict gave the man a bag of corn when he left. [24]

This story focuses not on the specific infraction or the offence (retributive justice) but on the needs and dignity of individuals (distributive and procedural justice). Serving as the path to justice is an active concern for the wellbeing of your neighbor.

Of course, theft and burglary are generally considered to be morally wrong. However, the ambiguity inherent in parables and stories, such as the one above, while escaping formalized creeds, allows for insight into service as the path to justice because they are examples of problem-solving that harms neither the transgressor nor the transgressed and construct desired virtues in the process of dealing with an imperfect social world. [25] Another way of saying this is that doing good by serving others is not simply abstract and systematic logic, it means engaging in fundamentally constructive dialogical interactions within a concrete social context. Serving others through such activities as voluntary service exists in particular historic circumstances to and with specific people.

Several millennia ago, Aristotle stated that doing good to another person is the inherent definition of friendship and is a central contribution to human happiness. For Aristotle, "We define a friend as one who wishes and does what is good, or seems to, for the sake of his friend, or as one who wishes his friend to exist and live, for his (own) sake." [26] However, this is far from universally applied in every situation, and too often we do not wish the good for others. More broadly, and in relation to justice, Aristotle believes that justice is prosocial, consisting of giving people what they deserve, and that a just society is one that enables human beings to realize their highest nature and to live the good life. For Aristotle, justice is a matter of rewarding and promoting virtue, and the ultimate measure of society is whether it produces virtuous citizens:

> "We see that all men mean by justice that kind of state of character which makes people disposed to do what is just and makes them act justly and wish for what is just; and similarly, by injustice that state which makes them act unjustly and wish for what is unjust." [27]

However, many respected contemporary social and political philosophers, such as John Rawls, expand Aristotle's position and evaluate society on the basis of whether or not social structures provide a fair framework within which individuals can pursue their own freely-chosen values. [28] These contemporary thinkers have languished over the procedural problem of what constitutes the good life (how is it defined and who gets to define it?) and are adamant that the *freedom or right to choose the good life for oneself* is generally of paramount importance over the good life. In contrast to Rawls and rights-based notions of social order, so-called communitarians, such as Amitai Etzioni, contend that this notion ignores a major sociological observation:

> "Movement from a high level of social restriction to a greater measure of choice, and hence enhancement of

SECTION I. THE CONCEPT OF DOING GOOD AND SERVICE

individual liberties, at some point becomes onerous for the actors involved and undermines the social order upon which liberties are ultimately based."[29]

Philosophers Michael Sandel and Charles Taylor have offered variations, but the essential core of this argument is that human individuality is itself a social construct, and therefore sustaining liberty requires social commitment and justice. Said another way, we believe that humans are deeply social beings and cannot be discussed without a sociology.[30]

Expanding upon Aristotle, the following will assert that doing good for others is necessary for individual and societal wellbeing. If justice, as Plato said, is giving a person her due, how do we understand and apply this ambiguous statement? Who is responsible to do what for whom? And how can we ensure that we do no harm in the process? Service as the path to justice acknowledges the strengths and insights of the contemporary rights-based discourse and the inherent problems in deciding what is the good life. Rather than continue confined within this "rights versus the good"[31] debate, the following emphasizes the prosocial activity of doing good for others as a necessary contribution to societal wellbeing. Here, service to others is defined as an essential component of doing good. The prosocial act of voluntary service has made valuable contributions to societal wellbeing and is uniquely qualified to bridge the debate between rights and the good.

The following will explore the history, practice, application, and promise of the prosocial act of voluntarily service as the path to justice in the promotion of the good life. An ultimate question, and one we can only approach but may not answer here, has dogged humanity throughout history: *Why should a person or group feel sympathy and compassion for others, or rather, why should a person or group not live basically for the welfare of the self or the group?* We are all too willing to pursue our selfish interests and antisocial values and actions. If we do so in this post-industrial age, we collectively (or even a few of us) may destroy humankind and the planet. We suggest that every person can and should engage in prosocial behavior. At this point, rather than jump straight into the further meaning of service and justice, we will steadily move from ambiguity to clarity, along the way incorporating and clarifying other ambiguous terms, such as love and responsibility. One way to tell this story of hope is by giving the unique account of the development of voluntary service and prosocial behavior directed at the "neighbor" by Anabaptists in the twentieth century.

A) The Thesis: The Duty of Love as Service and the Wellbeing of Society

The challenge of understanding the nature of our duty to *do good to our neighbors* has confronted humanity from earliest recorded history and provides the point of departure for our discussion. The ideals and values of individuals, families, communities, societies, and nations struggling toward the achievement of societal wellbeing are constantly undercut by natural forces, such as floods, earthquakes, and droughts, but most tragically by human self-aggrandizement and the misuse or abuse of others, social dysfunctions (intended and unintended consequences of societal institutions), and by accentuating self-interests or lack of concern of the common good. The central thesis is that service as the path to justice provides a guide for reflection and for prosocial action as a corrective for the harm of antisocial behavior.

Recent anthropological evidence demonstrates that antisocial behavior, violence, and war are not necessarily innate features of humanity and human social relations.[32] In fact, war and violence are socially constructed (just as service and justice). Aggression itself (despite the assumptions of many in the West) is not universal, and war itself is a relatively recent phenomena, closely connected to large-scale social organization. Anthropologist Douglas Fry, in a comprehensive comparative study of the potential for peace and prosocial behavior, states that a thorough reconsideration of the anthropological data suggests that this view of humanity as essentially violent and warmongering is simply wrong: "Warfare is no more natural than, say, slavery."[33]

There is thus an existential and ontological necessity for the interjection of service to others at an interpersonal and organizational level, which clans, tribes, and advanced, institutionalized social and political structures apparently can never fully achieve. In helping to meet the needs of others on an existential basis (such as the good Samaritan), that act is "salvific", or better understood as the healing, reconciling, and preserving forces in society. We propose that only these prosocial actions will keep human society from deteriorating. [34] This gap between the ideal of prosocial behavior and attitudes and the reality of existing antisocial attitudes and behaviors can only be narrowed by voluntary sharing and service (by individuals and organizations) to others, regardless of the cultural and sociological nature of any group or society.

The prosocial forces that have helped human civilization to survive, and that contribute to wellbeing, have been variously referred to as altruism, nonviolence, charity, compassion, cooperation, empathy, humanitarianism, helping, giving, mutual aid, sharing, social welfare, sympathy, and volunteering. We propose that though there are many other ways of defining and evaluating how and why the forces of service for justice have been able to stem the tide of the antisocial destructive forces, the phenomenon of doing good to our neighbor (the act of loving our neighbor as ourselves) is and has been a positive, prosocial, sociological phenomenon that contributes to individual and societal wellbeing. [35]

Service as the path to justice is also understood as *loving one's neighbor as oneself* by the attitude of acceptance of (and identification with) the other as being equal and worthy in God's sight, and is expressed in tangible ways such as sharing material, emotional and spiritual goods and gifts, and assisting by doing for the other what she cannot do.[36] This can be understood both in mundane and sacred ways.

The most common term for this omnibus concept has been "voluntary service". In the context of mass media, including cinema, drama, and literature, it implies that kindness, compassion and generosity, love, and "going the second mile" are considered uninteresting, naïve, primitive, or even weak themes. The romantic, naïve or bland fairy-tale type novel with a happy ending is considered banal. Fiction emphasizing love, compassion, harmony, and peace has not captured the imagination nearly as much as the focus on intrigue, deception, domination, violence, greed, exploitation, robbery, revenge, murder, revolution, war, political duplicity, and just plain nasty behavior.[37] A psychoanalyst in the same vein suggests that sanity "is something we can't get excited about... It is dull, uninspiring."[38] And it is precisely the sensational aspects of domination, struggle, conflict, murder, and especially war that have fed into the lack of interest in the significance of prosocial behavior: It is dull.[39] Dan Brown, author of the bestseller, *The Da Vinci Code*, admits that "Reason seldom worked [in discussing the achievement of the good], so the media always gravitated toward scandal."[40]

Prosocial actions, though they may seem mundane and even bland, help to stem the negative dimensions of the forces of tension and conflict and all social action. What could be a stronger plot? The remainder of this book describes the nature of service as the path to justice and how it contributes to the survival of the human species. Every human being has experienced acts of kindness, assistance, or help from a parent, a family member, a friend, or a neighbor (sadly there have been children who have been rejected by their parents, but this simply reinforces the universal reality of kindness in the "normal" human experience). This fact is further illustrated by the enduring idealization of heroic acts that exist in poetry and literature, which feature the devotion of caring for others, and risking or even giving one's life for another, but the context is often embedded in a larger story of antisocial behavior.[41]

B) The Duty of Loving Our Neighbor as Ourselves

The duty to love our neighbors as ourselves is perennial, not only in Christianity but in most religions and cultures.[42] In fact, Albrecht Dihle argues convincingly that the Jewish and Christian uses of the Golden Rule were actually derived from Greek popular culture.[43] Love is commanded, so love as a duty must be something other or deeper than an emotion or sentiment. This duty presents a social ethic and guide as a way of dealing with others. Of course, our interactions with others are not universally harmonious, and frequently contain elements of conflict. Our thesis is not that all conflict must be eliminated, but rather, as will become clear, that we can deal with others in such ways as not to engage in and promote unnecessarily destructive aspects of conflict and social interaction. All social conflict begins with one party wanting something that another party resists doing or giving.[44] We suggest revisiting the Golden Rule, with the prosocial action of service, as one way to curtail the destructive elements of social conflict. What does it mean to love our neighbors (and enemies!) as ourselves, and exactly what might this look like?

The Golden Rule and the duty to love one's enemies have both been the object of ridicule and praise, and also have "too often been accepted or rejected without much reflection about what it really means."[45] Keith Stanglin insists that they are complementary and require each to be properly understood, because these prosocial commands are the basic principles of the Hebrew and Christian Scriptures.[46] However, the Golden Rule does not supply complete concrete guidance for actions.[47] With this in mind, one conceptual framework is to fashion them in terms of ascending principles, from pleasure, sympathy, and reason to brotherly love, moral insight, and "God-consciousness."[48] Even Immanuel Kant concluded that the Golden Rule is "therefore…only indeterminate; it has a certain latitude within which one may be able to do more or less without our being able to assign its limits definitely."[49] While perplexing, this is not surprising.

Philosopher Peter Searles claims that rules cannot and do not specify exactly what is to be done in particular situations; rules always require interpretation. By what calculation, standard, or authority do we understand what is the right thing to do? Philosopher Marcus Singer proposes that we follow "good reason" to deduce "relevant" and "similar" categories for what we regard as "fair, right, [and] just" according to how we might treat the other person. In the end of his lengthy discussion of the contours of discourses and debates of the Golden Rule, Singer ultimately admits that "it would not at once tell everybody just what do in all the complexities of his relations with others…it requires interpretation and is consequently no substitute for an ethical theory."[50]

Philosopher Paul Ricoeur suggests that, with the Golden Rule, both the neighbor and "the enemy become the touchstone of the new ethics"[51] and this involves the substitution of generosity over self-interest and the substitution of the gift over reciprocity and obligation. In this helpful perspective, we might better say that the Golden Rule opens justice as anticipatory of the future, and therefore exceeds the confines of the reactive, historical, and proportioned *retributive* justice of *lex talionis* (eye for an eye). Said another way, this turns the focus from retributive justice to *procedural* and *distributive* justice. For Ricoeur, this new understanding of justice is an "irruption" of the "economy of exchange" and the "logic of equivalence" and therefore it is a valid moral principle for Christian and non-Christian alike.[52] Within this context, it is in the positive injunction to commit prosocial action (not simply the negative injunction to refrain from certain harmful actions) that the disorienting project of "loving the enemy" reorients ethical action to actions that are truly creative, and not solely based in the calculations of reciprocity and retaliations for past actions. This will be further developed, but for now, suffice it to say that it is doing unto others by anticipating what we would have them do unto us, and that this moves us from the spiral of retaliation to the prosocial reorientation of loving our neighbors and our enemies,

A note of caution and clarification is in order: Social and political theory commonly operates by constructed types and dichotomies. In social theory, the polarity is often between individual agency and freedom on one side and determining social structure on the other. In political theory, the polarity is between the individual and the collective. However, the Golden Rule complicates or challenges the emphasis on either the individual or the collective. First, we are not called to love ourselves less than our neighbors, which is fairly straightforward to comprehend. However, we are not called to love our neighbor more than ourselves either. We are to treat the other in the same way that we would like to be treated. In addition, we are not called to place higher value on the individual than the collective, or vice versa. So, if we perceive a conflict between ourselves and another, or between ourselves and a collective, what are we to do?

Since World War II, when examining conflict, psychologists have routinely emphasized the cognitive dimensions of human involvement in social situations, primarily focusing on the ways that human beings are motivated in conflict situations and ways in which they interpret conflict situations.[53] This research culminated in the classification of four strategies that individuals may employ when involved in social conflict. The first is *contending*: attempting to impose one's preferred outcome on the other party. The second is *yielding*: lowering one's own aspirations and settling for less than one had desired. The third is *avoiding*: not engaging in the conflict, through either inaction or withdrawal. The fourth is *problem-solving*: pursuing an alternative that clarifies and satisfies the aspirations of both parties.

To diagram these differences, social psychologist and conflict specialist Dean Pruitt uses the Dual-Concern Model [54] with a vertical axis of "other-concern" and a horizontal axis of "self-concern." When self-concern is high and other-concern is low, this leads to strategies of contending. When other-concern is high and self-concern is low, this leads to yielding. The dual concern model predicts that problem-solving is encouraged when parties have both a high concern for themselves and a high concern for others. Problem-solving involves careful integration of the self's concerns with the other's concerns, commonly creating a novel solution that was not foreseen at the onset of conflict. Problem-solving provides the most socially stable outcomes and brings the highest satisfaction for both parties.

In terms of loving our neighbors as ourselves, the Dual Concern Model suggests that to achieve stable and satisfactory outcomes, we should love ourselves and our neighbors equally. This adds complexity to the idea of service as the path to justice, since service is generally understood as action that promotes the needs of the other (altruism).

When we are serving justice, we must include ourselves in the calculus. This can be understood in terms of the Golden Rule. Paul Ricoeur (mentioned above) explains that the same rules and boundaries that can be applied to self-interest are also applied to self-sacrifice! [55] This insight remains underdeveloped in the literature on voluntary service. For our present purposes, it is sufficient to say that service is not simply perennial yielding, even though yielding to the other (if for no other reason than to hear the other's position) is the crucial first step. Pruitt and Kim suggest that the above strategies for dealing with conflict commonly call forth a combination and sequencing of these strategies. [56] The first and primary concern in this sequence is to limit one's own desires and address the needs of others. At the very least, we must be able to comprehend other-concerns. Conflict Transformation scholar-practitioner John Paul Lederach reiterates this point further in a number of his works.[57] Voluntary service promotes other-concern by taking the needs of the other seriously.

Another way of expressing this is to stress that voluntary service is less interested in status distinction and fulfilling our own desires and rather seeks to "bear one another's burdens" (Galatians 6: 2). Though this may not be the explicit purpose of voluntary service, psychologist Carl Rogers emphasizes the importance of empathy for relieving suffering, because it dissolves alienation.[58] For Rogers, empathy is not simply a condition of healing; it is the healing agent itself: "This in-tune-ness is in itself healing, growth-promoting."[59] In this process, empathy is both the means used to relieve suffering and the actual healing agent itself.[60] This empathic response is located in the creation of new values that follow in the wake of empathy. This interpersonal ethic holds equally for the friend and the most hated enemy and to the lowest social status. This radical idea, according to psychologist Erik Erickson, occurs in "the elemental sayings [of Jesus] … is the universal We."[61] While voluntary service is not necessarily designed with such therapeutic ends in mind, the effect can be positive since (as Heinz Kohut acknowledges) the mere presence of empathy has a curative, therapeutic effect.[62]

Though not always explicit, implicit in the conflict-resolution literature is that the means and ends of conflict resolution is to move from violence to politics, or from physical force and threats to mutual understanding, respect, and dialogue. Other religious traditions also promote variations on the theme of love and doing good to others. Buddha charged his disciples to "love all mankind with a mother's love."[63] "Let him cultivate love without measure toward all beings. Let him cultivate towards the whole world-above, below, around a heart of love unstinted, unmixed with the sense of differing or opposing interests."[64]

Kristen Goss agrees, stating, "Buddhism teaches that compassion helps one to achieve inner peace," and continues: "In Islam almsgiving to aid the poor is one of the five pillars of the faith."[65] Another version was expressed by Confucius' "negative golden rule" many centuries ago: "What you do not want done to yourself, do not do to others." He explained what he meant by saying, "To serve my father as I would expect my son to serve me. To serve my sovereign as I would expect a minister under me to serve me; to act towards my elder brother as I would expect my younger brother to act towards me. To be the first to behave towards friends as I would expect them to behave towards me."[66]

This philosophical tradition, which will be expanded upon later, defines the concept of "doing good" in varied ways, such as duty, justice, and obligation. Socrates understood that the "'just man' does what he ought to do because it is just, and because justice is essential to the very life and health of the soul."[67] Aristotle believed "it is justice alone, not virtue in general or any other particular virtue, which gives rise to duty or obligation ... It alone of the virtues is thought to consider 'another's good' because it concerns the relation of a man to his neighbor."[68] For Aristotle, "Justice always refers to the good of another, or to the common good of all."[69]

Briefly, the theme of empathy and respect for the neighbor, and considering the needs of others, is the theme of service as the path to justice. Service is not the loss of self but rather respecting the other as much as one respects oneself, de-emphasizing retributive justice, and emphasizing procedural and retributive justice. Understanding service as a path to justice involves exploring and unpacking different conceptions of what is understood as justice, and as already pointed out, further exploring different forms of service.

C) Prosocial Service and Justice in the Judeo-Christian Tradition

We now turn more specifically to *doing good to our neighbor* as a central tenant in Judaism and Christianity and reiterate and further explore the themes above. In Judaism "performing good deeds and acts of charity (*tzdakah*) is one of three core obligations of the faith and caring for parents is likewise obligatory."[70] As indicated above, according to Leon Kass, the most important events in the emergence of the Jewish people is God's giving of the Law. The first commandment demanding a human response is "Thou Shalt not Kill." Kass maintains that this sets the "negative" restriction on the implied positive relationship of "doing unto others" between human beings." [71] The positive implication is respect for the dignity of "the other" and above all, expressing and sharing love, which makes society possible. Kass admits that love expressed in these early forms was not yet a full expression.[72] "To be sure the problem of brothers will long be with us," by which Kass implies that genuine love of neighbor and the other is a goal to continually pursue but one that is never fully achieved.

The New Testament features Christ's central maxim: "Love thy neighbor as thyself." Jesus consistently taught service as the path to justice through parables such as the Good Samaritan. Jesus' ministry focused largely on tending to the sick, the weak, and downtrodden. This principle of service guided by love is clearly defined when Jesus was asked, "Which is the greatest Commandment in the Law?" He replied, "You shall love the Lord your God with all your heart, and with all your soul, with all your mind. That is the greatest and first Commandment. And a second is like it: 'Love your neighbor as yourself.' On these two commandments depend all the law and the prophets" (Matthew 22:36-37, RSV).

Jesus however expanded the definition of neighbor to the absolute limit by stating "You have heard that it was said, 'Love shall your neighbor, hate your enemy.' But I say to you 'Love your enemies and pray for those who persecute you, so be the sons of your Father which is in heaven." (Matt. 5:43-48, RSV) This is close to defining agape love—self-sacrificing love, as a parent has toward the child.[73] Parenthetically, many Christians throughout history have found it hard to believe Jesus was serious or believe that it cannot possibly apply in certain contemporary examples and have rejected it by way of a multitude of rationalizations. But this all-encompassing concept of love, service, and justice, even for the enemy, provides the foundation for the argument of this book. It is both a philosophical and theological axiom existent not only in the West but universally.[74]

SECTION I. THE CONCEPT OF DOING GOOD AND SERVICE

There are many representative illustrations of these convictions that find their ultimate sources and representations in the life and teachings of Jesus, but it seems the most succinct essentials of his teachings focus on the treatment of the neighbor. The following is representative:

> "You know that the rulers of the Gentiles lord it over them, and their great men make exercise authority over them. It shall not be so among you; but whoever would be great among you must be your servant, and whoever would be first among you must be your slave, even as the Son of Man came not to be served but to serve, and to give his life as a ransom for many" (Matthew 20:25 RSV) [75]

The implications of this axiom for family, economic, social, and political institutions are broad, profound, and pertinent to all human history. The early Christian Church expressed this orientation of love and compassion in the form of rejecting warfare and substituting it with service to the needy and generally doing good to others. Rather than submit to military service, Origen (circa 230) stated:

> "Christians do really co-operate in the business of the commonwealth, but as Christians, their manner of service is special. They avoid office, not in order to escape the burdens of public service, but because in the Church they are already committed to a better and more effective service of society and its rulers than that which either the soldier or the magistrate can render. This 'Divine and more needful service' consists in personal morality, intercessory prayer, in the task of education and influencing others for good, and in conquering the demons, who are at the bottom over breach of peace." [76]

A leading early-church historian suggests that Jesus laid down several important ethical principles, namely: love, truthfulness, prudence (to distinguish hypocrisy), right treatment of enemies, and humble service. [77] The early

Christian Church closely followed the basics of Jesus' teachings. In fact, one of the major sources of conflict between the young church and the state was over the refusal of the Christian church to "serve" in the military forces and engage in killing for the state. This issue reflects that the original interpretation of the concept of service is derived from military sources but that this understanding of service was being modified by the early church. As Cadoux suggests, the major emphasis and teaching of Jesus was love of the neighbor. [78] He states:

> "The fact that very many public offices involved the holders in participation in acts of judicial violence, such as imprisonment, torture, death-sentences, and executions, at once brought the service of the State into conflict with the Christian law of love, and not unnaturally caused the most thoughtful Christians to regard the former [serving in the State] as closed to them." [79]

This principle expressed itself most explicitly in the arena of military service. Although there was not universal acceptance of refusal to serve in the military, there were strong teachings against it by many early Church leaders. Thus Clement (150-220 CE) states: "We are being educated, not in war, but in peace. We, the peaceful race, are more temperate than the war-like races. We have made use of one instrument, the peaceful word, wherewith we honor God." [80]

D) Christian Responses.

Loving thy neighbor and the Golden Rule (service as the path to justice by doing good), as proposed by the early Christian Church leaders, seemed equally appropriate in later times. To the accusation of being parasites rather than serving the state, Minicius Feliz stated: "Even though we refuse your official honors and purple, yet we do not consist of the lowest dregs of the populations." Early Church father Origen argues the Christian accusation of being parasites in this way: "The Christians as such are already preoccupied with a higher and better service"—an alternative service. Tertullian, referring to the ancient Jews, maintained that "had they embraced the Gospel, they could neither have slain their enemies, nor sentenced criminals to death." Stating the essentials of the alternative service, Tertullian explains, "Yet to me also it will be to some extent allowed that I am an advantage to the public. I am wont, from every boundary-stone or altar, to prescribe for morals medicines that will confer good health more happily on public affairs, states and empires, then your works will."[81] And Origin summarized: "Christians do really cooperate in the business of the commonwealth but as Christians their manner of service is special."[82]

Much of the history of the Christian Church in the following centuries relinquished this strong "higher service" to the prerogative of the state and society, thus becoming part of the Constantinian alliance of the state and the Christian church. In fact, after Constantine, one had to be a Christian to serve in the military! The alliance of the Roman Catholic Church with ruling kings and princes, resulting in territorial or national churches, is well known. The classic account of this major historical catastrophe is G.J. Heering's *The Fall of Christianity*.[83]

In some cases, the alliances were so close that bishops also served as kings and princes. On the other hand, the papacy challenged the authority of the secular rulers over the Church, and the concept of heresy was used as tool of control from both sides. The decline of the Christian Church was palpable.[84] Heering is very pessimistic about the Church's alliance with power, but he concludes:

> "Perhaps there is still escape. God is at work today. He is active to restore Christianity from its fall, to restore to Christianity something of its original spirit, its moral abhorrence of war and bloodshed, its passive resistance, or better put, its spiritual readiness (Eph. 6:10-17) to withstand the pagan brute activities of this world, the 'camp of darkness.'"[85]

Latourette agrees:

> "Here and there in the darkness were gleams of light, which as the event proved, were the harbingers of a better way. As we are to see again and again, often in what have appeared to be the darkest hours for the Christian faith, movements have begun which, at the time affecting only small minorities, have later assumed major proportions and have brought revival and advance." [86]

The social and economic status of individuals and communities, from the beginning of the Constantine rule until the Reformation era, was generally understood as functioning within the state and church conjoint auspices. The Middle Ages were highly stratified and authoritarian, with little freedom for individual expression or social and economic life on the part of individuals in the general population. Though this period has often been romanticized, the life of most people was lived in a hierarchical feudal society, often very regimented and oppressive, even in religious matters, and provided services for the ruling political and religious leadership. It is no mere coincidence that the Constantine legacy contributed to the Crusades, the wars of the Reformation, and the violence of the Inquisition.

One of the best indicators of these conditions is the number and variety of counter traditions that emerged during this period. Protests, heresies, and reform movements emerged during the rise of monasticism. Soon thereafter, other reform groups solidified, such as the Bogomils, the "Poor Men of Lyons" (later the Waldensians), the Albigenses, the Brethren of the Common Life, etc., as protests to the hypocrisy and decay of the official church. [87] In fact, "Until the eighteenth century, religion was almost always the link between formal ideas and popular social and political protest. European aristocrats and frequently town burghers had a sense of local right and status that could be used to justify protests or even rebellion." [88] The number of insurrections in this sociopolitical context, such as the utopian tradition, is abundant and remains neglected as a focus of study. [89]

In the West, the conflict between the forces of self-centered individualism and the good of the collective has played itself out largely in the context of the Judeo-Christian traditions. Christianity, building on and adapting historic Judaism, wielded a very strong influence on the emergence of Western civilization. In reference to the central focus of this work, namely the antisocial and prosocial dynamics, Anabaptism first relied on nonresistance and separation for survival during its first several centuries, only later developing unique and active approaches to be engaged in the world—primarily voluntary service—while remaining true to the spirit of nonviolence and its general creeds. [90] With a new emphasis upon justice, many Anabaptists of the twentieth century developed and promoted alternative service programs and humanitarian-aid efforts that are adamantly prosocial by providing service to others, the logic and details of which are examined in the chapters that follow.

E) Radical Reformation Churches and the Praxis of Service and Justice in Recent Times [91]

What are appropriate ethical norms and how should people in general relate to society? These are perennial questions also facing the institutions of the Radical Reformation and for Anabaptist Churches, for whom they are especially relevant today. These questions contrast with the topics clarified by scholarship over the past several decades regarding identity (Who are we?), as were congealed primarily in the "pure church" doctrine of nonconformity and nonresistance. One view of the love ethic has been commonly understood and articulated, especially by Anabaptist Mennonite Church tradition, as nonresistance and nonconformity resulting in and relying upon the principles of pacifism. Withdrawal from the socio-political world is one option. [92] The commitment to their vision of purity, the true church of peace, and to separate themselves from a hostile and violent world, encouraged the Radical Reformation groups to pursue a strategy of relative ideological, geographical, and social withdrawal. [93]

However, during the tremendous socio-political upheavals of the early twentieth century, Theron Schlabach, from a Mennonite perspective, writes:

> "The forces distorting the vision were so strong that during the first half of the twentieth century Mennonite Church leaders would devote much of their energy to refocusing—to redefining and restating—what Mennonite Church people believed, who they were, what they stood for, what they understood to be the gospel." [94]

During the first decades of the twentieth century, while some members of the Anabaptists were moving into either the fundamentalist or modernist religious camps, many searched for a third way. Neither fundamentalist nor modernist, the alternative responses focused, on the one hand, on relief, service, and social justice, and on the other hand, the history and identity of the Anabaptists.

Here we follow the example of the Mennonite response to the circumstances of the twentieth century. Those favoring Goshen College professor and dean Harold S. Bender's historical-theological "Anabaptist Vision" failed to see beyond the sometimes rebellious and sometimes alien social-justice scholars and activists, who were part of the "Mennonite Community" alternatives to secular society and the state. Therefore, they did not fully appreciate the potential and the challenges of social ethics. In contrast to the ethical-community approach, espoused especially among Mennonites trained in sociology and social activism, Bender maintained the centrality of historical Anabaptism. [95] Whether intentional or not, Bender blurred (or ignored) the emerging Mennonite community and social-justice ideas back into the historical identity of nonconformity and nonresistance.

Like Bender, the chosen academic discipline for many Mennonites was history, and they viewed history as a fundamental source of authority. Optimistic that the solutions to the relation between Mennonite and the world would not be overly problematic, and perhaps unaware of the underlying paradoxes in ethics, Bender pronounced to the youth of the Mennonite Church:

> "The Golden Age of the Mennonite Church is not past; it is just ahead. The problems of the present are many;

they are difficult. But problems are challenges. They are opportunities for consecrated talent. The time never was and never will be when problems are not present. Let vision and faith see problems and challenges." [96]

History is crucial to the essence and understanding of the Radical Reformation and Anabaptist tradition. But it is not the only guide. In *The Way of the Cross in Human Relations*, Goshen College professor Guy Hershberger wrote that "Christianity is not primarily a system of beliefs or even a set of ethical principles, although these are included." [97] So, how are we to understand exactly what it is? A number of Mennonite scholars have pointed to the Radical Reformation community of believers and the local congregation as a guide to hermeneutical questions, to questions of how to interpret the meaning of the text. The hermeneutical community includes the epistemological dimensions that shift from "What does the text mean to me?" to "What does the text mean to us?" [98]

Are the answers in orthodoxy, fundamentalism, evangelism, modernism, or some other theological system? The crucial period from the beginning to the middle of the twentieth century was marked by tensions within the Radical Reformation member communities, as they struggled over whether to join one of the groups just mentioned or to retain a distinctive identity. According to Norman Kraus, most Mennonites chose to retain the Mennonite identity over assimilation: "The overarching issue for Mennonites following the rude awakening of World War I was the preservation of a consistent community of religious and ethical practice that would give them a distinct identifiable reference in dealing with the sociopolitical world." [99] It should be noted that Mennonites were divided in many ways on how to understand their own relationship to the modern world. Some emphasized nonconformity and separatism, others social justice, and many others some variation in between.

Like it or not, Mennonites were confronted with the geopolitical reality of the ever-present possibility of war and the reality of the modern social world. It is evident that developments, such as the industrialization of war, urged a response from the Radical Reformation churches. It is informative that many maintained the prosocial love ethic and the Golden Rule as a means for understanding how to act in the modern world. We present three case studies with analysis and commentary in chapters that follow. The Radical Reformation and Anabaptism's primary historical and theological emphasis and identity have been historically centered in peace and nonviolence, thus the "Peace Churches" identity emerged. This position has served the survival of the group in the face of persecution. There has, however, also been a strong subtext that emphasizes love, mutual aid, and service. Though less theologically developed, the subtext of societal wellbeing has been vigorously practiced.

Beginning in the early twentieth century, the emphasis on peace and nonviolence has increasingly included an emphasis on procedural and distributive justice. This is not without some added tensions and debate. Not all forms or conceptions of justice fit the peace and nonresistance perspectives. Therefore, the following chapters will argue that the emerging Radical Reformation/Anabaptism blending of peace and justice proves a challenging adaptation. The prosocial behavior of voluntary service to the neighbor is both consistent with its fundamental principles, and when practiced, provides a useful overall guide for promoting individual and societal justice and wellbeing. Achieving human wellbeing is based in and dependent upon doing good for the neighbor. Christians have maintained that the ideal and the motivation both come from God, who created humans with this desire. Other peoples, coming from non-Judaic/Christian traditions and non-theistic traditions, may conclude that collective action via the state is the best solution to the human wellbeing and flourishing, while still others on occasion have pragmatically concluded that the duty to love and serve simply works best. The motivation to serve others has many sources. The state has always played an important role in promoting the ideal vision. However, as too many are painfully aware, the state has too often contributed to antisocial forces. In fact, it is the state itself that is the principle oppressor and violator of human rights.[100] This problem will be dealt with later.

Glenn Paige, founder of the Center for Global Nonkilling, writes: "The surprise insight … is that what did not happen [mutual assured destruction] explains why humanity lives today."[101] He continues that "this turns upside down" the conventional view that history is the story of the struggle of good defeating evil in an epic (often violent) battle. In fact, Paige contends that in order for the human species to survive, killing attributes have somehow not extinguished non-killing attributes. Howard Zinn writes: "Most men everywhere agree that they want to end war, imperialism, racism, poverty, disease, and tyranny. What they disagree about is whether these expectations can be fulfilled within the old frameworks of nationalism, representative government and the profit system." [102] Zinn continues that the solution is to persist in open nonviolent dissent. This too will be further developed in upcoming chapters.

Conclusion

How is one to pursue justice in this context and engage in open nonviolent dissent? Sociologist Pitirim Sorokin's response is that citizens need to become more prosocial and cooperative, "unselfish, and creative, [as] ideally formulated in the Sermon on the Mount…in overt behavior." [103] The duty to love others as one loves oneself can be proposed as a universal axiom for societal survival. Humans are faced with the various forms that "responsibility for others" can take and understanding how and where it can be (and should be) applied. We will first, and primarily, deal with this concept as it has been expressed in the North American context. This will be followed by descriptions of how the three denominations from the Anabaptist tradition have understood serving justice as a central and special or even unique element of the Christian Gospel. [104] The last section of the book will present an ethical and sociological analysis of the relationship of service as the path to justice. Loving thy neighbor is therefore both a problem and promise for human wellbeing. Our thesis is that service to our neighbor is the better way to understand and practice what it means to love.

A caveat needs to be restated: This book examines the valuable role that service as the path to justice has played and continues to play in societal survival. We do not make the claim that the Radical Reformation has solved the problem of societal survival for all times. The specific historical cases of service as the path to justice that are presented here are not offered as the universal template applicable to all times and across all cultures. [105] We simply claim that similar service motifs, norms, values, and ideals around justice, which are present in other religious and cultural traditions, provide necessary illumination and should be nurtured as guides for the wellbeing of people. Though necessarily brief, it is hoped that our thesis will be a useful perspective first on the emergence of the idea of prosocial behavior through the act of serving others, and second, on how it became organized among certain marginal groups, both politically and religiously, and finally, how we might proceed into the future to enhance individual and societal wellbeing.

CHAPTER 2.
The Concept of Prosocial Service

"All knowledge and every pursuit aim at the highest of all good... which the general run of man and people say is happiness"

— Aristotle [106]

The nature of the omnibus concept of good and of doing good has been described and analyzed in many forms through the ages. The above quote from Aristotle suggests that the ultimate goal is happiness.[107] An enormous variety of terms have been used in defining "doing good," but in terms of the Golden Rule within various social and cultural structures, the idea of service is central. The concept, and the words service and servant are among the most universally used and yet variously understood words in human language.[108] Service has been used to describe the work of slaves in the building of the pyramids of Egypt. The millions of unknown servants who built the Great Wall of China or ministered to the Chinese dynasties, and the dynasties of other nations and empires euphemistically described as civil servants are examples. On the other end of the spectrum is the vast and extensive service provided by mothers and fathers throughout history for their children. These latter servants have been primarily responsible for the survival of the human race.

A) Service and Voluntary Action

Surveying all the dimensions and factors related to the concept of service cannot be adequately achieved here. Nevertheless, we attempt to provide an adequate understanding of the nature of service activity and its role in promoting human society and wellbeing. We will use the term service to help focus the discussion, but as the argument unfolds, we will develop a specialized view of service: prosocial service.

Service in historical usage has typically been defined circularly, as that which a servant does. At this level, service is a term that refers to a variety of meanings and activities of helping others, for some good, with no precise definition. Service etymologically derives from the Latin, (OF) as *servitium* i.e. "serv(us)" (slave) and "*itium*" (ice), defined as "condition of a slave, employment as a servant, providing the needs of others through some type of motivation, usually coercion." Ironically, the derivation of the word slave comes from the same root *sclavus* or bond servant. (ML)." [109]

The etymological evidence thus seems to indicate that service has been historically and ideologically derived from a specific status in political and military institutions. It is ironic, and highly suggestive, that the idea of service, and especially in an organized sense, should have been derived from political and military institutions! [110] In any case, in the common everyday language of many cultures, service is still highly associated with effort for the superior, whether in the state or the military structure. The timelessness of this observation is often still read in obituaries: "He was killed in the service of his country." Parenthetically, this statement is rarely met with the question: "What kind of service was she performing, and for whom or for what ultimate purpose?" [111] What is the good of the service?

Every society has had some form of obtaining the good and gaining service from its citizens. For example, a major force in the history of China has been the impressing of humans for the conduct of warfare by the emperors. It was the uncontested duty of everyone to serve the demands of the state. [112] However, there have been many eloquent objections to the destructive and antisocial uses of the term "service" in its military and political context. The

SECTION I. THE CONCEPT OF DOING GOOD AND SERVICE

incompatibilities between the different nature of military and humanitarian service has long been held up to critique. [113]

To illustrate this point, we turn to the work of William James. In 1910, William James opened a debate that still captures the popular imagination and remains unresolved. In a speech given at Stanford university, titled *The Moral Equivalent of War,* he proposed that American youth be conscripted into "an army enlisted against nature." [114] The context was the increasing resort to violence and war as a means to solving human conflicts. But James also acknowledged that war does promote some highly valued and social useful (prosocial) virtues. Among them is the idea that "our gilded youths be drafted off, according to their choice, to get the childishness knocked out of them, and to come back into society with healthier sympathies and soberer ideas." James admired the virtues of courage, devotion, hardiness, and commitment and service to the greater good. He found these virtues in the preparation for war; however, it should also be noted that James was a pacifist. Thus, James found the moral equivalent of war in an "army against nature" and not against other people. However, given the rise and importance of ecological sustainability in contemporary times, the "war against nature metaphor" is less appropriate.

We propose that voluntary service may provide an answer to his call for a moral equivalent to war. We suggest that these virtues can be best promoted in voluntary service. When virtue is discussed, actions are evaluated according to specified standards in a given social context. These standards often vary according to different communities and different time periods. For example, the "heroic" virtues of courage and bravery in battle and loyalty to the tribal and kinship groups in medieval times stand in stark contrast to the New Testament virtues of humility, meekness, cooperation, and service to others (including those not in one's own kinship circles). [115] *The Sermon on the Mount* characterizes virtues very differently than the military honor codes. While war may promote virtues for the good of one's own society, it fails to address the consequences of war upon civilians and the alarming rates of post-traumatic stress among returning veterans. Also, the impact upon neighbors and enemies in war is not prosocial.

The Biblical command is that we love our neighbors. Nazi-era German theologian Dietrich Bonhoeffer warned that having close, special friends may be a threat to the requirement that we love all equally. [116] Rabbi Yehoshua Leib Diskin warned against joining a group that pledged allegiance to help one another because "such a group is not a manifestation of loving one's fellow man. It is a manifestation of love for one's self" and goes against the Torah's commandment to love everyone, even those who are not members of the group."[117] The duties flow from the reality of the human relationship, not from our *feelings* about the relationship. Voluntary service is based on the virtues that provide an ethics rooted in the psychology of self-governance and the sociology and politics of how we respond and interact with those to which may not have kinship ties and with those we may not know nor like.

B) The Sociology of Service

Common usages of the word "service" branches widely into a range of institutions, uses, and meanings, including such terms as service station, service charge, and worship service. Therefore, service needs to be defined more narrowly to be useful as a focus of our analysis. Further, the concept of service, as it pertains to individual human actions, is often not willingly or *voluntarily* given. Hence the word "servant" refers to one who provides the service and is universally understood to mean actions given to the superior because of status differences enforced by power. Therefore, service generally (if not generically) is understood as an involuntarily act given by an inferior. [118] We are here concerned with voluntary service.

Before embarking on this more complicated journey, it is important to examine more closely the etymology and usage of the term "voluntarism". Voluntarism (from the Latin *voluntas*, meaning will) [119] is fundamentally a philosophical, theological, and ethical theory of action wherein *will* takes precedence over the intellect and emotion. The most elementary form is when will is typically understood as capacity and motivations for decision-making. This form of voluntarism appears in writings from St. Augustine and John Duns Scotus to Thomas Aquinas and William of Ockham. Along this path, the voluntarism of the will is eventually subordinated to the practical intellect, which refers to reasoned judgments. Much of the discussion of voluntarism is then taken over by theological concerns about the will of the individual in relation to the will of God.

Ethical voluntarism, on the other hand, deals more specifically with the degree of virtue in the intention of action. Ockham's example is of a person who attends a religious service with the intention of glorifying himself rather than glorifying God. For Ockham, the act (going to church) is identical in both cases, while the moral quality, the will, differs for the individual in each case. Immanuel Kant follows this line of thought: It is not the actions themselves but the fundamental ways in which actions are willed.

For our purposes, these discussions above of voluntarism seem mired in the ego. While will as intention has moral implication for the individual in terms of motivations for actions, actions committed around or with other individuals (can and often do) have impacts and consequences beyond the will of the individual ego. Much of the literature on volunteering and altruistic behavior examines the *will* of those volunteering.[120] The primary focus of much of this research is on the intentions and motivations of specific individuals to engage in altruistic, self-giving activities or otherwise commit prosocial acts.[121] The intrinsic quality of voluntary acts—motivations for giving of oneself and/or one's time—has been the focus of much research and reflects the terms in which voluntarism has been discussed, from Augustine to the present.

However, in terms of the discussion of voluntary service presented in the coming chapters, limiting the discussion of service in terms of the *will* of the agent misses crucial dimensions of the ontology of human social life. What is missing are the means and the consequences of social action. Discussions of justice are socially sensitive categories, not merely individual categories. Therefore, viewing justice in terms of the ethics of interpersonal responsibility (service) is to define justice in respect to *social* engagement with others. Stephen Carter refers to this ethics of recognition and engagement of the self and the other as "civility."[122] This expands the discussion of voluntary service beyond individual will and the intentions of the individual agent, as important as they may be, to the broader dimensions of participation in human social life. The point here is to examine the extrinsic prosocial effect of action from the focus upon the individual to the inclusion of the social community.

In regard to inequality in status, and the resultant involuntary obligations defined as service above, Georg Simmel proposes that this is not a normally desired position: "Typically speaking, nobody is satisfied with the position which he occupies in regard to his fellow creatures; everybody wishes to attain one which is, in some sense, more favorable." [123] Thus, this type of involuntary or coerced service is undesirable.

Human social organization typically involves super-ordination and subordination. In most social situations, there exists an inequality of power. [124] When there is inequality of status, the super-ordinate can demand compliance, and very often (if not always) it means service of some sort. The basic substance of this definition thus refers to obligation on the part of a subordinate to a super-ordinate, whether it be a parent, a tribal chief, a prince, a king, a boss of a business, an elected official, military service, or community official (we continue this discussion in chapter four).

We cannot pursue here the variety of normative structures in which this inequality operates and the conditions which lead to it, nor its sources. For example, being paid for services rendered is one form of service, so highly valued in capitalism, and is dramatically different from the "service" that was performed in the southern United States during slavery. But the key issues in both instances are the motives for the service and the nature of the social structure, which define the conditions of the service, whether voluntary, involuntary, or mutually agreed upon. Where the factor of superiority is not operative as a reason for the server's actions (at least not predominantly), where it is given free of any coercion (at least relatively speaking), where it is given consensually, and the server and the recipient(s) are in full agreement on the terms, we will define it as consensual service. This is the realm of institutionalized service or "contractual" labor, work, or employment, and it is culture specific, meaning each culture has developed its own system of norms and values regarding how humans serve each other. This includes religious, social, and economic organizations, where service is extensively institutionalized. The assumption is that all consensual service is for the welfare of the recipient and the giver, which we refer to in this book as "prosocial service." But the ambiguity of the concept of consensual service contains an inherent dilemma, because the distinction between voluntary and involuntary becomes complex and is not neatly demarcated when institutionalized transactions are involved. [125]

This is illustrated in the economic sphere, where the term "service" is used to refer to the intricate ways in which individuals participate through the production and distribution of goods and services, which affect everyone in the society—the so-called *service sector of the economy*. [126] Economics is a vast conundrum of individuals providing some service for other persons in exchange for the other's reciprocal services to them, often regardless of how mediated the service is. That is, the services an individual provides and the ultimate beneficiary of those services is often impossible to identify because of its complexity. [127] These transactions operate under the conditions of reciprocity: however, they may affect the servers differently, some positively and others negatively.

The disciplines of sociology and anthropology, especially following Emile Durkheim, have expanded the idea of service as the "division of labor" in society. Theories of society are commonly based on the premise that it is the interdependent and reciprocal activities of individual efforts that allows for the structures that function for the survival of the whole society, leaving the issue of whether the service is positive or negative unexamined. [128] The basic engine of the division of labor is the holistic interdependence of parts (the whole is the sum of its parts): "All human behavior above the level of the physiological must be regarded as sharply conditioned by society, by the totality of groups, and the norms and institutions within which every individual human being exists from the moment of his birth." [129]

No living entity, human or subhuman, regardless of the time, culture, or place, can emerge, function, or survive without prosocial service relationships and actions from and to other entities in the larger system. [130] Individuals need the collective's assistance to survive, and the group is also dependent upon individuals to perform their duties. The individual and the group were twin born, according to sociologist-philosopher Cooley: "'Society' and 'individuals' do not denote separable phenomena but are simply collective and distributed aspects of the same thing."[131] The diagram below describes the parameters of service, which includes the motives of service.

Table I

The Prosocial and Antisocial Behavior Continuum[132]

A. The Objective Description of Service

Prosocial	Neutral (adiaphora)	Antisocial

B. Motivational Indicators[133]

Compassion	Cooperation	Egotism	Aggression	Annihilation

The conditions under which service (however defined) is also a necessary aspect of all service and is illustrated in table II.

Table II

Conditions of Service[134]

Voluntary	Coerced	Consensual
Business/professional[135]	Indentured Laborers	Public service[136]
Religious events	Military Service	State and Federal programs
Parents/Family	Feudal/autocratic systems	Criminal restitution
Community work	Prison/ Slavery	Apprenticeship

This categorization is not fully adequate because human thoughts, relations, and social structures are immensely complex. For example, charity has a long tradition in Christian history and is involved in the expression of prosocial voluntary service. Thomas Aquinas maintains that charity "is based on the fellowship of happiness, which consists essentially of [as coming from God as] the First Principle, while our neighbor is loved as receiving together with us a share of happiness from Him."[137] Love as a motivation for charity, and more broadly stated as service, indicates the complexity of the idea of

SECTION I. THE CONCEPT OF DOING GOOD AND SERVICE

service but assumes that service is consensual, and for the benefit of the recipient. Love and charity do not necessarily challenge or erase status and power differences, which create injustices, and may even exacerbate them; charity may be an expression of totally unmitigated love but may on the contrary actually accentuate the senses of obligations or superiority, and/or power differences, and result in hostility or resentment.

One such nuance is Georg Simmel's proposition that a spontaneous gift (prosocial voluntary service included) can never be freely or fully returned: "The reason is that the giver's gift, because it was first, has a voluntary character which no return gift can ever have. For, to return the benefit we are obligated ethically; we operate under a coercion which, though neither social nor legal but moral, is still coercion." [138] Though service may be compassionate (motivated totally by love), any kind of gift given in return cannot be totally voluntary or totally compassionate. This complicates the issue of service. The meaning of service therefore is complicated, and it is not possible to address this variety comprehensively at this point. There are psychological and generic factors as well as sociological factors involved in any act of service. [139] All cultures have their own stories and perspectives regarding good or positive service. [140]

The treatment of service above suggests that the conscious, volitional, and especially moral and ethical forces in human behavior have been largely overlooked. Increasingly, however, scholars are focusing on empathy and altruism as factors in the non-biologically derived prosocial behavior. [141] Others, such as Pulitzer Prize winning author Edward O. Wilson and primatologist Alex De Waal suggest that hereditary and biological forces do promote cooperation. It is logical to propose that the explanation of behavior based on reductionist biological factors (for its survival function) does not need to exclude the emergence of humanitarian (ethical) impulses to contribute to ethical pro-social behavior.

Recent psychological and sociological literature indicates that the academic community is increasingly wrestling with the difficulty of understanding the role of prosocial forces in human society from a non-materialistic reductionist perspective. One such example is the recent *Encyclopedia of Community:*

From Village to the Virtual World, first published in 2003.[142] This encyclopedia represents a comprehensive survey of the positive psychological and social forces that contribute to the survival of the human community.

We introduced the concept of prosocial and antisocial acts, which form the basis of our analysis. Thus, we begin with the idea of humanitarian service to the human being in the specific context in which the person(s) is situated. The cooperative and altruistic phenomenon ("giving" in Simmel's terms) thus brings us very easily and quickly to the concept of doing good or prosocial service, especially in its voluntary form. Prosocial or humanitarian voluntary service is significantly motivated to contribute to the welfare of others, and by definition, typically involves effort and cost on the part of the person volunteering, putting the welfare of the other above the individual's self-interest and benefit.

The forms and contents of prosocial actions are legion and pervasive. The foremost examples, mentioned above, are mothers and fathers who almost universally sacrifice their energy, resources, and time for the benefit of their children or immediate family for most of their lives. Significantly, this kind of service has largely been unrecognized in the institutionalized system of rewards and benefits in almost all societies. Why? Because of its massive scale, from the miniscule to the societal, it cannot be objectively measured and evaluated. It has, however, been noted and indirectly noted and indirectly studied from biological, genetic, and psychological perspectives.[143]

Specific examples of service exist everywhere. We include a contemporary example, which has numerous dimensions and implications that cannot be analyzed here. During the winter of 2008-2009, more than 20 percent of the workers in Goshen, Indiana were unemployed. In the city's north-side neighborhood, the situation was worse. Staff at the neighborhood school, Chamberlain Elementary, learned that children in the school lacked food on weekends. The school started sending food home with the children on Fridays. Across the street from the school, employees of Maple City Health Care Center noted that, even with a 90 percent income-based discount, unemployed patients with diabetes or high blood pressure felt they couldn't afford care and were missing appointments. "Since the beginning of the center in 1989, our mission has been to foster healthy community in our neighborhood by providing and promoting affordable accessible health care," said James Nelson Gingerich (MD and founder). "We decided that, if our patients used their asset of time to volunteer for these organizations, they would be helping us accomplish our mission of fostering a healthy community. In return, we would offer patients a $10 credit for every hour they volunteered. In this way, patients who had no cash could still contribute to their health care." The program has been so successful that another healthcare center under MCHCC has already been constructed.[144]

C) The Problem of Justice and Government

We have maintained that no society or state has been able to develop a full range of social institutions and social programs to adequately serve the weak and the poor. This is illustrated in the contemporary United States. The richest nation on earth does not care for or treat its citizens equally, and some of the richest people on earth play less taxes proportionately than the poor because of economic, political, or financial influences. Its health care is even more shameful.[145] Rousseau cautioned that if "empathy" is lost in the civilization process, laws would develop ultimately to serve those with power, because those with power would make the laws to serve their own interests. Whether or not Rousseau is accurate, this caution should at the very least cause pause for reflection, since (in the United States) we are witnessing an increasingly massive gap between the rich and the poor.

Individuals, groups, and societies everywhere and throughout history have given time, energy, and resources to their neighbors, communities, and those in need. One of the primary forms this has taken is through the government of the collective. Among the most ubiquitous institutions, collective governing has taken many forms, including tribal structures, clans, principalities, nations, and (more recently) nation-states.[146] This prosocial activity appears in one of the earliest formal governing statements: the Babylonian Code of Hammarabi which dates to approximately 1750 B.C.E. Prosocial action has been based on tribal myths, traditions, constitutions, and charters, which guarantee basic rights, such as citizenship, protection, rights of property health, and emergency assistance. More specifically, almost every organized community has enacted policies that contribute to the welfare of its citizens.

It is not possible to illustrate them here, but throughout history, civilizations have produced formal codes of conduct concerning social welfare. Most of these social-welfare efforts are clearly prosocial. However, traditions, norms, codes, and policies can be either prosocial or antisocial and can impact individuals differently (and often contain elements of both). These can be formal or informal. A vast array of human actions are not part of the formal or official charter of the state. Many times, service is given presumably without any expectation of personal material or societal reward and is not sanctioned by an administrative position. Rather, it is freely given because of compassion or concern (or the duty of love) for the wellbeing of the recipient, who had not received needed or fair treatment in the larger community or social system.

Is the idea of prosocial action not merely a palliative, compassionate response to a deeper issue, namely the injustice that exists in all societies, for which the solution is not compassion and palliation prosocial service but fulfilling justice? Is justice not what we look to human government for, and would it not largely mitigate the need for prosocial service?

We propose that government cannot be the final or ultimate solution. In a review of literature that analyses the increasing numbers of poor people in the United States, Robert C. Lieberman states: "the financial rewards are increasingly concentrated among a tiny elite whose risks are born by an increasingly exposed and unprotected middle class." He then states the reason: "The dramatic growth of inequality, then, is the result not of the 'natural' workings of the market but of four decades worth of deliberate political choices."[147] In other words, the state's political and economic policies, including its taxation policy, determines to a large extent how the wealth of a nation is distributed, to whom, and how much shall be allocated for various social purposes.[148] This raises looming questions about human social and economic rights, resource distribution, and responsibility for poverty and unmet human needs. In short, it raises fundamental questions of procedural and distributive justice. Who is involved in these decision-making processes, and how are the costs and benefits of living in a society distributed? So, how can we better speak to the need for prosocial action, even though the language of human rights and needs now dominates international law? [149]

The implicit question behind rights and needs relates to who bears the counterpart obligations or responsibilities to deliver on those rights and needs. [150] Or (said more succinctly), "Who must do what for whom?" [151] If justice is "giving a person what she deserves," who or what is to do the giving? Onora O'Neill reminds us that most contemporary approaches to rights and the satisfaction of human needs assume that *states* are the primary agents, and view all other agents as secondary in accountability. The main problem with a state-centric approach to the delivery of human needs is that it unburdens the private individual agent from responsibility. [152] If the state-centric approach is accepted, then private individuals are basically free to pursue their own (perhaps selfish) interests, with their primary moral responsibility simply to elect state leaders who pursue policies that work towards fulfilling human rights and needs. [153] What is the case if private individuals have responsibilities that exceed a strictly state-centric approach? [154] It matters greatly whether needs and rights are postulated as negative duties (not to coerce others), or whether existing human needs and rights may impose positive obligations and responsibilities (to protect and/or aid) that go beyond the institutions of the state. [155] Voluntary prosocial service as designed and practiced by the historic Peace Churches is one answer to this dilemma of possible interpersonal responsibility.

D) What Are We to Do?

Influenced, perhaps both by the socio-political environment of the 1960s and 1970s and by the writings of church leaders, many Mennonites and others of the Radical Reformation church family have begun to question the traditional church-state separation. In fact, several recent surveys of the shift from non-participation to involvement in political affairs provide credible evidence that there is clearly a shift in paradigms taking place. [156] For many denominations in the broader Christian community, the shifting emphasis from peace to justice has been expressed not in quiet pacifism but instead now promotes nonviolent direct action. [157]

Our emphasis on direct voluntary action—prosocial service—brings us squarely to the question of large-scale social and political change. It points to achieving justice and overcoming oppression in the revolutionary achievement that "has put down the mighty from their thrones and exalted those of low degree." (Luke 1:52-53, RSV). By now prioritizing justice over peace, one choice of action is for the revolutionary overthrow of the powers of injustice and thereby ushering social change. Liberation theology, popular in many Latin American revolutions, is an answer to questions of duty in the face of injustice. One answer to the call from injustice is to demand social justice through (possibly violent) revolution. However, when asking what we should do, another answer is provided in Luke's Gospel, wherein the revolutionary question is answered in this way: "The man with two shirts must share with him who has none and anyone with food must do the same." When we see others (and perhaps even ourselves) suffer, what are we to do? What did Jesus do?

The questions of large-scale social and political change face us today just as they did in Palestine during the life of Jesus. Mennonite theologian John Howard Yoder describes "the four ways" available to the question of revolution: realism, withdrawal, revolutionary violence, and finally, new forms of interpersonal relations. [158] For Yoder, these options were available in the time of Jesus and are also the options available to us today.

The first option is realism: accept the reality of the given socio-political structures. This was the strategy of the Herodians and the Sadducees in the first century CE. Accepting possibly slow evolutionary change while living with (and possibly benefiting from) the realities of "the establishment." The second option, withdrawal, comes in two forms: "desert" or absolute physical separation and contact from systems of injustice, such as the monasteries around the Dead Sea or some of the Amish sects; and "Separation", which is to live in the midst of social systems but to maintain purity by segregating themselves in a distinct community. This is the approach of the Pharisees

SECTION I. THE CONCEPT OF DOING GOOD AND SERVICE

and distinguishes a clear line between the sacred and the profane; this is echoed in Jefferson's "wall of separation" between religion and the state.

The third option is the most dramatic and is the starkest alternative to the establishment: righteous revolutionary violence. In Jesus' time, these were the Zealots, comprised of military and underground political groups in clandestine warfare with the Roman Empire. For Yoder, this was the real temptation for Jesus. This was the temptation in the desert and the temptation in Gethsemane. In fact, most of the disciples came from the Zealot group and many had these expectations. Scholarship has clarified the extent to which Jesus' ministry must be understood as representing a constant struggle with the social option of revolutionary violence. [159] Jesus was executed under the pretense that he was a Zealot. But he rejected the Zealot option, as Yoder explains: "What is wrong with the violent revolution according to Jesus is not that it changes too much but that it changes too little; the Zealot is the reflection of the tyrant whom he replaces by means of the tools of the tyrant."[160] For Jesus, the Zealot is immature, unreflective, and lacks knowledge of the workings of history. The Zealot is blinded by righteous arrogance. Jesus chose none of these options. Instead, Jesus followed the fourth option of inclusive and loving interpersonal relations. Rather than build a violent uprising, Jesus washed the feet of the disciples. No doubt, this was as perplexing to the disciples as it is to many of the followers of Jesus today. Jesus did not violently confront the state.

The state does a great amount of good work, which can be defined as prosocial. But tragically, as the taxation issue indicates, the state apparatus (including its government policy) has also been involved in some of the most serious antisocial behavior conceivable: war and mass atrocity. Caused by economic factors, land pressures, perceived security needs, or military aggression, states have produced the most destructive violence and on the grandest scale. "War is Hell,"[161] Karl von Clausewitz's classic definition, affirms unequivocally that "We can never introduce a modifying principle (i.e., that there is something good about war) without committing an absurdity." [162]

The issue of war is problematic, and Michael Walzer presents a very sobering paradox: "The dream of a lion lying down with a lamb...will not come, so we have been told, until the forces of evil have been decisively defeated and mankind freed forever from the lust for conquest and dominion. In our myths and visions, the end of war is also the end of secular history." [163] In other words, the war to end war is still the only unrealized hope and may never come. We will deal with this issue of why war is still "practiced" in Chapter 9, although there is no way to understand fully why something so absurd persists.

Two conclusions can be drawn from this discussion: 1) states and their governments provide many services and social programs for the common good; 2) states and their policies also contribute some of the greatest antisocial actions, including oppression, killing and maiming of soldiers and citizens, destruction of property and material and social infrastructures—in short, massive antisocial actions. Thus, the state and government can be classified on both sides of the pro and antisocial classification, and ironically provide the best argument for the thesis of this book: *There will always be a need to tip the balance toward prosocial ends regardless of the state and government's contributions.* [164]

E) Voluntary Prosocial Service: A Summary Conclusion

Analysts tell us that most social relations, from small groups to nation-states, are socially asymmetrical, meaning that an individuals' status and rights are not equally distributed among all the members. There have always been vulnerable and needy people in every society, regardless of whether the reference is the families, the community, the county, the state, or nations. We are reminded by Jesus, whose life was an example of ministering to others, that there has always been and continues to be a great need for "second mile" service. In one context, Jesus said, "The poor shall always be with you." There have always been persons who have fallen victim by the wayside, in every society.

There are always some individuals, groups, and communities who (for a myriad of reasons) have not received equal and fair treatment and in fact have been unjustly treated. Life in human society has never been fair. [165] In

SECTION I. THE CONCEPT OF DOING GOOD AND SERVICE

this treatise, the specific focus of voluntary service is the human response to the needs of the "neighbor", such as personal and family needs resulting from health crises, mental disabilities, economic catastrophes, communities suffering from natural disasters such as floods, earthquakes, tornadoes, droughts, and political crises such as civil war, inter-ethnic warfare, and international conflicts. But this list does not encompass the entire universe of needs. The North American scene, in the specific organizations, is described in the pages that follow, beginning with Chapter 3.

We therefore repeat (and expand) here a more nuanced version of the role for voluntary service presented in Chapter 1: *In every social system, human interdependence is not equally and fairly distributed. Institutional structures favoring the powerful and the rich will always demand a response by providing specific, needed "services". In addition, due to individual differences in personal endowments, unpredicted and uncontrolled events, accidents, tragedies, and economic uncertainties, there will always be people who are left "by the wayside" requiring the good Samaritan.* [166] *And we propose that it is this situation or tragic condition that the principle of compassionate prosocial behavior expressed as voluntarily serving others emerges as a relevant response and a solution—not the entire solution, but at least a partial one.*

Relating this concept directly to prosocial action, through the centuries, the persistent and urgent needs call for voluntary service action that will insure human survival, and beyond that, wellbeing. It is this realization that provides the source of motivation for finding remedies, which ultimately are based on an ethical principle—the Golden Rule—and requires the actions of individuals, in whatever sociological structures they exist. Generally, it has been assumed that most efforts at remediation require the reforming of social structures and institutions to solve these needs, especially by the government. For example, when theorists think about the topic of peace, they predominantly focus upon states and empires as its main building blocks, "thus broadly discounting the role and agency of individuals and societies in its construction and sustainability." [167]

Every society and culture has a gap between the ideal and the reality on the ground. Voluntary service, we contend, is a crucial human dimension in the solution to both acknowledging and reinforcing the role of individuals in the construction and sustaining the approximation of the ideal. However, the fact that utopian literature (and attempts to create a just community) typically end in failure is a continuing reminder of the fact that social solutions are not easy or even achievable.[168] Human social life is constructed, not predetermined: "Man lives not only with the reality that confronts him but with the reality (the ideal) he makes."[169] However, this assumption has not been extensively evaluated by comparing cultures and societies.[170] We turn now to how the prosocial activity of voluntary service, broadly defined, has emerged and has been expressed in particular aspects of American cultural tradition in order to put the Radical Reformation or Anabaptist response into perspective.

CHAPTER 3.
Perspectives on Service and Justice

> *"Hold thou the good: define it well for fear divine philosophy should push beyond her mark and be procurers of the Lords of Hell. Oh, yet we trust that somehow good will be the final goal of ill."*
>
> – *Tennyson* [171]

Human beings have an almost universal desire to serve others, which has been understood as "volunteering" in most human societies, though each culture uses a different term. One of the great love stories in the Jewish tradition is Jacob's love for Rachel. Jacob was on his way to visit his uncle Laban when he saw a beautiful woman drawing water at a well. When he drew near, he kissed her and wept aloud. He was so smitten by Rachel that he volunteered to serve her father Laban for seven years in order to claim her for his wife. Like most romances, the story requires dismaying difficulties. Thus, conniving Laban reneged on his agreement with his nephew, but Jacob's love persevered and he accepted the injustice and served another seven years! What Jacob must have thought about the idea of service is not clear, but we believe it supports our contention that service has many subjective and objective meanings and thus requires further defining and historical understanding. [172]

The following brief historical and analytical review of the emergence of the general concept of serving others and its social expression will help to understand its essential genesis and genius in order to analyze its present status and importance.

A) Historical Sources of Service

The socio-cultural-religious revolutions that were taking place in Europe, beginning with the agrarian Middle Ages, accelerated and expanded during the Renaissance and Reformation, and grew dramatically in the subsequent socio-economic-technical transformations. These changes have been variously characterized, depending on the author's perspective and discipline, but they all can be subsumed under global terms, such as industrial, scientific, capitalist, socialist, communist, and technological societies/cultures. [173] One engine of massive change was the development of the printing press, and later forms of communication, which provided freedom for individual expression in religious and social issues, especially during the Reformation.

Not only did the printing press make the Bible more accessible but also literature in general, especially by pamphleteering, which encouraged social revolution, with major consequences.[174] The corresponding innovations in science and the technical applications of the free-market capitalist system produced more individual initiative and wealth than any other system in history. [175] However, these changes produced winners and losers, as the long-term social and economic evolution benefitted the privileged far more than the majority of the population. [176]

Thus, the protest and rebellion regarding the economic inequalities, poverty, exploitation, and oppression that followed the Reformation was precipitated at long length in the Marxian and other related socialist revolutions. All of these developments must be couched in the context of a civil society, on which all these innovative social forms were based, namely negotiating personal rights and advantages for the sake of the others' benefit. The idea of voluntary giving up of some minimum of self-interest has been included in most (if not all) discussions of the emergence of civil society (however defined). The most obvious example of this is the social contract advocated by Hobbes, Locke, and Rousseau.

However, other theorists, such as Adam Smith, promoted a radical form of the deliberate pursuit of self-interest and viewed that the more self-interest was achieved the better society would function. However, this benefited the privileged far more than the majority of the population, leading to outbreaks of protests and rebellions. Protests about economic inequalities, poverty, exploitation, and oppression will continue to intensify. As developments in recent centuries have demonstrated, the flowering of capitalism has failed miserably in providing the things normally associated with the good life for all people, namely health care, retirement benefits and security, and access to capital and political power, especially in the United States. Nor has capitalism been any more successful in solving the issues of alienation, deprivation, impoverishment, marginalization, domination, and oppression, resulting in the continuing creation of classes, rich and poor.[177]

However, not everyone followed the advice of Adam Smith. All of these developments must be couched in the emergence of the idea of a civil society and the search for procedural justice in how decisions are made, and in distributive justice in the allocation of costs and benefits of living in society. The idea of voluntarily giving up some minimum level of self-interest has been included in most (if not all) discussions of the emergence of civil democratic societies, however defined.[178]

Whatever one may believe about the relative prosocial quality of the major socio-economic philosophies, and the political systems which resulted from them, the problem of social and economic inequality expressed via individual rights, social status, power, and wealth has not been solved.[179] In the context of these major paradigms of the good life or the ideal social system, which were emerging in the West, Christianity has also been directly confronted with the issue of social and economic inequality: "Since its fledgling origins as an obscure sect within the Roman Empire, Christianity has been forced to consider the problem of its proper relationship to the larger social world. Within this broad context, much discussion in Christian ethics and in other disciplines has focused on Christianity's assessment of economic life."[180]

Especially since the Reformation, emerging dominant religions and sectarian religious movements have also been assertive in facing the problems of inequality based on a unique interpretation of God's purposes and goals for human life, and how they are to be achieved. [181] As such, the Anabaptists took an early lead in this process, which is analyzed more extensively in Chapters 8 and 9. [182] But we turn now to an analysis of American society and the concept of prosocial service to provide a context for the analysis.

B) American Society and Serving the Neighbor

In the 1830s, Alexis de Tocqueville travelled the United States and produced a significant study of American society, summarized in *Democracy in America*. In his observations in the United States, he discovered a major trait of the American people, which he considered almost unique: the penchant to form voluntary community organizations, to solve problems from the mundane to the profoundly general without depending completely upon the state or government to do it for them. [183] He states:

> "Those Americans are the most peculiar people in the world. In a local community in their country, a citizen may conceive of some need which is not being met. What does he do? He goes across the street and discusses it with his neighbor. Then what happens? A committee begins to function on behalf of the need. You won't believe this but it's true. All of this is done without reference to any bureaucrat. All of this is done by private citizens on their own initiative." [184]

Alexis de Tocqueville continues, "In no country in the world has the principle of association been more successfully used, or more unsparingly applied to a multitude of different objects, than in America." [185] de Tocqueville's perspective proposes that American individualism expresses itself in "group individualism." [186] This characterization is probably partly due to the generally accepted interpretation that the United States was a new world, where the traditional patterns and institutions had not yet fully developed. [187]

SECTION I. THE CONCEPT OF DOING GOOD AND SERVICE

In the early twentieth century, Pitirim Sorokin conducted sample-survey research on what he termed "good neighbors" in the United States. He began the research by defining a good neighbor as follows: "Their altruism is plain and fairly ordinary. It is however, real. Each of our 'good neighbors' has rendered real help to his fellow men and has done so freely without any legal duty or without expectation of any advantage or profit." [188] The book that resulted from his research was published as *Altruistic Love*. However, Sorokin discovered that contemporary Western society is increasingly focusing on the "negativistic and pathological types of human beings and human actions." [189] Sorokin's growing concern was that the spirit of cooperation and prosocial service that de Tocqueville described and celebrated was being replaced by antisocial dynamics of self-interest.

Sorokin's research found, contrary and to the surprise of the expectations of religious people, "Eighty two percent [of the interviewees] state that the religious Christians whom they know personally practice Christian love for the fellow men only to a slight extent. The survey confirmed the well-known fact that most professed Christians have been negligibly Christian in their overt prosocial behavior and relationships. A series of other tests and studies have shown that during these past centuries, the overt behavior of many Christians exhibits little if any application of the Sermon on the Mount or the other teachings of Christianity." [190]

An interesting sequel to the idea of prosocial service pertaining directly to the subject of this volume is found in Sorokin's *Forms and Techniques of Altruistic and Spiritual Growth*. A chapter titled "Altruism in Mennonite Life" by three Mennonite authors cite numerous examples of prosocial behavior expressed by Mennonites, and conclude by suggesting: "Mennonites conceive of their church as a brotherhood which seeks to practice the New Testament teaching of love and neighborliness. Prosocial service is part of that purpose. Prosocial service concerns are less the product of conscious or formal cultivation than a derivative from a disciplined brotherhood way of life." [191]

In any case, prosocial voluntary service has an honorable history in the United States and Canada. North Americans have been recognized as having a penchant for voluntarily associating together for public good. This focus, however, may place less emphasis on the voluntary-service aspect, with which we are ultimately concerned, than it does on the association for the purposes of achieving personal, group, or national ends.[192] Of course, voluntary associations may not promote prosocial service for people beyond their own membership.

More recently Robin Williams proposed that "humanitarianism" was "an important value cluster in American society," which he defined as "any type of disinterested concern and helpfulness including personal kindliness, aid and comfort, spontaneous aid in mass disasters, as well as the more impersonal patterns of organized philanthropy."[193] Williams, however, reminds the readers that "America" has been very un-humanitarian in the treatment of the native Americans, the imported African slaves, and various immigrant groups. Williams' survey of voluntary associations therefore runs the gamut from The Aaron Burr Association to the Women's International Bowling Congress, most of which reflect self-advancement goals.[194]

Two narratives or competing paradigms are formed to describe the essential character of US society. On the one hand, the emergence of increasing individualism has resulted in an individual's basic concern for themselves with less concern for the welfare of "outsiders." According to Williams, "In American Culture, there is very great emphasis upon monetary success… [but] there is not a corresponding emphasis upon the legitimate avenues on which to march toward this goal."[195] He suggests that the goals and means in the highly differentiated value system and individualism can best be integrated in community associations, thus "The proportion of people isolated from opportunities for stably recurring interaction in family, neighborhood, work group, and church has increased."[196] The trend toward individualism has increased.

On the other hand, the deep analysis of a New England community in the late 1950s, found in *Yankee City* by W. Lloyd Warner, illustrates the significance of associations in the life of the community and ferreted out nineteen different types of community activities covering a range from "the most sacred to most profane and secular, from extreme forms of competition and opposition to the most intense cooperative efforts."[197] Warner's analysis of the purposes and functions of these associations provide extensive insight into the fabric of any community: "Structural and membership interconnections, our interview and observations tell us, organize and express some of the feelings, attitudes, and values of the people who belong to the various associations."[198] He concludes, "It seems likely that [voluntary associations] will continue to be important in the lives of Americans, for they serve their members well and conform to the way Americans do things."[199]

In a path-breaking recent study of American culture, Robert Bellah and associates propose that individualism and commitment are the two great opposites in American life.[200] Among the many examples of the balancing of selfish individualism and community service, the authors describe Howard Newton, who "sees a natural harmony between his self-interest and the public good of his community. In the long run, his prosperity depends on the prosperity of the community as a whole."[201] Another interviewee states, "Generosity of spirit is thus the ability to acknowledge an interconnectedness—one's 'debts to society' that binds one to others."[202] Bellah and others propose that this "sustaining one another in the pursuit of the common good" remains a powerful element within the American tradition.

This contributes to balance the strong individualism that Bellah and associates maintain is a necessary characteristic for America's economic success, while emphatically maintaining that "Absolute independence is a false ideal."[203] Interestingly, they also maintain that "The great contribution that religion can make today is in its emphasis on the fact that individuality and society are not opposites but require each other."[204]

"What would you want me to tell my students about how to fulfill their responsibilities as citizens?" One of us used to ask this at the conclusion of the interviews with community leaders. Almost always, the characteristically American answer was, "Tell them to get involved."[205]

One of the most specific studies of the idea of prosocial service from the perspective of the American context is *National Service: What would it Mean?* [206] The book's argument is that "In 1984 the Gallup organization reported that 65 percent of the American people favored a program in which all young men and women would serve for 1 year in the armed forces or in civilian social work in return for unspecified educational benefits. It is not surprising that the concept of national service should exercise such appeal; it is one of the few innovations on the political horizon that, if adopted in comprehensive form, might transform the conditions of life in the United States." [207]

Danzig and Szanton provide a vast review of the history of various service programs that have been conducted in the United States. These include the major types of service: military and national service (non-national draft); military draft service (required of everyone), school-based national service, voluntary service, and universal service (required of all youth). The pros and cons of the varied forms of service, in reference to competition with employment of the general population, the costs of administration, and the implications for the National Service Participants (NSP), are detailed. This is important because these prosocial forces have kept the antisocial forces from destroying the human race.

In the 1960s, a new interest in community involvement and service emerged, which is best expressed by the "New Frontier" of J.F. Kennedy, made a famous by the campaign slogan, "Ask not what your country can do for you. Ask what you can do for your country." A recent review of Kennedy's influence states, "Kennedy, for all his cool, ironic detachment, showed a genuine passion for public service and yes for politics too." Dionne continues, "Kennedy's defense of politics and his celebration of service went hand in hand with his assumption that individual success found its roots in social arrangements that made prosperity and achievement possible. No wonder so many heeded his call to join the Peace Corps." [208]

Kennedy left the implementation to his brother-in-law Sargent Shriver, who symbolizes the broad interest in service. Of the many organizations he nurtured, the *Peace Corps* has provided emergency and longer-term assistance in every continent in the world, and the young men and women who served in it have benefited in unfathomable ways. Even though, ironically, he was a highly placed government official for much of his life, he initiated Legal Services, Head Start, Jobs Corps, Community Action, Vista, and Upward Bound, all of which were designed to fill a gap that the prevailing social

SECTION I. THE CONCEPT OF DOING GOOD AND SERVICE

and economic institutions and his own government could not fill. His accomplishments focused on closing that gap for many Americans. [209]

The success of the Peace Corps has shown the importance of the service idea in the American psyche. Though it was initiated under a liberal Democratic president, John F. Kennedy, it has survived the changes in political parties and political orientations through the years. Thousands of young people have served in virtually every country in the world. This service has not only transformed the lives of the volunteers themselves but has also contributed greatly to the human conditions of countless individuals and families around the world. This significant idealistic movement was further solidified by the Clinton administration's formation of the AmeriCorps in 1993.

Today more than 709,000 persons join AmeriCorps every year, and since its founding, it has attracted over 400,000 volunteers. Another service arm, which predated AmeriCorps (1965) but was subsequently absorbed by AmeriCorps in 1993, is VISTAS "Volunteers in Service to America." "Vista volunteers work for local non-profit and government agencies to help address issues related to poverty. Currently over 6,000 VISTA members are serving in the United States." [210]

Over the past decades, data has been gathered on the amount of service provided in the United States in the 1980s: "In 1983, an estimated 92 million American served as volunteers in churches, schools, hospitals, political action groups, and a vast range of civic organizations. A 1974 study concluded that the United States have about 40,000 voluntary organizations directly or indirectly involved with environmental problems alone." [211] This report does not distinguish between associations focusing on voluntarily serving personal goals and the public good, but obviously includes both.

Most recently, the Bureau of Labor Statistics reported that for the year 2010, 26.3 percent of the population had volunteered that year, a decline of 0.5% from the prior year. "About 62.8 million people volunteered through or for an organization at least once between September 2009 and September 2010. The volunteer rate in 2010 was similar to the rates observed in 2007 and 2008." [212] The variety and magnitude of people giving voluntarily of their time, energy, and material resources in North America is vast. Volunteer services in fire departments, emergency rescue and ambulance work, community symphony orchestras, fund raising for uncounted community chests, organizations and institutions like the Salvation Army, hospitals, and nursing homes, cover almost the entire social fabric. [213]

This interest in being "good neighbors," is reflected in the recently published *Encyclopedia of Associations*, which lists over 151,000 organizations spanning the gamut from ethnic organizations to public affairs groups, environmental associations to fan clubs, all performing important non-governmental functions or services for the common good. [214] Nevertheless, there continues to be a flood of criticism in America regarding the selfishness and individualism of American people.

C) Religious Groups and Service

Most world religions accept the premise that a difference must be drawn between the moral principles that are prosocial and those that are antisocial. "The theological doctrine, that there exist two principles or powers, eternally opposed and conflicting—good and evil," exist in all religions. [215] In the introduction to *The Predicament of the Prosperous*, Bruce C. Birch and Larry L. Rasmussen make the following conclusion: "In the face of the gluttonous appetite of American industrial society [there is] a corresponding chasm between the rich and poor." [216]

Birch and Rasmussen maintain that the problem lies not so much with the moral and ethical teachings of Christianity but rather with the possibility that Christian believers have imbibed the culture of individualism, selfish consumerism, and antisocial behavior (described in chapters 1 and 2), and therefore are not promoting and expressing the prosocial behavior promoted in Christian teaching. [217] However, in spite of considerable negative tendencies, it is still true that humanitarianism, compassion, altruism, mutual aid, and simple good neighborliness have a long and pervasive history in North America. And it has further been generally observed that altruistic behavior is more widely practiced among rural and religious groups, such as the well-known "barn raising" of the Amish and the ubiquitous humanitarian service responses to disasters such as war and natural disaster, conducted by the Church of the Brethren, the Mennonites, and the Quakers.

One source that describes only one small segment of the global service theater, in one time period, is the classic book *International Relief in Action 1914-1943*, which describes thirty-nine voluntary service organizations in the United States that were organized to help with the massive needs during the two world wars. [218] Kraus' extensive survey describes other major religious groupings, such as Roman Catholicism, the Reformed, Presbyterian, Lutheran, Anglican, Baptist traditions, and what they have accomplished in alleviating the problems inherent in the social and economic institutions, values, norms, and ethics operative in the world. [219]

The various Christian traditions' testimonies and responses to the poor, the unfortunate, the weak, the handicapped, the neglected, the disenfranchised, and the marginalized have been powerful and inspiring. However, some Christians have rejected humanitarian service as "socialism" or anti-Christian humanism. [220] Nevertheless, the obvious (though rarely stated) reason for the Christian rejection is that the various socio-politico-economic systems never fully solve the human issues of hunger, illness, poverty, homelessness, deprivation, and the seemingly fundamental rejection of so many human beings whether by nature or human actions. *So, they determined something must be done about it.* Their response is derived from the ethic of Christian compassion. Almost every Christian denomination has produced a paradigm that presents what they feel is the will of their "God and Creator" regarding the above-listed conditions.

D) The Emergence of Work Camps

All groups accept the basic role played by the socio-political-economic systems in providing the basic needs of humanity, but they also obviously believe that no system is totally adequate, neither the free-market capitalist nor socialist or communist systems. It is this gulf that provides the opening for religious groups to develop a teaching and practice to the fill the gap. [221] The increased emphasis on voluntary prosocial service for justice, especially in the West, ironically emerged (at least partially) as a reaction to the increasingly destructive consequences of social and economic strains due to international conflicts in which religion played a significant part. [222] The general promotion of peace, and the reconstruction in Europe after World War I, provided a major push for the transformation of the idea of service to humanitarian to just ends, among the Radical Reformation in particular.[223]

Danzing and Szanton's significant review of the service camps in the United States during and after the great depression, which followed the First World War, reflects this influence. The almost universal revulsion to the carnage of World War I, which many observers have maintained could only lead to World War II, also energized movements for peace and justice. Among the many agitators and promoters of peace and humanitarianism was Pierre Ceresole (1879-1945). He was an engineer, pacifist, organizer, writer, and lecturer.[224] "He demanded a 'peaceful revolution' sustained by the spirit of authentic Christianity and leading to an immediate and unilateral disarmament." He believed this would lead to an end to war. [225] Working with the *Fellowship of Reconciliation*, he invited others to help him put these ideas into practice.

Hence, the first international alternative service program in lieu of military service took place at Esnes, near Verdun, in 1920. Young men from various European countries performed reconstruction work under Ceresole's leadership. This resulted in the formation of *"Service Civil Internationale"* (SCI), which survived until recent times and inspired many similar organizations around the globe. SCI was known for its service work camps not only in Europe but in other parts of the world as well, including India in cooperation with Mohandas Gandhi. SCI also became the inspiration and model for the many voluntary-service organizations that sprang up in Europe after the Second World War.

Inspired by this spirit, "One of the first religious volunteer reconstruction units to serve in Europe [during World War I] was organized by the American Friends Service Committee (AFSC). Under the general direction of the American Red Cross, the AFSC sent fifty-four Quaker men and one Mennonite to Europe on September 4, 1917 to do reconstruction work in areas of France devastated by World War I. The volunteers understood that if any of the men were to be drafted [into the US army] they would return to stateside immediately."[226] These units built and repaired over five hundred homes. The program ended on April 1, 1920 with fifty-four Mennonite men having participated. The reasons that Mennonite men served in this pioneer venture was Christian service.

"During the last war [World War I] Mennonite Church leaders came more strongly to the feeling that there should be avenues available for young people which would enable them to give their talents and time to worthy projects without compulsion on the part of the state."[227] The Quaker pioneering work in relief and service in Europe subsequently inspired many religious groups, especially the "Peace Churches" to engage in voluntary service activities.

After the horrors of World War I had dimmed, the agitation for international peace and disarmament receded somewhat, though the *Fellowship of Reconciliation* and other peace movements continued to promote peace. The volunteer emphasis had taken root in the American Peace Churches, along with a shift toward including justice among their concerns, along with peace. Among the expressions for peace and harmony were "peace caravans" and work camps promoted by M.R. Ziegler, leader of the Church of the Brethren: "When I see so much that the war makers are doing and so little that the peace makers are doing, I wonder why the difference. Find me one hundred Dunkers between the ages of twenty-one and thirty who will [join a peace caravan and] give as much for peace as a soldier gives for war, and we will change the thinking of Congress in three years' time."[228]

After World War I, especially during and after the great depression, a quasi-military service-camp idea emerged in the United States with the Civilian Conservation Corps (CCC). These camps combined some of the elements of military service (such as administration and discipline) with more peacetime objectives of serving in the national interest but providing useful peace-time functions, as well as employment. The inspiration for these programs were derived partly from military service structure, but were also indebted to the moral discussions, such as that of William James, and the religious agitation for peaceful uses of human power. The work camps emerged with the same goals: "To achieve social justice without violence." [229]

Soon, during and after World War II, the flood gates to volunteering were opened. [230] The prosocial motivation in voluntary service, as a direct rejection of war as a solution to human conflict, has continued to gain traction and has been extensively treated by Charles Moskos in *The New Conscientious Objection: From Sacred to Secular Resistance*. [231]

Attempts to alleviate poverty and promote the "Brotherhood of all peoples" expanded greatly. The Society of Friends (Quakers), the Church of the Brethren, and the Mennonites were among the early proponents of the "peace caravan and work camp" idea. These efforts resulted in the development of the *Peace Corps* in the United States. [232] The Peace Corps is one of the best-known results of the volunteer-service movement, while the Peace Corps in turn contributed to many other volunteer organizations that are active today. [233]

E) Voluntary Service in Reconstruction and Development.

Another major field of socio-economic activity in the last hundred years is termed "post-catastrophe reconstruction" and "international development". Post-war reconstruction has a massive history, and it is not possible to adequately develop the topic in these pages. Development is a "fairly recent phenomenon, beginning perhaps, when the United Nations identified the 1960s as the 'first development decade'." [234] In any case, an immense number of development activities have been undertaken, especially in the interests of helping impoverished countries improve their living conditions. Most developed nations sponsor development activities, as illustrated by the Canadian International Development Agency, which allocates much of its funds through NGOs (non-government organizations).

Unfortunately, a concise definition of this sort of development has never been universally accepted: "There are many ways of describing the problem of 'development and how to get there.' What does seem to be clear is that there is no blueprint." [235] Denis Goulet has proposed that development means helping peoples achieve sustenance, self-esteem, and freedom from servitude."[236] As a process, it refers to the governmental and private organizational efforts in assisting communities and states achieve greater control of their own destinies, socially politically and economically—in other words "doing good."

The political, philosophical, and ethical implications of development have been aggressively discussed and debated. [237] One of the critical issues has been the degree to which development has been conceived, initiated, and implemented by so-called developed nations and peoples rather than involving the recipient peoples or nations in the processes. [238] There is an emerging consensus that development programs are helpful but that there is considerable "wastage." Some of the major criticisms of government-run reconstruction and development practices is that it is mounted and managed by professionals who do not identify closely with the peoples who are the recipients, and sometimes are more concerned with monetary rewards and personal achievements. [239]

The relevance of reconstruction and development to our discussion is that much of the national and international reconstruction and development work on the ground has been done by volunteers serving in religious NGOs. They are motivated by the same values and motives as service volunteers in general. [240] On the national level, the American denominational disaster service has evolved into a massive program. For example, the decedents of the Radical Reformation, namely the Church of the Brethren, Quakers, and Mennonites, have developed disaster-service programs, nationally and internationally known for their humanitarian aid and reconstruction work. [241] Other denominations are just as actively involved. In fact, all disaster-service organizations are well respected and work cooperatively with the Federal Emergency Agency (FEMA) and other governmental service organizations.

Thus, regardless of the political appropriateness of development work or meeting the global needs, especially in preventing disasters, reconstruction and development service is motivated by prosocial concerns, and though it is largely unrecognized nationally, it is profoundly appreciated by the recipients who are helped. [242] All that being said, because of its massive scale, organization, and sponsorship, this aspect of service is not one that can be pursued further here. We are concentrating on the far-reaching, interpersonal, grass-roots humanitarian service that does not make the headlines.

Some non-Western religions and faiths, such as those of many African and Asian nations and the indigenous people of North America, include nature in their "love one's neighbor as one's self" cosmologies. Their individual and group salvation includes nature in its reverence and faith. Increasingly, these religions have been more constructive in producing a holistic love of neighbor, since it is now increasingly accepted that one cannot love the neighbor without including love of nature in the formula. [243] No one has been more emphatic and articulate than leading environmentalist Thomas Berry. However, this issue cannot be ignored in any comprehensive discussion of the "peaceable kingdom." The Radical Reformation tradition has long been involved in prosocial voluntary service, but it is slowly giving thought and action to including the connection between humans, nature, and environmental sustainability by including the "redemption" of humanity and stewardship of nature in its theological structure. [244] "God's purpose in Christ is to heal and bring to wholeness not only persons but the entire created order. For God was pleased to have all his fullness dwell in him, and through him to reconcile to himself all things." [245] The next frontier in Christian thinking regarding good service is bringing nature on the stage as the director of the narrative.[246]

F) Voluntary Prosocial Service and the Ubiquitous Gap: A Brief Re-statement of the Thesis

Philosophical traditions in America and elsewhere have proposed that there are dimensions of good and bad in many human actions and relationships. **"The theory of good and evil crosses the boundaries of many sciences or subject matters. It occupies a place in metaphysics. It is of fundamental importance in all the moral sciences — ethics, economics, politics, and jurisprudence. It appears in all the descriptive sciences of human behavior,**

SECTION I. THE CONCEPT OF DOING GOOD AND SERVICE

such as psychology and sociology, though there it is of less importance and is differently treated." [247]

Robert Redfield, American anthropologist-philosopher, long taught a seminar on Social Ethics at the University of Chicago, which specifically analyzed the problem of good and evil in human society. "The social structure can be seen as an ethical system. It is an orderly arrangement of conception as to what good conduct is the ideal, the desired, the expected."

This laconic statement by Robert Redfield referred to this ethical system as the "great tradition." A few sentences later, Redfield presents the other side:

"To describe the social structure [the ideal] is one thing; to describe the usual social conduct of its people is another thing." Redfield then continues to describe and analyze the ubiquitous gap between the great tradition (the aspirations of the people) and the failures (evil). But the closest he comes to explaining how the negative or "evil" emerges is to say that "The social structure seems to be a set of ethical paradigms...an ideal system of demands that men can follow only if all things go as the social structure provides." [248]

But things rarely do go that way. Somebody acts in a negative way and begins a chain of consequences in the course of which other men are forced to make decisions with ethical consequences. Redfield proposed that the reasons for "deviance" are conflicts between rules of specific roles, or conflicts between the ethical rules themselves. [249] Redfield avoids a "spiritual" answer to the causes for the "falling short of the ideal," but clearly believes that ethical behavior is aimed at closing the gap between the ideal and the real.

A more pragmatic approach to the gap between the ideal and the real is proposed by Danzig and Szanton, who assume that there are needs that the public is not willing to pay for. "Needs currently unmet must, by definition, be needs that neither the marketplace nor our political processes have so far found more pressing than other claims on private or public resources." [250] These "unmet needs", which the authors define as the benefits minus the costs (for example the jobs that voluntary service takes from workers) thus forms the rationale for "filling the gap" that exists (in the prevailing economic and political system in the United States) between the ideal and the real. In other societies, different assumptions and values would provide the basis for filling the gap between the ideal and the real.

The literature on this topic is extremely complex. We deal with it more extensively in chapters 8 and 9, where we present the contribution that Radical Reformation have made. The issue of the "needs" that must to be filled to achieve any type of acceptable body politic thus demands sociological, philosophical, theological, and ethical paradigms, whose role it is to explain the meaning of reality and the source of good and evil.

This brings us to the basic foundation of doing good voluntarily, as understood in the West and especially in the Christian community. There will always be people in need and suffering, expressed in different ways in every culture. It was stated as a universal fact when Jesus famously said, "The poor will always be with us." [251] Giving a "cup of cold water" is a universal axiom that speaks to this issue. And we maintain that prosocial service is reflected in the "second mile" spirit of Jesus—responding to the humanly created flawed social, political, and economic systems. The poor and weak have always been unable to compete or achieve, for many reasons, including personal, family, community, economic, political, and religious factors. [252] We want to be very clear that "the poor are always with us" is not a justification for inaction but rather a call for continual prosocial service!

Our thesis, which was presented in chapter 1, is now expanded to include these ethical terms: *In all socio-political-economic systems, the "going the second-mile" response is inherently required as the glue that keeps any system from collapsing under its own weight of inefficiency, competition for goods, greed, cruelty, and finally "evil," that is, unjust actions and structures.* [253] There is no doubt that prosocial service was no less needed in the former Communist Soviet Union than in today's socialist Sweden or Great Britain, or than is needed in the market capitalist society in the United States. [254] In every society at every time there is the opportunity and the need for a good Samaritan to help someone. [255]

A graphic example of the gap is described in a recent study of the impact of hurricane Katrina in the United States:

SECTION I. THE CONCEPT OF DOING GOOD AND SERVICE

"Then Katrina hits. They are lucky, as their children move in quickly to evacuate with them to a public shelter. But they have never been in such a place and feel uncomfortable among thousands of strangers. Though there is adequate food, it is unfamiliar and at times hard to digest. A volunteer comes by and encourages them to get on the Internet (something they have never done) to view the damage. As they watch, the maps zoom in, and they realize with dismay that water has claimed their home. She leans over, exhausted, and he hangs his head in disbelief. Anxiety increases, and before they even leave the shelter, he is taken by ambulance to the hospital and then transferred to a nursing home. Through a combination of insurance, federal funds, and donations to the community, the couple's local recovery committee brings in a volunteer team to clear debris, gut the house, and start repairs. The gap between recovery and permanent displacement narrows, because volunteers cut the cost through contributing personal labor." [256]

Each religious tradition has defined this social obligation in its own way. It is difficult to present a unified description of the various Christian denominational views of theological salvation, which is often referred to as *The Kingdom of God*, or as prosocial behavior in sociological terms. [257] One leading interpretation, of the Radical Reformation Churches, holds that the community that developed around the historical Jesus was motivated by the "Good News"— a new way of relating justly to others in community. "You know that the rulers of the Gentiles lord it over them. It shall not be so among you. But whoever would be first among you must be your slave… even as the Son of Man; came not to be served, but to serve, and to give his life as a ransom for many." (Matt 20:25 RSV) [258]

In this re-conceptualizing of power, recalling the earlier discussion of the four options available, Jesus constructs a new community based in the inversion of the customary understanding of social status. In the spirit of the Sermon on the Mount, the new way of life offers robust irony in dealing with others:

- Forgiveness for offenders

- Radically democratize leadership

- Build a new society rather than destroy a corrupt one

- Universal equality

Jesus did not bring a new religious symbol, ritual, code, theory of God, or dogma; rather, Jesus brought a new way of understanding others and living together. Unlike the other revolutionary approaches, Jesus was willing to associate with "the impure, the sinner, the publican, and the Roman."[259]

One way of expressing this is to say that Jesus brought an ethic of justice, not a cosmogony or metaphysics. The rewards are not the Good News; they are *products* of the Good News, though they are often confused. The ethics lead us to build the New Kingdom by thinking and acting in new ways in the process of social interaction—in the process of the revolution itself. The desired end is built during the process of revolution. In more contemporary terms, the New Kingdom provides a new understanding of social responsibility that institutionalizes moral responsibility outside the political state—a just society.

This proposition illustrates the new understanding of causality: **Injustice increases the injustice; prosocial service reduces the gap and assists justice. Only with justice is peace possible.**[260] The New Kingdom is a renewed way of living in the present (I Cor. 7:20) marked by the servant-hood example and teaching of Jesus. This is called "revolutionary subordination", which asks of the disciple to live without resentment and that the person in the super-ordinate position must denounce the domineering use of power and social status.[261] John Howard Yoder, echoing similar claims made earlier by Mahatma Gandhi and many who participated in the nonviolent struggle for civil rights in the United States, summarizes the new gospel: "The willingness to suffer is then not merely a test of our patience or a dead space of waiting; it is itself participation in the character of God's victorious patience with the rebellious powers of his creation."[262]

This ethical irony of Jesus' teaching and life-example was transmitted into the early church and recovered prominently by the Radical Reformation. [263] Rooted in love, subordination is different from obedience: "Love does no harm." [264] Obedience to unjust laws, such as laws supporting slavery, harms people. Jesus' radical position is not rooted in brute force or retribution (an eye for an eye) but is exercised in irony and being open and vulnerable: "But I say to you. Love your enemies, and pray for those who persecute you, so that you may be sons of your Father who is in heaven." (Matt 5:39 RSV) These empathic relations extend beyond accepted status distinctions and reorder human relations with disregard for status. The question is not whether or not the new kingdom is coming, but what we do about it here and now.

Summary and Conclusion

Without delving into the theological differences and emphases, we accept the essentials of the Christian spiritual life and social responsibility as evidenced by the expression of various Christian humanitarian organizations—most broadly the prosocial service foundation. [265] Thus, most denominations have developed a deeply held pro-social and humanitarian service commitment. These are illustrated in the following groups: American Friends Service Committee (Quakers); Brethren Service Commission; Church World Service (composed of thirty-seven Coptic, Catholic Orthodox, Protestant etc. communions); Islamic Relief, USA; Lutheran World Service (The Lutheran Church); (CARITAS) Roman Catholic Church; Universalist-Unitarian Service Commission; Mennonite Central Committee; and the Salvation Army. These are only a sampling. Further, many internationally renowned relief and service organizations have emerged from religious Christian impulses such as CARE, OXFAM, and the Red Cross.

Numerous studies have been produced that analyze and evaluate humanitarian efforts. One such is Thomas H. Jeavons' book, *When the Bottom Line is Faithfulness*, which evaluates the effectiveness and integrity of seven charitable humanitarian service organizations. [266] It is literally impossible and unproductive to attempt to describe accurately the depth and breadth of this plethora of humanitarian agencies, and to analyze these many religious (not necessarily Christian) efforts, this "second mile" thesis, on a comprehensive scale. Appendix A presents a basic review on the variety of service organizations and some statistical information to demonstrate how extensive and diverse the humanitarian drive in the West has been. Additionally, its persistence is because of the gap between what the socio-political-economic structures and systems intend to provide and the concrete needs of the people, because the "poor are always with us." Jevons' study, and many others, point to the similarity in goals and structures of prosocial voluntary service in concrete and revealing ways as the path to justice.

CHAPTER 4.
Science and Prosocial Forces

> *Scientific solutions, in the long run, carry with them their own compulsions for acceptance. The demonstrated superiority of scientific methods has been in the last analysis, the major reason why they have triumphed over the vested interests that opposed science."*
>
> -- George Lundberg [267]

Aliens from space are commonly depicted as threatening and violent. But it is probable that this violent theme is merely a projection of the hostile fears that inform the denizens of planet earth itself. [268] However, the various sciences have observed that many individuals, on the contrary, often engage in prosocial behavior, loving their neighbors and many times risking their own lives for them. [269]

To underscore these antisocial perspectives, a number of recent studies report how violent humans really are. For example, primatologist Michael Ghiglieri, in *The Dark Side of Man*, argues that "warmongers lurk in every human landscape." Lawrence Keeley, in *War before Civilization*, argues that warfare is ancient and widespread. And finally, in *Evolutionary Psychology*, David Buss contends that warfare is pervasive across all cultures worldwide.

However, in stark contrast, there are more optimistic scientific narratives. While violence tends to grab the headlines, according to anthropologist Douglas Fry, "violence constitutes only a minute part of social life. To focus too much attention on aggression is to totally miss the 'big picture'." [270] According to Fry, "the anthropological data do not support the validity of a…bellicose human nature for war." [271] The scientific debate continues, but there is strong and pervasive evidence that serving the neighbor is gaining and deserves increasing attention.

Based in comparative, cross-cultural studies, Robert Hinde assures us that humans "have propensities to behave pro-socially and cooperatively, with kindness and concern for others." He continues, reiterating almost word-for-word, our thesis: "Social life would not be possible if these prosocial tendencies did not predominate over selfish assertiveness and aggressiveness." [272] It is important to challenge the self-fulfilling war prophesy, as conflict scholar William Ury expresses:

> "Perhaps the principle obstacle to preventing destructive conflict lies in our own minds—in the fatalistic beliefs that discourage people from even trying. The story that humans have always warred, and always will, is spread unchallenged from person to person and from parent to child. It is time…to question and refute this story and its embedded assumptions about human nature. It is time to give our children—and ourselves—a more positive picture of our past and our future prospects." [273]

We can choose.

A) Social Science Perspectives

From the social scientific point of view, there is intimate intertwining and interdependencies between competition, conflict, domination, oppression, enslavement, conquest, war, and murder—the antisocial. Cooperation, mutual assistance, deference, service, and sacrifice—the prosocial—remain one of the major enigmas of human history. As indicated in chapters 1-3, the nature and problems of *good and evil* informed the early Greek philosophers and political thinkers, the Jewish religion, and the Eastern religions and

SECTION I. THE CONCEPT OF DOING GOOD AND SERVICE

philosophies, including Confucianism, Taoism, and Buddhism. Most world religions and philosophical proposals have produced texts and prophets that weighed in heavily for love, justice, mercy, and righteousness, which was used to protest and resist the ever-present exploitation and miss-use of the neighbor.

1. *Historical and Philosophical Perspectives*

From the Jewish point of view, scholar Kass has proposed that it was the giving of the "Noahide law" that set humanity on a prosocial direction:

> "The institution of [Noahide code/law] transforms the human world, and thereby the world altogether. It creates new relationships between man and animals, man and man, and the cosmic order, and between each man and himself. It requires and promotes new powers of mind and heart. It makes possible a new form of sociality, civil society, founded on shared explicit expectations and agreed-upon notions of justice and punishment. Precisely as it restrains human impulses, it liberates human possibility." [274]

However, Kass also observes that the Noahide code and law was basically negative, though it paved the way for the positive Decalogue to emerge later. The general discussion by leading scholars maintains that human society has produced two major streams of social thought, each of which emphasize a single theme. The first theme emphasizes the struggle for dominance of some over others, while the second theme emphasizes cooperation.[275]

The concern with the good is exemplified by the early Greek philosophers, such as Aristotle, who promoted the principle that "Every art and every inquiry, and similarly every action and pursuit, is thought to aim at some good; and for this reason the good has rightly been declared to be that at which all things aim."[276] This philosophical tradition has produced an enduring discussion, proposing assumptions and theses upon which an analysis of human society can be evaluated and should operate. But the understanding of good was also not consistent.[277]

As noted earlier, a very influential theoretical-ideological system emerged, which accepts the drive for domination, violence, and exploitation of others as innate to human nature. This provided the basis for the *struggle-competition* school of Western thought, described by intellectual giants such as Thomas Hobbes, Niccolo Machiavelli, Charles Darwin, Sigmund Freud, J. Novicow, Karl Marx, and Adam Smith, to name only a few.[278] Some theoretical thinkers who helped pioneer the sociological tradition suggest that human beings, and the structures they create, are basically antagonistic and antisocial, and if left unchecked, will destroy each other. The following quote by Hobbes (1588-1679) illustrates the antisocial thesis:

"So that in the first place, I put for a general inclination of all mankind a perpetual and restless desire of power after power, that ceaseth only in death." [279] Hobbes concludes that this exercise of power over others for his own benefit will injure his fellows: "Competition of riches, honour, command or other power inclineth to contention, enmity and war, because the way of one competitor to the attaining of his desire is to kill, subdue, supplant, or repel the other." This will result in resentment and hatred. "He must expect revenge or forgiveness, both which are hateful." [280]

Because of this "hopeless conundrum," Hobbes proposed the "social contract," which he believes is the only way out of this dilemma: "Fear of oppression disposeth a man to anticipate or to seek aid by society; for there is no other way by which a man can secure his life and liberty." The social contract suggests that each human can achieve his own selfish and aggressive ends only by agreeing to relinquish control over some of these "urges" to the common will (society), thereby becoming protected from the same ravages of others. That this interpretation is based on a negative self-preservation motive rather than a moral or ethical one is rather obvious and distressing. [281]

One of Hobbes' most important descriptions of the essential nature of human beings is his analysis of the role that desire and power play in human behavior. Hobbes posits that human nature has an unquenchable desire "from one object to another. The cause whereof is that the object of man's

SECTION I. THE CONCEPT OF DOING GOOD AND SERVICE

desire is not to enjoy once only, and for one instant of time, but to assure forever the way of his future desire. And therefore the voluntary(!) actions and inclinations of all men tend not only to the procuring, but also the assuring of a contented life."[282]

It is this need for an assurance that desires will be satisfied that Hobbes attributes to the issue of power: "So that in the first place, I put for a general inclination of all mankind a perpetual and restless desire of power after power, that ceaseth only in death. And the cause of this is not always that a man hopes for a more intensive delight, but because he cannot assure the power and means to live well, which he hath present, without the acquisition of more."[283] Based on this interpretation of man's basic motivation, Hobbes continues: "The right of nature, is the liberty each man hath to use his own power as he will himself for the preservation of his own nature (i.e. his own desire); that is to say of his own life; and consequently of doing anything which, in his own judgment, and reason, he shall conceive to be the aptest means thereunto."[284]

It is clear from this construction that human beings would thus be in a continual struggle (more commonly described as a war of all against all) with others in the satisfaction of personal desire. He states, "Hereby it is manifest that during the time men live without a common power to keep them all in awe, they are in that condition which is called war; and such a war as is of every man against every man."[285] Hobbes concludes that if every person were to give up a certain amount of personal rights, and everyone else would do the same, then where would be a possibility of peace. It is here that a subtle yet significant shift occurs for another view of human society.

Hobbes resorts to the biblical record and suggests that this demands nothing short of the "Law of the Gospel: Whatever you require that others should do to you, that do ye to them."[286] Hobbes states that voluntarily giving up some individual rights is based upon the hope that the other person would do the same, which then would provide security for both (or all, if everyone were to engage in it). "The motive and end for which this renouncing and transferring of right is introduced is nothing else but the security of a man's person, in his life. The mutual transferring of right which men call contract."²⁸⁷

John Locke (1632-1704), born about thirty years after Hobbes, expanded on Hobbes thesis and developed the idea of a civil society. Beginning with pre-history, Locke assumes that humans were organized sequentially into a variety of forms, from the family to the extended family, developing into organizations including vast variations from siblings, clans, to tribes: "Thus the natural fathers of families, by an insensible change, became the politic monarchs of them too...[and] laid the foundations of hereditary or elective kingdoms under several constitutions and manors, according to chance, contrivance or occasions happened to mold them."²⁸⁸

With the formation and evolution of "larger groups and collectives", a number of structural types emerged, namely priestly orders, monarchies, oligarchies, religious-political states, dictatorships, and finally (in recent centuries) democracies. ²⁸⁹ In the "state of nature," each person, to protect his own interests, was forced to act in her own interest; this resulted in the "law of the jungle." Locke defined it in this way: "All government in the world is the product only of force and violence, and that men live together by no other rules but that of beasts, where the strongest carries it [laying] a foundation for perpetual disorder and mischief, tumult, sedition and rebellion, a total lack of control of human urges and aggression and violence."²⁹⁰ Locke developed Hobbes' famous dictum that "human history is the naked and brutal struggle," into his theme of civil society and proposed that the beginning of "politic society depends upon the consent of the individuals to join into and make one society (and) when they are thus incorporated, might set up what form of government they thought fit," and thus be protected from each other in the state of nature. In this form, the individuals give up the rights inherent "in nature" and allowed the civil society to apply the rules and regulations of that society, arrived at by majority approval. This protected each person from the aggression of the other.

This counter thesis—the concept of human duty to give up personal rights for the sake of the community—began to increasingly interest and intrigue social philosophers. Immanuel Kant (1724-1894) is well known for the role of duty, which he defines as an absolute moral obligation, which he maintains is a universal law.[291] He states, "It is a duty to do good to other men according to our power, whether we love them or not, and this duty loses nothing of its weight, although we must make the sad remark that our species alas! is not such as to be found particularly worthy of love when we know it more closely." Then he provides a psychological reward and even justification for exercising the moral duty, which rings true everywhere: "Beneficence is a duty. He who often practices this, and sees his beneficent purpose succeed, comes at last really to love him who he has benefited."[292]

2. Recent Sociological Perspectives

One major approach to understanding the conflict is to assume that humans have a natural self–interest, which provides the basic motivation for social and economic action. This perspective has become an ideology and the main bulwark of modern free-market capitalisms. Among the recent propositions is rational-choice theory, which proposes that all humans ultimately make decisions based on the best "cost-benefit" equation. This has been popularized by the Nobel Prize winner Gary S. Becker.[293] It has been widely criticized, but in a subtle way is a major boost for the defenders of free market capitalism. This theory is valuable in that it is candid about the understanding of "human nature," which many of the social philosophers discussed above also assumed but did not have the scientific documentation to make it a more convincing argument.

Modern social-science theorizing has accepted the idea that "social evolution" has produced the conditions to accept the benefits of civil society. Many other theories concerning human nature and the civil society, including the concept of natural law, and the derivative "basic human rights" have been proposed.[294] Possibly, as at least a partial reaction to the domination school, there is also a long tradition that has emphasized the reality and importance of nurturing love in the human community, expressed in concepts such as sympathy, empathy, compassion, cooperation, agape (Greek for self-giving love), mutual aid, altruism, helping, and sharing, often called the *"sociologistic school."*[295]

The idea of voluntarily giving up personal rights in the "state of nature," as the only way to be assured of protection from the aggressive rights of others, is a major insight. But the dubious assumption that it can be voluntarily done continues to face a huge hurdle: believing and trusting that the other people would also give up their "natural rights." How this social contract could emerge in situations where individuals or groups existed in a state of nature, in which self-defense was the way of survival (to protect and respect the individual rights of each individual vis-a-vis others), is an even greater mystery.[296]

Sorokin believes "There is no doubt that, side by side with the phenomena of the struggle for existence, there exist the phenomena of mutual aid, cooperation, solidarity, and ultimately compassion. These phenomena, although in opposition to the struggle for existence and domination of others, are as general in human and the animal world as the relations of antagonism and war."[297] Ironically, from a philosophical point of view, some claim that *conflict* and *mutual aid*, serve to complement each other, but this point cannot fully be explored here.[298] Briefly, the tradition dating back to at least James Madison accepts that productive conflict is the engine that drives a healthy democracy. That is, ontologically speaking, both interpretations reflect the nature of human reality, and each are resultant from the existence of the other. Even logically, these two states cannot exist without each other (i.e. dominance implies subservience, whether willing or unwilling as Hegel brilliantly described). We can therefore assume that prosocial behavior has somehow emerged and flourished because of the existence of antisocial behavior, namely that of selfishness, domination, subordination, exploitation, and oppression of others. We suggest, but cannot further explore here, that the irony of unintended consequences drives and is derived from this tension between prosocial and antisocial behaviors and attitudes.

Therefore, it is equally convincing to argue that the existence of either prosocial or antisocial behavior somehow causes the emergence of the other?[299] The contemporary academic field of sociology has produced a variety of sub-fields and the closest area related to the concept of voluntary service is voluntary association and voluntary organizations. However, the idea of serving others as considered here has unfortunately remained remarkably underdeveloped.[300] How and why the competing forces of exploitation of others and compassion have emerged and operated in human history has never been persuasively answered, even though most religions are based on a "cosmology" that attempts to explain it. [301]

To restate, but not completely answer, the ultimate question that has perplexed humanity throughout history is: *Why should a person or group feel sympathy and compassion for others, or rather, why should a person or group not live basically for the welfare of the self or the group?* Almost all cosmologies or mythologies, religious or not, begin with stories of the conflict between good and evil—usually referencing a "golden age" that was later contaminated. As late as the 1970s, the *indigenes* (natives) in the Paraguay Chaco recited stories to the senior author of how the world was created. One tribe's (*Nivakle*) account states that "The earth was nauseated at the filth and stench (of man's habitation). The heavens fell upon the earth and covered everything up. Only one family that had fled to the safety of a large tree was saved."[302] We do not struggle with the display of prosocial behavior of a mother for her child, or a family member for another family member. What is more perplexing is why a stranger would choose prosocial behavior over antisocial behavior? We slowly and ambiguously explore this question as we proceed.

3. Religion and Conflict

It is widely recognized that the violence found in the Old Testament story was a major problem for most Christian traditions. Scholars are becoming more convinced that the Old Testament reflects a cosmology based in retributive justice and practice, and evolved, reflecting new conceptions of justice that developed as prophets proposed a counter-vision of compassion and love—procedural and distributive justice.[303] It should be noted that, according to Kass, *eye for an eye* retributive justice was meant to positively *limit* retribution, to make sure that (at the very least) it would not add more harm. The apparent success of the prophets' appeals to modify the Old Testament cosmology is intriguing. In contrast to the Torah and 'the law," the New Testament and the early Christian church predominantly rejected the degrading domination or oppression of others as a natural state of humans, as recorded in the Old Testament, and emphasized instead the sympathy, empathy, and love of the neighbor promised in the New Testament. The love of the neighbor, through the modification of the meaning of justice, represents a substantial shift. While not yet fully developed and realized, retributive justice is diminishing, and procedural and distributive (sometimes called social) justice is being further explored.

This tension between the two forces was increasingly illustrated in the West in the warfare between the Christian West and Islam of the Middle East.[304] It continued with successive internal social and political upheavals of the Renaissance and Reformation periods, illustrated by horrible religious wars that lasted for decades. As periods of peace emerged, giving people time to reflect, the scholarly community, increasingly freed from religious auspices and dominance (i.e. dogma and theology), began to recognize that there were some very strong forces operating in human society, namely selfishness, greed, aggressiveness, the struggle for power, domination, oppression, and exploitation, or even extermination, but increasingly countered by forces of social compassion and healing.[305]

The breadth and depth of this religious theological and social dialogue on conflict still persists. It hardly needs to be repeated that many wars in history were motivated by religious factors. In any case, many explanations and rationalizations of the religious antisocial and prosocial forces in human history have been proposed, and it is not possible to enumerate them or evaluate them adequately. The argument of the Anabaptist traction eschewing violence in any form is one example of the many religions that promote this perspective.

B) Natural Science Analysis of the Prosocial and Antisocial Polarity

To restate and briefly summarize the distinction between the natural sciences—with a preference for a single cause—and the type of social sciences we support which view humans as mailable and having predispositions, formed by nature, nurture, and by their own learning and agency—determinism and free will intersect and interact. Among the central concerns that have occupied the reflections on the reality of these two forces and traditions have been these questions: Is there not an original or natural human nature that causes persons to help and love other humans, or on the other hand, to exploit and subordinate them? If not, why do people take either stance?[306] The available records dating back to antiquity document the fact that the antisocial forms of aggression, violence, and oppression have always been present, but are not the only forms of human behavior. Prosocial forces counter these negative forces. However, given the possible resources and tools of force, it is now increasingly more urgent to acknowledge and promote prosocial forces.

The present growing drive to understand human behavior has been most clearly expedited by the emergence of centers of learning and universities in many nations, and even more importantly, as a result of economic surplus and general wealth in many societies.[307]

Several major "causes" of human behavior have been promoted: training, environment, and heredity. Each view has developed strong supporters and evidence. At one time or another, each of these has been promoted as the sole causative determiner for human behavior, which has resulted in loss of credibility. This mode incidentally tends to corroborate the time-tested axiom that any proposition or position driven to its extreme becomes a heresy.

There is an enormous amount of research being done, and literature being written, in this burgeoning field. Over time, we started to understand that human behavior can be determined by chemical, biological, and even genetic factors. There is now robust discussion of a "selfish gene" which explains human behavior.[308] This position states that behaviors are determined by biology and genes and transmitted and accentuated through natural selection. This direction of research has developed some intriguing and instructive insights, though the empirical proof is still open to debate. After reviewing the extant research on this subject, Samir Okasha states, "…However, human behavior is obviously influenced by culture to a far greater extent than that of other animals and is often the product of conscious beliefs and desires (though this does not necessarily mean that genetics has no influence).

Nevertheless, at least some human behavior does seem to fit the predictions of evolutionary theories reviewed above."[309]

Ironically, however, no consensus on the essential nature of the human being (biologically, socially, culturally, or otherwise) conclusively emerges. In fact, there seems to be growing doubt as to whether a definitive understanding of "human nature" will ever be achieved. As indicated above, human nature is now thought to be a vast and complex configuration of biological, chemical, and genetic factors (i.e. nature) interacting with the vastness of experiences and environment of the human individually, and the group itself through the emergence of culture (nurture).

Still, the exact role that either or both plays remains unresolved. Classically, this is stated by Miller: "The nature of human nature has been debated since antiquity. Since humans are capable of both good and evil behaviors and amply exhibit both types, and since it is conceptually and ethically impossible to conduct an appropriate experiment to resolve the issue, the nature of human motivation will no doubt be debated for many more centuries."[310] This raises a logical question: Can a subject analyze an object (totally objectively) when both are the same entity?"[311]

However the issue of nature versus nurture is ultimately resolved, one still cannot solve the problem of the *origins of motivation* for pro-social and anti-social behavior based on biology alone A vast number of factors are non-biological, according to scientists (as noted above). Finally, an added problem complicates things even further: Which comes first, or which is more determinative, heredity or environment?[312] Human behavior, regardless of whether it is environmentally, biologically, or pedagogically determined, or the extent to which individuals have agency, has both prosocial and antisocial attributes.

A relatively recent statement, by the eminent sociobiologist W.C. Allee, presents this general conclusion regarding these two forces:

> "The conclusion that emerges from cumulative studies of social biology is that co-operation and its opposite, dis-operation, both exist. There are egoistic and altruistic

tendencies in nature, and both are important. Considering the evidence available, contrary to Herbert Spencer and the conclusions of Social Darwinism, the co-operative forces are biologically and sociologically the more important and vital. The balance between the co-operative, group-centered tendencies and those that are dis-operative and egoistic is relatively close. Under many conditions, the co-operative forces lose. In the long run however, the group-centered more altruistic drives are the stronger."

Allee concludes, "If co-operation had not been the stronger force, the more complicated animals, whether arthropods or vertebrates, could not have evolved from simpler forms and the more complex social levels could not have arisen and persisted. Finally, the weight of the evidence from the sociology of other animals strongly indicates that, despite many appearances to the contrary, human altruistic drives are as firmly based on an animal ancestry as is man himself."[313]

This stream of thinking leads one to believe that it is reasonable to accept the conclusion of W.C. Allee's above statement, that there have been at least as many expressions of altruism in human history as the opposite. This is succinctly described by E. Gil Clary, in a helpful discussion entitled *Altruism and Helping Behavior*. While human beings are clearly capable of extreme cruelty and violence toward their fellow human beings, people also display extraordinary acts of kindness, generosity, and sacrifice on behalf of others. Amidst the horrors of Nazi cruelty, which dominated Europe, were cases of Gentiles rescuing and hiding Jewish victims of the "Final Solution". In 1992, in the riots sparked by the verdicts of the four Los Angeles policemen involved in the Rodney King beating, we saw four black men and women rescue a white truck driver being beaten by a group of black youths.[314]

From a natural-science perspective, prosocial behavior (as a characteristic of human behavior) has been understood as rooted in evolutionary determinism, and thus a major factor upon which culture depends. "Helping behavior has been explained within a variety of theoretical frameworks, among them evolutionary psychology, social learning, and cognitive development. One socio-biological approach maintains that helping behavior and altruism have developed through the selective accumulation of behavioral tendencies transmitted genetically. Three mechanisms have been suggested: kin selection, reciprocal altruism, and group selection."[315]

At present, it can be argued that the major scientific paradigm of human history is the evolutionary idea of survival of the species, which includes the altruistic tendency, but the role of culture continues to "temper" the genetic conclusions, since human motivation continues to confuse the issue. "The key point to remember is that biological altruism cannot be equated with altruism in the everyday vernacular sense. Biological altruism is defined in terms of fitness consequences, not motivating intentions."[316]

The predominant contemporary drift tends to be reducing the causes of human nature to the physical, biological, and evolutionary realities. The hereditary sources of human behavior have received renewed attention with the disciplines of evolutionary biology and sociobiology, which have focused on the biological and genetic evolutionary sources of animal and human social behavior. "Very recently, however, we have begun to see empirical findings that demonstrate the importance of natural selection in explaining cultural myths, taboos, or practices. Perhaps the most important of these is the powerful taboo (West Africa) against eating newly ripened yams. It provides an archetype of self-denying behavior of a sort essential for the survival of human cultures." So, we may not need to resolve the exact cause of human behavior in order to maintain that two opposite behaviors exist simultaneously in humans.[317]

C) Capitalism and Prosocial Action: A Special Problem

Capitalism has become a dominant ideology and socio-economic engine in modern times, especially in the United States, it deserves some special attention in regard to prosocial and antisocial life. Capitalism has been proposed as a solution to the problems of economic life, including production and distribution, but its social contract seems to not have functioned well enough to seem fair to many as wealth is disproportionately concentrated.

SECTION I. THE CONCEPT OF DOING GOOD AND SERVICE

To protect those who cannot compete, other systems, organizations, and programs are struggling to co-exist with it. Perhaps an even more disconcerting thought emerges in the context of a capitalist economic system and its close association with war and violence. Who profits from aggression and war? Direct military spending by the federal government accounts for approximately one fourth of the U.S. budget.[318]

More than half of *Fortune* magazine's Top 100 companies are directly involved in defense production.[319] In a capitalist system, anytime the citizens are asked to approve a war, the question of benefits to private industry is relevant. Richard Rubenstein, Professor of Conflict Resolution and Public Affairs at George Mason University, asks: "Who stands to gain from war? How many military careers, civilian jobs, executive salaries, and stockholder dividends hang in the balance, as we decide whether or not to fight?"[320] Rubenstein cautions that the US economy may be so dependent on war spending that giving it up may jeopardize entire local economies. Should something as destructive as war be guided by economic interest and gain?

Thus, Mennonite economist Henry Rempel states, "There is nothing just or moral about capitalism. The driving force of the system is human selfishness."[321] He continues: "The capitalist system is like a massive eighteen-wheel truck barreling through history. It is an excessively powerful motor driven by the sum of all human selfishness. It has no brakes. The steering mechanism is clearly at fault. As a passenger on this truck, are you inclined to ask where we are going?"[322] Ironically, the ideologies of both Capitalism and Marxism (and variations of them both) have special relevance, since it is the Christian tradition, which has (in large part) been the source of values as well. The origins of these beliefs or ideologies are the only way to understand the militancy and aggressiveness of capitalism, socialism, and communism. Their evangelistic and even harsh and brutal methods in trying to impose their views on the masses reflect the Christian tradition.[323]

Capitalism has become the reigning social, economic, and political philosophy and has created many defenses and adaptations. Adam Smith's theory of the "invisible hand" in economic behavior has had very profound implications for the concept of service. Smith accepts the basic selfish and individualistic nature of humans as axiomatic, and under minimal social regulations, the basic personal self-interested motives end up working best for the common good: "By pursuing his own interest he frequently promotes that of the society more effectually than when he really intends to promote it. I have never known much good done by those who affected to trade for the public good."[324] Smith argues that those who earn a living or "trade" for the common good, ironically, seldom realize or promote public good.

This proposal to harmonize or integrate the dismal view of human nature and behavior into a positive consequence for human society is a fascinating paradigm, for it transforms the drive for self-centeredness and the exploitation of others into the "miraculous" social wellbeing of all. This theory seems to be the most ambitious attempt to solve the riddle of individual selfishness and the common good: that self- interest and struggle for self-gratification in the long run turns out for the best of all! This theory has been enthusiastically greeted by disciples who have created a vast philosophical ideology derived from this theory and in support of it, not to mention the wealth they have accrued.[325]

Most social conservatives propose that this is the historically correct view of human history, for it integrates basic (natural) selfishness into producing the common good—that individual selfishness is the law of the kingdom of peace.[326] In short, it turns the vice of self-love into the virtue of the common good.

Regarding the contemporary "stranglehold" of market capitalism on the Western mind, social commentator William Greider states that:

> "The great paradox of this economic revolution is that its new technologies enable people and nations to take sudden leaps into modernity, while at the same time they promote the renewal of once-forbidden barbarisms. Amid the newness of things, exploitation of the weak by the strong also flourishes again."[327]

SECTION I. THE CONCEPT OF DOING GOOD AND SERVICE

Empirical proof for the inability of capitalism to fully meet human needs is provided among many others, such as Charles Allan McCoy, who has marshaled comparative data on the ineffectiveness of capitalism to meet human needs, such as poverty, illness, class differences, and general well-being. When compared with other nations and economic systems the United States, the leading free-market society, demonstrates lackluster records that are indeed disturbing if not appalling.[328]

But an interesting counter-trend is appearing in the ideological discourse regarding self-interest capitalism, which has long been conveniently ignored. In his latter days, even Adam Smith became "increasingly alarmed by what Hirsch has called the "depleting moral legacy of commercial society."[329] Ironically, McCoy states that "even Smith recognized that the state was essential for providing a degree of infrastructure beneficial to the accumulations of capital, those necessary services which they could not provide for themselves or for others at a profit."[330] Smith's later (and almost embarrassed) concern seems to be derived from his belated realization that, for a market-driven society to function properly—in a positive and civilized way—it would have to maintain a high degree of collective vigilance, trust, and "propriety" with regard to its morality. Put simply, Adam Smith, the evangelist and prophet of the capitalist age, began to realize that selfishness without social constraints based on some moral code would lead to disaster. He realized that trust based on some moral system is the basic foundation of any economic system.

Smith's theory that self-interest is good, resulted in an overarching belief system that is a totally self-contained and self-justifying concrete knowledge system, attempting to prove the superiority of its position to that of any other. There is no doubt that the material, scientific, and social results of the capitalist system is unprecedented. In fact, it is precisely the overwhelming success of free-market capitalism in producing material wealth, technological breakthroughs, and the consequent development of a powerful wealthy class and the ability to wage wars that has produced so many reactions, tensions, and conflicts.[331]

One generally accepted conclusion is that the self-interest perspective of Adam Smith paved the way for the historically most violent rejection of this ideology, namely communism as introduced by Karl Marx. The creation of the growing super wealthy, and the impoverishment and inequalities of the lower classes that resulted, has created a major socialist reaction. For example, one of the most famous and consequential dictums ever uttered came from the *Communist Manifesto*: "Hitherto every form of society has been based on the antagonism of oppressing and oppressed classes. The modern laborer, on the contrary, instead of rising with the progress of industry, sinks deeper and deeper below the conditions of existence of his own class."[332] It is also generally agreed that the various applications of Marxism have (at least in some sense) derived from the teachings of Christianity regarding the concern for the weak and care for the neighbor.

Although it is clear that Marx and his disciples originally set out to bring about freedom from oppression and domination, it is equally true that the human and social cost of the Marxist visions of the good society, such as the implementation of Stalinism and Leninism are in need of critique.[333] However, in spite of all of the violence and inhumanity these forms of Marxism created, his basic contention (that human equality is not achieved through unrestricted individual freedom to pursue selfish ends) stands confirmed. Tragically, though it has been eradicated in the former Soviet Union, his analysis of capitalism's shortcomings introduced various forms of socialist and communist agitation, which is still being applied in China, North Korea, and other "satellite" nations who are still trying to free the masses from capitalistic imperialism through often violent means.

Thus, several ontological and philosophical problems connected with unrestrained free market capitalism remain and are antithetical to the broader application of prosocial action. The basic problem is well stated by Yergin and Stanislaw: "Market systems, by their very nature, confront the question of fairness. Because of their dynamics, and indeed the very nature of the incentives on which they depend for motivation, they generate a much greater range of inequality of income than more controlled societies in which egalitarian values are so strong."[334] The shortcomings of capitalism thus include the following:

SECTION I. THE CONCEPT OF DOING GOOD AND SERVICE

1) The capitalist free-market system demands a coexisting civil society that provides explicit rules and conditions, such as honesty, decency, and truth telling, in order for it to function and operate fairly. Thus, paradoxically, the emergence and functioning of capitalism demands external limits to control the excesses of capitalism, otherwise it will quickly destroy itself, as well as society itself, as Marx and others have shown.[335] But, again paradoxically, the capitalist system strives for less governmental controls, because it gives more freedom for personal accumulation.

2) Unrestricted market capitalism does not serve the best interests of all, since the basic competitive self-interest inevitably increases the gap between the successful and those who cannot compete on an equal basis (the unvirtuous circle), which incessantly increases the disparity, thus setting the conditions for distrust, deception, corruption, and oppression, finally promoting violent revolution or revolt.[336] Further recent evidence, since the global recession of 2009, makes it clear that free-market capitalism has no built-in ethic regarding its extractive assault on the environment, which ultimately may join capitalism in the undoing of our planet.[337]

3) A new unintended consequence of the contradictions of free-market capitalism is the environmental reality limiting growth. The "material" of the environment is the stuff upon which capital and capitalism are built, and only in recent decades has the reality of a limited world begun to be realized. The fact that the environment has been considered an "externality" in the cost of production is very reluctantly and painfully conceded by the proponents of capitalism as a major flaw in its paradigm. The vehemence with which this reality is being resisted is the best proof of its importance. Extracting limited capital from the environment in

the process of producing capital but not including it as a cost of production is believed only by those who have only immediate self-interest at heart and no concern about future generations. [338]

4) Finally, capitalism is not based on a moral/ethical foundation, as for example the "just price" ethic that was promoted in mercantilism. Thus, it is not concerned about the normal "anti-social" consequences of the "rational market" dynamics of supply and demand. Probably the best support that this contradiction bothers even the purest "Adam Smithers" is the fact that even Adam Smith admitted as much by stating that a society must have moral concerns about equality of distribution of wealth or it cannot function.[339] And in recent times, the increasing destruction of the environment has emerged as another reaction against the ideologies of unlimited capitalism.[340]

Nonetheless, supporters and apologists of the capitalist free-market ideology have developed an intense debate resulting in competing ideologies, such as anarchism, socialism, state capitalism. Ideologies have been defined as abstract "secularized and rational belief systems [which] embody and rest upon a unique secularization that is linked in the West to the last great revival of religious zeal, the emergence of Protestantism."[341] Ideological claims are thus dependent more on psychological and political persuasion than material facts derived from experience. Much more could be (and has been) written about capitalism. We have only acknowledged a few of the perverse consequences of capitalism and a few of the ironies and inconsistencies. We will move on.

SECTION II.
Radical Reformation Participation in Service

CHAPTER 5.
Mennonite World-Wide Service to the Neighbor

> *"Anabaptism had little to say about the great questions of faith in relation to divine acceptance. The question of the Anabaptists was, 'What does it mean to follow Christ as disciple?' Hence ethics was central in emphasis and inseparably tied to faith.*
>
> —J. Lawrence Burkholder [342]

A lively debate continues concerning the exact intent and meaning of the terms *Anabaptism* and *Mennonite;* ironically there is currently a counter discussion as to whether there is an "identity crisis".[343] Mennonite Scholar Hans-Juergen Geortz believes "The Mennonite world has found itself in deep crisis of legitimacy and identity. The Mennonites' cognitive center has dissolved and created a vacuum in to which outer, nontraditional viewpoints have flooded and are struggling with one another to become the determiner of a new center."[344]

"Crisis" may be a bit overstated. Still, a brief description of the generally accepted nature of the Anabaptist movement and its basic intentions (as understood today) is necessary to understand the values and beliefs of Anabaptism. A very condensed review of especially relevant issues of this topic follows.

The Anabaptist movement began as a specific challenge to the Zwingli-led Reformation in Switzerland and its rejection by Roman Catholic religious authorities in the 1520s. The precipitating factors included baptism of adults rather than children (hence called Anabaptists), refusal to bear arms, rejecting any involvements with or interference by the state in religious affairs, and strong emphasis on following Jesus in a life of discipleship. A strong sense of fellowship and mutuality emerged, with ultimate authority couched in the body of believers who interpreted the biblical faith in the life of the Anabaptist community. Intense persecution resulted in a dispersal into the hinterlands and centuries of living in separated enclaves, but slowly the movement reentered the mainstream world.[345]

A) History of Mennonite Service to the Neighbor

Mennonite conferences, deriving from the above tradition, have stressed strong commitment to peace, mutual aid, and economic sharing. But they have also become widely known because of their active voluntary service.[346] For example, for the last number of decades, Mennonite Disaster Service (MDS) has become a household word in many localities across the United States and Canada. MDS, composed entirely of volunteers, except for a skeleton management staff, has responded to tornado, hurricane, and other natural disasters in North America, helping to clean up and rebuild damaged homes or build new ones. One recipient, whose home was destroyed by a tornado in 1994 in Georgia, wrote, "Dear Friends, I've always believed in God and that he does answer prayers. But I have never seen him send so many angels at one time, Thank you for all your great assistance, especially the angels from Plain City, Ohio. Warmest regards, Don."[347]

Mennonites were early sponsors of voluntary service. In 1917, the Quakers provided a model for organized service programs in Europe.[348] In 1924, "Gerhard Friesen presented a paper to the Oklahoma Convention of the General Conference Mennonite Church, in which he proposed an organization to provide a practical means to live our confession of faith. Friesen relied heavily on the American Friends Service Committee (AFSC) program proposals for 1925."[349] It took some years before the first organized voluntary service project organized by Mennonites materialized. In 1935, a work camp was conducted in Chicago, led by Carl J. and Martha Landes, who had also worked for the AFSC. "The work camp was a project of a Bluffton-based Mennonite Peace Society of which Landes was executive secretary."[350] The work assisted a Mennonite mission in the inner city of Chicago, renovating buildings or doing surveys to investigate social injustices and [to] study ideas for nonviolent reform."[351]

The concept of a "term of voluntary service" was thus beginning to germinate in the Mennonite world.[352] Harold S. Bender notes that the first formal discussion of Mennonite voluntary service in the Mennonite Church (MC) "arose initially early in 1943 as the result of the request from the Virginia Conference to the Peace Problems Committee in late 1942 to provide some type of service as an alternate to civil defense work which at time was being pressed upon Virginia Mennonites by the Government Civil Defense Agency."[353] Consequently, in February, the Peace Problems Committee of the Mennonite Church requested that the Relief Committee "undertake the setting up of a program for Mennonite service units" in 1943.

The memorandum stated several principles, in addition to meeting present emergency needs: 1) we should think of a long-range program of Christian testimony; 2) we should organize Mennonite service units which will be distinctly Mennonite in their personnel, work and practice;, 3) the service should be voluntary; 4) should provide opportunity for expression of Christian faith and Mennonite practice; 5) should be initiated through our church schools and through other church organizations where there is sufficient interest and personnel to undertake it; 6) the service should utilize existing skills in the church as well as prepare them with new skills for service in the church; and 7) the units should be integrated into our whole church and missionary program.[354] The proposal was that service should become part of every aspect of life. Service should be holistic and purposeful, supported by a plan of preparation and training for service, and should be guided by principles of Anabaptism.

The next year, "voluntary service was first undertaken as a summer service program. The first unit of four worked in Chicago, May 2 to July 2, 1944, in connection with the Mennonite (MC) Mission work there. In 1945, three units were set up in connection with the Canton and Detroit city missions..."[355] The coming of World War II and the implementation of Civilian Public Service (CPS) increased attention and interest of all the Mennonite groups in voluntary service. With the beginning of the induction of many young men into alternative service, many young women felt the obligation of contributing their fair share along with the men. Thus, a number of voluntary service units for women were also established during World War II, in connection with CPS (1944, 1945, 1946).[356] These camps were established near the CPS units, to accommodate the women married to CPS men, as well as single women.

The conference of the General Conference Mennonite's had been discussing the launching of a voluntary service program that would not compete with the developing Mennonite Central Committee (MCC) program.[357] Therefore, General Conference Mennonites initiated their first voluntary service program on February 20, 1946, when nine volunteers were assigned to the Woodlawn area of Chicago doing community service work. The Mennonite Church, as indicated above, launched its program in 1948 with four volunteers who served at the Kansas City, MO. General hospital.[358] That year, the Mennonite Brethren were discussing the necessity of conducting a voluntary service program, and produced clear purposes and guidelines for such a program but an actual program did not materialize until 1960.[359] A number of smaller Mennonite denominations and conferences also launched their own voluntary service programs but cannot be listed here.[360]

Elmer Ediger states that "Functionally, voluntary service is a direct outgrowth of CPS and relief. MCC summer service units began in 1943, when some young women of our constituency volunteered to render a service in Mennonite hospitals parallel to what the young men were drafted to do."[361] These units were sponsored by local CPS units in conjunction with MCC, so the timing of MCC and MRSC work camps were practically simultaneous.[362]

Summer service units were also initiated in 1944, with two units composed of sixty-one girls. In 1945, there were five units with seventy-eight girls in the camps. Robert Kreider reports that "the great majority of the girls favor a continuation of this type of service in the future. They speak appreciatively of the opportunity to serve others in need." They also appreciated the Christian fellowship and enriching educational experiences. [363]

Rachel Goosen suggests that women's role in voluntary service has been largely overlooked: "By 1943, so many Mennonite women were requesting peace-oriented service opportunities that MCC opened an eleven-week relief training unit for women at Goshen College. The following year, MCC developed a Women's Summer Service Program at Ypsilanti, Michigan and Howard, Rhode Island, where CPS men were working in mental hospitals."[364] Not only wives and sweethearts of CPS men were encouraged to put greater emphasis on voluntary service, but single women were as well. Harold Penner reiterates that the first service camps for women "who were not part of the CPS program, were begun in 1944 at the Ypsilanti State Hospital and the State Hospital for Mental Diseases and Howard R.I."[365]

Albert Keim describes the work the CPS men were assigned, and writes, "There were also many frustrations with make-work and a lot of lost motion. The Poet Milton's line, 'They also serve who only stand and wait,' was a popular CPS phrase."[366] In informal discussions and "bull sessions" in the dormitories, there was a very general agreement that much of the work was not important, and in some cases of very little significance.

The CPS service program had grown so rapidly that, in 1946, the MCC administration proposed a survey of the CPS experience to see what its effects had been, before the program was discontinued on March 29, 1947. This extensive survey was administered to a sample of six hundred and thirty-four CPSers. "Of the total sample, 71% thought the work in CPS was generally significant, while the remainder felt it was insignificant, or they were undecided. Another question touched on using skills and abilities. Some 28% felt their skills were not used sufficiently, while 58% felt they were used "quite well." [367]

This report reflects the CPS men's awareness of their context. They were very aware of the general public's derision for the CO position. It was not popular to be a CO. Thus, the men desired to make an equivalent or even greater contribution to the nation, to show the world that the CO position was not a "slacker" position. At first glance, it seems that this was an urge on the part of the COs to serve the nation as patriotic Americans, similar to those who served in the military. This suggests a problem of interdependence of military service and voluntary service in the minds of many.

There was criticism that "CPS [is full] of men who were comfortably isolated from the suffering of war when the men in uniform were dying in supreme sacrifice." In response, Don Smucker admitted, "It is true CPS has not been as dangerous and sacrificial as the army. But, please note, this is not according to the wishes of the men themselves. By action of Congress, the men were kept away from the foreign nations where relief and reconstruction work is urgently needed. The desire to serve overseas amid danger and hardship is the ardent desire of most CPS men." [368]

This emphasis/thrust is clearly stated in the newly released film *A Life of Peace in Time of War*. [369] The film maintains that young men who wanted to do something of national importance subjected themselves to become human guinea pigs, were infected with diseases for which there were no cures, or eagerly signed up to join the smoke jumpers, etc. They wanted to show their sincerity in taking the CO position and wanted to sacrifice on par with the soldiers in the military. The public, as well as the official Mennonite evaluation of the significance of CPS, was different from CPS men's informal evaluation. The official concern about not rocking the boat regarding the US government, resulted in a muted criticism.

In addition, the objective of the Mennonite church leaders was keeping the non-resistance witness strong among the young people. Making a significant contribution to the nation was evidently not as important as making a peace witness to the state and its war machine. The research questionnaire itself, which focused largely on the "spiritual welfare and growth" of the men, and on how effective the men thought the CPS program was for expressing the non-resistant principle, contained only several questions regarding the significance of the work itself! [370]

Donovan Smucker states:

> "It would be grossly unfair to many very sensitive men in Mennonite Central Committee camps to wholly ignore their criticism of Selective Service and MCC itself. (In response to these criticisms) the National Service Board for Religious Objectors and the various administrative agencies have made numerous changes in response to these criticism, constantly seeking special projects called detached service, setting up specialized schools of relief training, rural life, Christian service, etc., within the camps, placing units outside the borders of the United States such as Puerto Rico and seeking for assignments to service in foreign lands as soon as Congress permits." [371]

One of the difficulties, Gingerich proposes, is that "It may be that it is too early to evaluate the CPS program accurately. The CPS evaluation questionnaire might be answered differently now by some of the men than it was answered in 1946." [372] The evidence tends to support his evaluation. Even some administrators of the CPS program admitted "there was considerable 'made work' and that in the closing months of the program the efficiency of the CPS labor declined." [373]

After peace was declared, MCC sponsored voluntary coeducational service units consisted of six summer units in the summer of 1947. One camp was conducted in Chuauhtemoc, Mexico, and another was conducted in Gulfport, Mississippi. This latter camp evolved into the first year-round voluntary service camp. These camps were co-ed in nature and had a large contingent of women volunteers. For example, the Gulfport VS camp served in a variety of ways in the local black community. Appropriately enough, the Gulfport VS project grew out of the CPS Camp Landon, established in 1945, which was terminated in 1947. The voluntary service idea was on the way to becoming a viable movement.

The CPS experience had taken the young men, and some women, from their home communities and helped them to look outward to a larger world—a world which proclaimed a new agenda of needs and opportunities. How would they respond? Wilfrid Unruh states that "The years [culminating in] 1945 gave rise to many questions and observations. Why not continue this service program in post-war years? What will MCC's mandate be if conscription were to end?" [374] At a special meeting of MCC, in October 1946, a "Report on Standards and Plans for a Possible Voluntary Program during 1947" was submitted to the MCC, which began by asking, "Why such a program?" The rhetorical question was answered thus:

> "We live in a world of need and confusion. A growing consciousness of the suffering, the hopelessness, and the evil of a war-torn world has caused us to become restless in our own favored situation. The realization of the love of God and the fruits of His blessings constrain us to give ourselves to a greater service of love during peace as well as war time. The Kingdom of God requires that all of its citizens serve with their time and talents."[375]

The report then proceeded to present six major aims: to provide channels of Christian Service for young people; to provide a means of testifying to the Gospel of love and non-resistance; to provide projects that will help alleviate human need, tension, and spiritual confusion; to provide an experience of internship in Christian service; to provide for the Christian servant an opportunity to express his(sic) appreciation for material, religious, and general well-being; and finally to provide an opportunity of the person serving to better understand the world of need and a clearer understanding of the "good news." [376]

A section on "Standards for Volunteers" included the following qualifications: A volunteer should be a Christian; a volunteer should give of his service without consideration of financial remuneration; should be interested in growing spiritually and in love for others; should be in good standing with his congregation; and should be willing to respect other convictions including those of other religious groups.[377]

The next section suggested some "Standards of Voluntary Service Projects," which included rendering the program in such a way that "God will be glorified," balancing the program and projects to provide as much opportunity as possible to serve for varying persons' abilities; avoiding exploitation of volunteer labor as much as possible; cooperating with government agencies wherever advisable and feasible for maximum effectiveness; using group activities to "nurture the purest Christian motivation"; and providing adequate leadership for the project and the religious and educational life of the unit. [378]

This report assumes a "Charter" of voluntary service as an "action movement" in the American Mennonite Community. This charter, created by the Mennonite Central Committee, generally represented the broad Mennonite constituency, with the provision that several of the constituent groups of MCC developed their own voluntary service organizations. They were decentralized, not because of differences in theology but because of a desire to protect denominational emphases, polity, and practices, such as "close communion", evangelical stances, attitudes toward certain behaviors, such as smoking, movies, etc. For example, the Mennonite Brethren General Conference passed a resolution in 1957, which stated, "We stand in approval of Voluntary Service whenever and wherever it remains in line with the evangelical policies of the church."[379]

This tension between preserving the pure motivation of impartial service and sharing while witnessing to the gospel with the goal of evangelizing the recipient has plagued members of the Anabaptist/Mennonite community from the early beginnings of voluntary service. Thus, in one of the first proposals for voluntary service, cited above, the second in the list of "Aims of Voluntary Service" is: "To provide a means of testifying more widely to the Gospel and its way of love and non-resistance." Point four repeats the theme: "To provide an experience of internship in Christian service in finding purer service motivation, a more effective witness..." [380]

Further, in the formative stages of the voluntary service projects, MCC sent a message with the extensive title: "Message from the Mennonite Central Committee to its Constituency Regarding Voluntary Service by our Young People in the Light of the Recent Emergency." This was adopted at MCC Special Meeting on October 7, 1950. Included in the eloquent call for voluntary service is the following statement: "Why should not all eligible young people seriously face the question before God whether they should not now offer themselves for a substantial period of direct social service, both to meet the needs of their fellow humans and to give further witness for Christ and his Gospel."[381] Soon after, in 1952, Paul Erb (an influential churchman) proposed that "every I-W will be a lay evangelist, extending the front line of Christian witness."[382] Voluntary service moved with accelerating speed, and by 1947, MCC had created a voluntary service office headed by Elmer Ediger, who had been the last director of the CPS program.[383] The Voluntary Service Report to the annual MCC meeting in 1955 presented a ten-year summary of voluntary service activities: "Since beginning of VS, most VSers have served in mental hospitals; since 1953, the trend is downward; gradual increase in participation of smaller MCC constituent groups; since 1948 the number of women in long term VS has remained around 35; after 1950 the men have reflected draft legislation; 1951 Korea legislation resulted in the 1952 1-W decision, the beginning of 1-W program in 1953 while by 1954-55 there were fewer draft calls.[384]

Meanwhile the voluntary service program in the United States and Canada expanded in types of work, number of volunteers, and number of units. Elmer Ediger, then MCC voluntary service director, describes the growth: "During 1950 the total Mennonite Voluntary Service program, aside from the regular relief program, including at least 125 one-year volunteers and 800 short term summer and winter volunteers. If we were to visualize this in an institutional figure, it would be the equivalent of a college student body of more than 300 for a nine-month terms."[385]

Ediger lists the projects, which included "orphanages, delinquent homes, prisons, mental hospitals, in mission work in the cities, mountains, and rural areas...among Europeans, the Mexican and the Paraguayan people...and in various other types of teams."[386] The types of projects, structure, and contributions they made covers the gamut of social services, and each Mennonite conference had its own program. A general overview of the development of the programs of the various groups is found in H.A. Penner's "Voluntary Service" in *Mennonite Encyclopedia*.[387] The voluntary service programs and projects for the various Mennonite groups were normally listed in the *Denominational Yearbooks*. For example, the 2001 *Mennonite Directory* lists forty-five voluntary service units in the United States, of which ten are in Canada. There were four major sponsors of voluntary service programs: the Mennonite Central Committee; The General Conference Mennonite Church; The Mennonite Church; and the Eastern Mennonite Mission.[388] The service parameters include short-term service, such as a summer or year-long commitment to several year terms. Most of the service units are in urban centers such as Winnipeg in Manitoba, and Reedley, California.

The Church Membership Profile (CMP) research of 1989, sponsored by the five major Mennonite groups, included several questions regarding voluntary service in its random interview sample. Around 6 percent of the Mennonite population had served in short-term VS, while 9 percent had served in VS or MCC overseas for more than one year. Another 14 percent had served in Mennonite Disaster Service. The responses were much higher when the question dealt with service in the local communities, in programs such as Mennonite Disaster Service, retirement homes, etc. Over 77 percent reported they had been involved in such service. This suggests that voluntary service is deeply entrenched in the life of the community.[389]

B) Voluntary Service in Paraguay: A South American Example

Gradually, the organized voluntary service programs began to be exported to other countries as well. One of the most interesting is the voluntary service program initiated by Mennonites in Paraguay. The first Mennonite settlement was the result of a migration of conservative Mennonites from Manitoba and Saskatchewan in Canada to Paraguay in the late 1920s. This group of 1,765 persons settled in the Chaco of Paraguay in order to be free from government regulations of their schools, and to be freed from compulsory military service in Canada.

A second group, numbering 1,437 persons, settled in adjacent sections of the Chaco in March 1930, coming from Russia. The Mennonite Central Committee was very helpful in negotiating with Paraguay to relocate these refugees, and then helped them significantly in becoming economically and socially established. This group had escaped Soviet Communism in Russia, and settled in Paraguay because no other country would take them. A third group of similar background was able to leave Russia as a result of the German military occupation and retreat from the western part of Russia to Germany, and arrived in Paraguay in June 1947.[390]

A major factor in the successful resettlement of these three groups of Mennonites was their philosophy of cooperation and mutual aid. All three settlements immediately established mutual-aid structures, including orphans' funds, fire insurance, dairy and produce marketing cooperatives, and even banking. In addition, beginning in 1941, MCC sent thirty volunteers to help the Mennonites in becoming established, when Vernon Schmidt was sent to Paraguay to assist John R. Schmidt, a medical doctor.[391]

As the communities flourished, a number of social and economic needs emerged, which MCC felt could best be met with the structures of voluntary service. Thus, in August of 1949, MCC sent two young men to Paraguay to service with STICA (*Servicio Tecnico Interamericano de Cooperacion*), an organization which was founded by the United States and Paraguay to assist in the technical and economic development of Paraguay.[392] Because there was a great need for a road between the Mennonite colonies and the main commercial center, Asuncion, the MCC helped in the planning and building of such a road, nearly three hundred miles long. One of the most important aspects of the assistance was the provision of some thirty young North American young men—"Pax Boys"—to help build the road by running heavy equipment, including huge earth movers. The project was begun in 1954 and completed in 1961.[393]

The Paraguayan Mennonites were duly impressed, especially with the trans-Chaco road project by *Pax* volunteers, and there were sporadic attempts to apply the principle in other areas. The specific impetus for an indigenous voluntary service program emerged when the Mennonites, in cooperation with the MCC, established a Leprosy Sanitarium at Kilometer 81, east of Asuncion. The purpose of this hospital was not only to help with the large number of lepers in Paraguay but also to thank Paraguay for having become a welcoming country (including exemption from military service) for the Mennonite refugees.

The *Gemeinde Komitee* and MCC worked together and provided some of the personnel, including Dr. John R. and Clara Schmidt, who were the leaders of this renowned project for many years. On November 6, 1956, they formally organized *Christliche Dienst* (CD) (Christian Service), reflected in a logo including a cross and a helping hand. Many young people volunteered for terms from a few months to a year in duration. The organization flourished, and by 1959, the MCC was asking the CD of Paraguay to help in other Latin American countries, such as in Chile during the major earthquake there. Paraguayan voluntary service has become a very extensive and successful program, which includes working with homeless children, in mental hospitals, and with youth career training.

In his article "Praxis: The First Act of a Diaconal Theology", Alfred Neufeld lists the extensive voluntary service organizations and projects that have been operating in Paraguay for decades, such as Kilometer 81. But he cautions that "Although there has been a most impressive diaconal praxis, almost no theological and missionary reflection has taken place that would make it fruitful to mission and service endeavors outside the immigrant community."[394] His proposition is based on the fact that it was community cooperation and mutual service that allowed the Mennonite settlement in Paraguay to succeed as a society. But Neufeld insists that even though the "praxis" of cooperation and mutual aid was extensive, the needs in Paraguay are overwhelming, and the service program needs to be expanded.

C) Voluntary Service in Europe

The Mennonite voluntary service program in Europe emerged as a result of post- World War II relief and reconstruction. In 1946, the Council of Mennonite and Affiliated Colleges (CMAC) started a Foreign Exchange Program, having become aware of the needs and opportunities in Europe due to the war's devastation. One of the first actions was to invite European Mennonite young people to study in the United States. Thus "the various

Mennonite and Brethren in Christ colleges opened their doors in the fall of that year to Mennonite young people from Europe for a year's study."[395]

This ignited the interest in more contacts with European young people, and in 1947, the CMAC sent a "group of young people from the American Mennonite colleges [that] toured Western Europe and listened to lectures arranged for them at universities in Holland and Switzerland."[396] The response was very positive, and the CMAC decided to expand the program, but strong feelings emerged that demanded more direct interrelationship and interaction between European youth and the American students. "One of the most feasible means of bringing this to pass was through the avenue of short-term reconstruction and repair projects in devastated Germany."[397] Thus, in the following year (1948), two units were set up through the co-operative efforts of the council, voluntary service administrators, MCC personnel, European Mennonites, the military government of the British and American zones, and local authorities.[398]

Concurrently, in December 1948, a "permanent" voluntary service unit was established at Espelkamp, Westfahlen, in northern Germany. This unit was the vision of a German Lutheran pastor, who envisioned a destroyed munitions bunker as a potential home for thousands of German refugees returning from the east.[399] In subsequent years, a number of the European VSers, beginning with ten volunteers in 1949, were assigned to the Espelkamp project. The project immediately attracted European youth, and a continuing stream of German, Dutch, Scandinavian, and even Spanish long-term volunteers arrived. Milton Harder, the first director, reported that by "the end of two years (1948-1950) of camp operation, ninety-five young people had helped in Espelkamp's work camp. Of these, twenty-seven were American, sixty were Germans, four came from Holland, two from France, and one each from England and Switzerland."[400]

This is not to imply that the voluntary service idea had not already taken root in Europe. There had already been some work camps operating, beginning in 1924. Under the leadership of Pierre Ceresole, the vision of international voluntary service for conscientious objectors survived during the War II years, and his vision influenced most of the work camp activities

SECTION II. RADICAL REFORMATION PARTICIPATION IN SERVICE

in post-World War II Europe.[401] But obviously the social turmoil leading up to and during World War II had slowed the development of service projects. As soon as the war was over, the work-camp movement, sponsored by a variety of organizations and traditions, gained incredible momentum in Europe (especially in Germany) and soon resulted in an association of work-camp organizations coordinated by UNESCO.

European Mennonites in France, Germany, Holland, and Switzerland had become distanced from their compatriots in North America as a result of the war. But because of the very significant relief and service the MCC had given to the refugees, including Mennonites, as well as many others who had been seriously affected by the war, the European Mennonites became reconciled with their American brothers and sisters, and offered to help in the relief and service activities where possible. In this context, the European Mennonite Voluntary Service work-camps program expanded rapidly.

On the basis of this new openness to participate, a *Mennonite Voluntary Council* was formed, representing the Mennonite churches from France, Germany, Holland, and Switzerland, with the MCC as a fifth member. The four conferences were not able to provide much financial help, but helped in the recruitment of Mennonite youth for the camps' leadership positions and other logistical issues. From the time the organization was finalized, in April of 1951, the program took off. By 1956, an average of fifteen work camps were in operation each year.[402]

The French and Swiss Mennonites withdrew from the MVS organization in 1971. The German and the Dutch Mennonites, however, continued to operate voluntary service projects, although both are operating separate programs. Reasons for the separation and terminations were differing theological emphases on whether "social service" plays any role in the witness of the Christian faith. An interesting parallel activity to the European Voluntary Service emerged in 1950, when the Frankfurt MCC voluntary service office began to consider the implications of the conflict in Korea, which was then just beginning.[403] The question of whether the European work camp program might become an alternative service option for American conscientious objectors, who were not satisfied with the rather mundane work many of them were doing in North America, energized the discussion.

In the meantime, the vision of foreign service was presented to the MCC executive committee, and an experimental project with twenty-one young conscientious objectors was sent to Europe in April of 1951. Ironically, in June of 1951, the US Congress passed the "Universal Military Training and Service Act "[404] With the experience gained in the work camps, MCC officials offered to provide young CO volunteers as volunteer labor, if the German government would provide the land and material for the construction of homes for the thousands of refugees streaming back from the East. This "long shot" idea was accepted by the German government, and the Pax program was born. Beginning in Espelkamp in April of 1951, Pax (with the cooperation of the German government) built literally hundreds of refugee homes in at least ten different locations in Germany before the program was terminated in 1975, when the refugee crisis had largely been settled. [405]

D) Summary and Conclusions

The voluntary service sector of Mennonite church life continues to expand and change. The book *Mennonite Disaster Service*, which appeared in 2014, provides the history and maturation of one major sector of Mennonite voluntary service up to the present. The motivation for service reflects the fundamental ethos of Anabaptist-Mennonite *love ethic directed by service as the path to justice*, which was stated so clearly by Burkholder in the heading of this chapter, namely the centrality of ethics, not doctrine. But the consequences for the recipients described in the book are equally impressive and inspiring. The other continuing forms of voluntary service are reported in the official reports of the Mennonite Central Committee's publications.[406]

Specific statistics on the numbers and percentages of Mennonites who now participate in voluntary service are hard to obtain. The comprehensive survey conducted by Conrad L Kanagy et. al. indicated that 73 percent of the respondents felt that "doing both evangelism and social ministry" was the "most important thing Mennonite agencies should be doing in the United

States and abroad."[407] A significant conclusion from the survey indicated that only 11 percent believed that "evangelism" alone was desirable.[408]

In his concluding paragraph, summarizing the North American voluntary service program, Penner described the concept of voluntary service:

> "(It) has gained wide acceptance in the churches as a way for persons, especially youth, to commit their lives voluntarily and sacrificially for a period of Christian service in situations of human need. As a result, significant learning about the world, the meaning of Christian discipleship and servant-hood has ensued—a process both enlightening and enriching the churches around the world."[409]

To this fine summary, we add several additional dimensions or consequences (which form the basic arguments of this book): "enlightening and enriching the churches" means 1) the fundamental changes in the world views of the participants; 2) the changes in the world views and theologies of the sponsoring congregations, especially in regards to justice issues; and 3) the increasing responsibility for the world beyond its own boundaries by "putting faith into action." [410]

In other words, an emphasis is placed on ethics rather than promoting a doctrinal or dogmatic basis for cohesion.

CHAPTER 6.
Quaker Multi-Faceted Service to the World.

Most persons familiar with the American Christian denominational family will agree that the Society of Friends, also known as Quakers, are widely known for their manifold prosocial service activities. The testimony of Quaker service, both domestic and global, is probably unsurpassed by any other group, especially when based on membership.

Although known for their modesty, it is appropriate that in 1945, Gerald Littleboy (a Quaker) more forthrightly described its achievements:

> "In its history the Society of Friends has produced many people whose lives of conspicuous service have profoundly influenced their times. John Woolman, Elizabeth Fry, Joseph Sturge, and many others would have made for themselves no claim to a special dedication to service, but they were none the less able, out of the depth of their love for their fellows, to take great opportunities that came to them" [411]

The source of this expression of human service "sprang directly out of their religious faith, but ... was itself stimulated and fostered by the religious atmosphere in which they lived. To this atmosphere, the lives of many Friends, now nameless and unknown, contributed by their faithfulness in inconspicuous **service,** and so made it possible for the greater spirits to grow to their full stature." [412] The religious faith of Quakers is considerably different from other denominations, however, which will be discussed more explicitly in chapter nine.

A) An Historical Survey of Quaker Approach to Service

An adequate account of the Quaker contribution to the idea of service and its fulfillment requires reaching back to the origins of The Society of Friends. "From their earliest days of radical religious dissent in the seventeenth–century England, Quakers [have] remained dedicated to the proposition that men can and must be both effective and compassionate, tough-minded and tender-hearted in matters of social change. At certain moments in history, [they] have been able to combine the goals of 'doing good' and 'getting things done'."[413]

The connection between faith, doctrine, and social service was clearly stated as the service mission was being formed. "We are deeply impressed by the thought that this world service and widespread missionary effort (are) of the very essence of the life of a religious community following the path of Christ…It was John Wilhelm Rowntree who told us that the 'Gospel must be social' and that Christ would 'lay on us the burden of the world's suffering and drive us forth with the apostolic of the early Church."[414]

We restrict this review to a few activities of "doing good" predating the American Friends Service Committee (AFSC), which is almost synonymous with feeding the hungry, reconstructing homes in war ravaged regions, or working for peace domestically and on the global scenes.[415] Elton Trueblood has proposed that, "the work of relief and reconstruction, the best-known single aspect of Quaker life, so far as the general public is concerned, has reached its peak in the periods of war, but is not limited to such periods."[416] But Trueblood continues: "though there are many examples of Quaker work in previous wars, the organized service[417] work as it is known today began when in October, 1870, British Friends, who were deeply moved by the sufferings of civilians in the Franco-Prussian War, set up a Friends War Victims Fund."[418]

SECTION II. RADICAL REFORMATION PARTICIPATION IN SERVICE

This action was followed by the formation of the Friends War Victims Relief Committee, set up by the London Meeting for Sufferings in September of 1914. At the same time, the Friends Ambulance Unit (FAU) was formed, especially "appealing to young men who, though convinced that they were led not to fight, wanted to make sure that they were not following some safe or easy alternative."[419] The FAU was a volunteer ambulance service founded by Quakers, and served between 1914 and 1919, and again from 1939 to 1946, after which it became the Friends Ambulance Unit Post-War Service and expanded into twenty-five different countries around the world.[420]

The concern of British Quakers to alleviate suffering continued when in "April 1916 a small group of English Quakers visited Russia in order to investigate conditions there." They were able to establish a hospital for Russian orphans in the Samara district, and supplied personnel for several other hospitals in the district. "District nursing centers were established in Effimovka in December of 1916 and Bogdanovka in March 1917. Nurses were in charge at each of these centers and a dispensary was open during the mornings."[421] Later, six American women (all trained social workers) reached Russia in September 1917, one year after English Friends started their work. The work was closed in October 1918, due to increased pressure from the Russian government to leave.

It is apparent that American Friends were also becoming involved in the organized service work that originated in Britain, since there were numerous spontaneous service projects already operative in the United States. The generally accepted timeline and impetus for the formation of formally organized Quaker service activities in North America was in response to the consequences of World War I, which ended in 1917. A group of American Friends met in Philadelphia, Pennsylvania to consider the major crises looming on the horizon. "No one dreamed in the sharp crisis of 1917, when the first steps of faith were taken, the we should feed more than a million German children, drive dray loads of cod liver oil into Russia, plough the fields of peasants and fight typhus in Poland, rebuild the homes and replant the wastes in Serbia, administer a longtime service of love in Austria."[422]

Rufus Jones stated that though "The Quakers had always from the time of their rise in the period of the English Commonwealth been sensitive to the ills of humanity and ready as occasions arose to take up the burden of the world's suffering...(the) American Friends Service Committee, as its name implies, was from the beginning, and has all along continued to be, a corporate activity."[423] This reference to a "corporate activity" is especially significant in the light of the well-known Friends' respect for "that of God in everyone", which requires that corporate decisions cannot be taken until there is "common consent" or "consensus" among all the participants.

This requires "a high degree of 'like-mindedness' and a great deal of humility all around." Jonas further maintains that "even at best, the consensus process is time consuming and exhausting, and would seem to be a heavy cross to bear for a religious congregation, much less for a far-flung corporate entity like the Service Committee."[424] Nevertheless, the Quaker meeting in Philadelphia, in June 1917, exhibited remarkable unity, and Rufus Jones remarked upon it, after he was called to be chair:

> "We have met together a few times and already we are deep in plans for a piece of relief work which will demand sacrificial lives and consecrated hearts. We are, all of us, dedicated to this task to which we have set our hands and we are dedicated to our beloved Society of Friends. There are only a few of us but I hope we shall be able to keep ourselves free from prejudice while men are torn with bitterness and hate."[425]

The first order of business was to change their name from Friends' National Service committee to American Friends Service Committee, which was approved.[426]

The issues at the organizational meeting included accepting Quaker women applicants and involving seven British Friends "who are to work with their relief committee in France." The decision was made to "begin training of one hundred men to comprise Reconstruction Unit number one at Haverford College as soon as possible after Commencement."[427]

Bernard Walton asked, "Will the Unit of a hundred men be made up of Friends, only, or do we expect to welcome conscientious objectors from all denominations?" Chairman Jones replied, "There will be many, especially among the Mennonites and the Brethren, who will share our testimony concerning war. I hope that we can co-operate with other sects (sic) in every way that is possible but I feel that we ought to make this first Unit primarily a Quaker group." [428]

B) The Growth of American Friends Service Work

Though the primary motive for the historical Quaker's service activities was compassion for all humans in need, the formation of AFSC had been specifically initiated by the desire to help the victims of war in Europe and Russia. Thus, the plans were "made in the office at Twenty South Twelfth Street to organize a Unit of one hundred men to be trained during the summer at Haverford College under the direction of Dr. James A. Babbitt and to reach Paris early in September." [429] After strenuous preparation in "road building, plowing, lessons in French and first aid and other necessary information," the unit was ready to sail. Though the first ship could not accommodate all the men, the first forty-nine arrived in Paris on September 7, 1917. "These were followed by fifty-one men and three women a week later."[430]

The AFSC continued to expand its work in France. It included "medical, agricultural, transport, building and relief" work. It involved an amazing variety of reconstruction, such as "the rebuilding of the destroyed Verdun region, and it was at this time they tried two daring schemes." This involved buying several "army dumps which were now useless to the army, and which contained tools of all kinds, machines, barbed wire, everything which the Mission could use for its task of rebuilding." [431] The second daring thing was to hire German prisoners to assist in the rehabilitation work, with the "wages" going to their families. By the end of 1919, the AFSC had performed "relief in some form or degree to 1,666 (sic) French Villages and over 46,000 families (and) planted 25,000 trees, mostly fruit trees in the Verdun area." [432]

Relief work spread to Germany in February of 1920, focusing on feeding children but expanding into massive feeding programs, lasting into 1924, involving the purchase and distribution of food, finally being transferred to the German Central Committee for Foreign Relief. With this ambitious beginning, Friends service work spread to Russia, beginning with the English Quaker work in 1916, and joined by AFSC in September 1917, with intermittent disruptions, focusing on the devastating famine and disease in until 1922. "In almost every instance, the Soviet Government was extremely co-operative with the Service Committee and gave them help whenever it was possible." [433]

But the service commitment could not be restricted merely to strictly relief.

> "In 1917 the American Friends Service Committee had been created in order to do relief work abroad. As this work developed and it was found that actual relief was not the only contribution which Friends could give to Europe [several] members of London Yearly Meeting came to America and shared their concern that there should be a committee formed to foster religious work in Europe." [434]

This impetus for a vastly expanding view of service Quaker organizations could do resulted in the sending of Quaker representatives to variety of countries "to find out what opportunities it might have for work in that country." [435] Thus, a variety of operations were opened in China, France, Russia, Poland, Austria, and Geneva (sic), consisting mainly of Friends Centers in various localities, which performed numerous services including guest houses, student hostels and services, study groups, teaching cooking, crafts and trades, and organizing youth work camps. [436] It is apparent that many of the "centers" were located in areas where a Quaker presence already existed. But it also obviously served to strengthen a Quaker religious presence in each specific location. [437]

Though an itemized account of the growth of Quaker service through the AFSC and related structures is beyond the scope of this survey, the operation of the Quaker service outreach was originally international, and

SECTION II. RADICAL REFORMATION PARTICIPATION IN SERVICE

is now global. A brief overview of the expanding work and scope of Quaker service is presented here: [438]

- Feeding thousands of children in Germany and Austria after World War I

- Helping distressed Appalachian mining communities find alternative means to make a living in the 1930s

- Negotiating with the Gestapo in Germany to aid Jewish refugees

- After World War II, sending aid teams to India, China, and Japan

- Giving aid to civilians on both sides of the Vietnam War and providing draft counseling to thousands of young men

- Sponsoring conferences for young diplomats in emerging African democracies

- Establishing economic development programs in Asia, Africa, and Latin America from the 1970s to the present

- Providing extensive support to the modern U.S. civil rights movement and public-school desegregation

- Working with numerous communities such as Native Americans, immigrants, migrant workers, prisoners, and low-income families on education and justice issues

- Building peaceful communities all over the world

In 1947, along with British Quakers, AFSC received the Nobel Peace Prize, which recognized our work "…from the nameless to the nameless…."

But another aspect of Friends and service needs to be briefly noted, and that is the peace emphasis that motivated almost all AFSC work. Working for peace has been a central tenet of Friends from its beginning, long before the AFSC was born. Thus, Mary Hoxie Jones' chapter on the origin of the "Peace Section" begins with the question "Will the church outlaw war or condone is as a necessary evil? The spectacle of Christian nations fighting each other has turned a great many thinking men and women in these nations, as well as the great majority of the non-Christian world, away from Christianity."[439]

The annual report of the AFSC in 1925 asked "if we were each asked to name the thing that we considered to be the greatest piece of work to be done in the world, we should reply without question, perhaps, that it was the abolition of war. The problem that confronts the Society of Friends, therefore, is encouraging Friends to work actively for the abolition of war in times of peace." [440] This concern about the "abolition of wars" reflected what George Fox had enunciated in his prophetic witness, "I live in virtue of that life and power which does away with the occasion for all war." This clearly seemed as urgent as the call to serve others, and also helps to explains the emergence of the Peace Section in the AFSC [441]

Its goal was stated by Sherwood Eddy: "We must not let the present generation pass until we have made war impossible." [442] The means to achieve these goals from the originators of the Peace Section were: "1) work in Yearly meetings; 2) work among colleges and college students; 3) send literature to Friends' papers; 4) work with young people; 5) work with other churches; and 6) arrange for deputations of Friends to inter-visit."[443]

That the scope, depth of the work, and accomplishments of this committee sponsored by the AFSC was presented in abbreviated form above does not deny or ignore the massive, complex, and extensive activities, but an insight can be gained by the report Jones gives in 1937, regarding the institutes the AFSC and Peace section held in American colleges and universities in the 30s: "It is not possible to quote an exact figure but it has been estimated that the total membership of the Institutes since their beginning in 1930 through 1936, has been forty-five hundred persons and this number does not include many thousands more who have attended the public lectures only." [444]

The interaction and co-operation with other organizations and groups ranged from colleges and universities, including various student organizations, and foundations such as the Woodrow Wilson Foundation, the Carnegie Foundation, labor unions, and the like. The enthusiasm generated the formation of "Peace Caravans" that traveled to various communities, including the YMCA.[445] A total compilation of all of the work related to or administered by the AFSC is probably not possible, since the modest Quaker culture and milieu has discouraged displaying its own achievements. But to offer an idea of its scope, the operating budget for AFSC in 2014 was $33,853,122 [446]

[447] "Boasting about observable achievements was avoided out of their fear it might imply subtle proselytizing of others to their faith. "There is a widespread view that the purpose of missions is to win people to the Christian way of life, whereas Quaker service has been in the name of Friends, but not for the purpose of proselytizing." [448] One Quaker opined, "I have a fear that Quakerism cuts least ice when Quakers receive the world's approval. People speak well of us today, more than ever before." [449]

C) The Broadening of Service Activities

The records of Quaker activities working toward the relief of human suffering, and the records of activities aimed at the abolition of war, are indeed amazing. The Quaker relief and service activities begun during and after World War I were greatly expanded following World War II. AFSC activities after the war included providing food, clothing, medical help, and other emergency necessities, especially in Germany, France, and neighboring countries. Similar services also extended into India, China, and Japan. In 1948, Quaker workers helped Arab refuges in the Gaza strip. The Korean War, the Hungarian Revolution, the Algerian war all witnessed AFSC relief and social-service assistance. For example, medical care, emergency child care, and prosthetics were provided to victims of the Vietnam war, both from the North and South. [450]

The contemporary profile of Quaker service-related activities have evolved and differentiated to include well-known organizations such as Friends Committee on National Legislation (FCNL), Quaker Peace and Social Witness, Friends Committee on Scouting, Friends Disaster Service, and Alternatives to Violence Project. [451] A random selection of other more specialized Quaker organizations that include voluntary service includes the following: Association of Friends on Indian Affairs (ACFA); Bolivian Quaker Educational Fund (BQEF); Christian Peacemaker Teams (CPT); Friends Peace Center, San Jose, Costa Rica; work camps in Burundi; and, finally, Peace Brigades International. [452]

As may have been noticed, the causal connections between service and the peace witness, based on the strong Quaker conviction of conscientious objection to war, are not very extensively stated and explicated. This is explained to a considerable degree by the reluctance of Friends to express their faith in theoretical and theological terms. In other words, creeds and doctrines are not centrally a part of the Quaker self-identity. Nevertheless, Quakers generally accept the stance George Fox took: "We do believe that they (the holy scriptures) were given forth by the Holy Spirit of God, though the holy men of God…we believe that they are to be read, believed, and fulfilled." [453]

Nevertheless, Rufus M Jones maintained that the "original message of George Fox which gathered the Society of Friends was never systematically formulated by him. It was essentially the faith, based on personal experience that God and man have direct relationship and mutual correspondence. This was not, in the first instance, a doctrine, but a live and throbbing experience." [454] Similarly, regarding creeds, the "True basis of Christian unity" (1917) states that creeds "tend to crystallize thought on matters that will always be beyond final embodiment in human language, they better the search for truth and for its more adequate expression, and they set up a fence which tends to keep out of the Christian fold many sincere and seeking souls who would gladly enter it." [455]

The fact that Quakers have not strongly and extensively voiced the philosophical and theological reasons for their immense service and peace witness, and how it is related to their faith, will be more fully discussed in chapter 9. The society's work in Europe helped bring about the creation of United Nations Relief and Rehabilitation Administration (UNRRA). This new organization agreed to provide cattle transportation to Europe, if Brethren Service would recruit livestock attendants for all their shipments. Brethren and their neighbors donated the animals and hundreds of Brethren (and some of their neighbors) served as "sea-going cowboys." By 1948, the project

SECTION II. RADICAL REFORMATION PARTICIPATION IN SERVICE

was directed by an interfaith committee representing Brethren Service, the American Baptist Churches, and the Evangelical and Reformed bodies.

One aspect of the Quaker movement, which seems to imply organizational unity, is challenged when the actual Society of Friends is closely analyzed. There has been tremendous diversity and disagreement since its origins. For example, "in Great Britain, the model of active effort by Friends which would be institutionalized in the various service Committees of the new century was emerging at the close of the 1880s" This refers only to the service organization in Great Britain. Then, in 1917, "The various English war relief committees were both the examples and testing ground for the development of the American Friends Service Committee that was formed in Philadelphia I April of 1917." [456]

An attempt to form a unified structure was the "All Friends Conference" of 1920.

> "This gathering after the conclusion of World War brought together in London over one thousand Friends representing almost every Yearly Meeting in the world and coming from the United States, England, Canada, Australia, New Zealand, South Africa, Scotland, Ireland, France, Germany, Australia, Switzerland, Norway, Denmark, China, Japan, India, Syria, and Madagascar.[457]

This listing of the Quakerism in the world provides considerable information on the spread of Quakerism and the obvious problems deriving from such a polyglot collection of national Quaker meetings, and the obvious central role of service played in the faith and ethics of the Friends movement. The proliferation of Quaker Meetings by separation and division is not broadly discussed in Quaker literature. Because of the unusual egalitarian structure of Quaker Meetings, it is nevertheless true that many divisions have emerged between evangelical and progressive groups. The structural chart of divisions resembles most Evangelical Christian groups. [458] Trueblood states: "During the last century, there has been a repeated concern for wider unity among Quakers. One form is represented by the planning and conduct of

123

Friends World Conferences. [another is] The Friends World Committee for Consultation." The amazing reality is that though there has been great variety of Quaker theology and polity, the centrality of service is unmistakable. [459]

In conclusion, the Quaker relief service was closely intertwined with the issue of witnessing to peace, via conscientious objection to war. This is why, at the June 1917 AFSC organizational meeting, Rufus Jones stated, "We want to make it clear from the start that this Unit is not being formed to give Friends a way of escaping hardship. It is to offer an honorable service to those whose consciences will not allow them to defend their country by carrying arms…As was said at our first meeting of this committee on April 30th, 'We are united in expressing our love for our country and our desire to serve her loyally. We offer ourselves to the Government of the United States in any constructive work which we can conscientiously serve humanity.'"[460]

CHAPTER 7.
Church of the Brethren Serving Human Need

Introduction

The Church of the Brethren traces its roots back to 1708, when eight people were "rebaptized" in the Eder River flowing through the "Valley of Peace" in Schwarzenau, Germany. Influenced heavily by Anabaptist and Pietist friends, neighbors, and teachers in south Germany, they were convinced that even those who had broken away from the Roman Catholic Church in the sixteenth century had gone astray from the true teachings of Jesus Christ. Alexander Mack, Sr., who sold his home and half interest in the family mill he owned with his brother, led these eight dissenters. He then moved his family to Schwarzenau, because it was known that Count Henrich Albrecht had continued his father's policy of religious toleration in the county of Wittgenstein in the state of North-Rhine-Westphalia.[461]

Alexander Mack set the example by sharing his considerable means to assist others who were in need. This was so obvious that a "Radical Pietist sneered that when Mack's money ran out, the movement would fall apart." Seen as "mutual aid", service to others seldom reached beyond membership in the community of faith. After the death of Henrich Albrecht, persecution reappeared in Schwarzenau. The separatists moved to Kreyfeld and then to Surhuisterveen in the Netherlands, where sympathetic Anabaptists (Mennonites) welcomed them. Religious tensions, the glowing prospects of religious freedom, and abundant fertile land caused the early Brethren to look across the Atlantic. By 1740, most of the founders and members of the new body of faith had immigrated to Germantown, Pennsylvania. They built homes and a church building, while sending glowing letters back to Germany describing how pleasant it was to live in the new land.

Not everyone prospered, however, which was why a "poor box" was a prominent feature of that first meeting house. The famous printing press operated by Christopher Sauer, Jr., an elder of the church, carried the slogan, "To the Glory of God and my Neighbor's Good." As early as 1747, the poor box was a fixture in the Germantown church, and the congregation also supported a home for the elderly.

A) The Origins of Church of the Brethren Service

From the beginning, this reform movement (which later came to be known as "Church of the Brethren") has had a tradition of service to others. While the Brethren's efforts, during the eighteenth and nineteenth centuries, to care for their neighbor's good were largely seen as assisting fellow believers in the faith (mutual aid such as providing food for the ill, rebuilding a barn or house that had been destroyed, or doing the field and barn work of a brother who was injured or ill), the terrible results of World War I caused the Brethren to have a concern for any who were suffering, regardless of faith, color, or nationality. By 1916, the Church had established a peace committee. It reported to an Annual Meeting that the Church should encourage the president and congress to take an initial step toward ending all war, by having the government make a significant appropriation for the relief of suffering humanity throughout the war zones.

Encouraging the government to contribute money was easier than the next step. By 1917, it had become known (in the United States) that Armenian Christians were suffering, as did the early church martyrs, at the hands of non-Christians. In 1918, the Annual Meeting in Goshen, Indiana, appointed the War Relief and Reconstruction Committee to supervise the efforts of the Church in the field of foreign relief. Men who elected to become conscientious objectors, instead of entering military service, saw this as an opportunity to engage in relief and reconstruction work overseas, but the government would not allow draft-age men to leave the country.[462] A program of relief services was developed, including support of orphanages and schools, and the reconstruction of vineyards, gardens, buildings, and homes.

World War I had a dramatic effect upon the Church of the Brethren, in that there was no option for conscientious objection, although there was an option for non-combatants. Brethren leaders, such as M.R. Zigler and Dan West, who were faced with military conscription for World War I, gave leadership in finding alternatives in any future war. [466] In 1919, members of the Church of the Brethren raised $267,000 for relief to the Armenians who were being systematically deported and exterminated during the early years of the twentieth century. This was the first significant outpouring of relief from the Brethren to a faraway land. [463]

This optimistic endeavor was dampened, however, when the 1920 Annual Meeting was informed that the Brethren were not allowed to work as an autonomous unit in the Middle East. The Relief and Reconstruction Committee assured the Brethren that they would seek to work through organizations already established to work in the region, such as the Red Cross and the YMCA. In 1921, Michael Robert (M.R.) Zigler of Broadway, Virginia, was appointed to the Relief and Reconstruction Committee. At the Annual Meeting that year the committee was dissolved, and responsibility for overseas relief was assigned to the General Mission Board.

The outbreak of the Spanish Civil War in 1936 galvanized Brethren to engage in service work overseas. Clarence E. Pickett, executive secretary of AFSC, wrote to M.R. Zigler, informing him that the Quakers had been urged by different groups to organize a relief program. Hoping that at least one person from the Church of the Brethren would serve on a committee to determine program and policies, he asked if the Brethren would be interested in participating. Zigler responded enthusiastically, and the Board of Christian Education appointed Sara Florence Fogelsanger Murphy, president of the organization of women in the church, to represent the Brethren on this interchurch committee, which also included Mennonites.

In addition to personnel and money, the Brethren joined their ideological partners, the Mennonites and the Society of Friends (often referred to collectively as the "historic peace churches"), in sending for the first time "gifts in kind," later to be called "material aid." The first Brethren material aid consisted of two cases of shoes, shipped in May 1937. By the end of 1937, Brethren had given $1,330 worth of material aid, while the Mennonites gave $8,600 worth and the Friends $11,000.

Soon an appeal for aid was also heard from the other side of the world. China was then in the throes of the Sino-Japanese War. Careful to avoid charges of partiality, Brethren workers provided needed assistance to both sides of the fighting factions in both Japan and China. The Church supported them by sending close to $40,000 for China relief. Brethren leaders such as M.R. Zigler hoped that the record of service to suffering people would be a guide for future action in case violence increased.

With a view to the complexities of future service work, Brethren officials felt the urgency to create a new organization to administer the program. Therefore:

> "During the late 1930s, with service workers already in Spain and China...Brethren decided to form a separate service arm in the church organization. Responding to the recommendation of a committee made up of M. R. Zigler, Dan West, and A.C. Baugher, the Council of boards decided in November 1939 that the General Mission Board and the Board of Christian Education should form together as a committee, which would later become known as the Brethren Service Committee in the field of relief and reconstruction work."[464]

The newly created board met in late 1939 and 1940 to discuss the operating procedures of the new board and "discuss ways of keeping the urgency of relief needs in the minds of Brethren." At the Annual Conference in 1941, delegates adopted the report of the Brethren Service Committee, which included a statement of purpose, later referred to as the "Charter of Brethren Service." The statement began by quoting the words of Jesus: "I was hungry

SECTION II. RADICAL REFORMATION PARTICIPATION IN SERVICE

and ye gave me to eat...I was a stranger and ye took me in; naked and ye clothed me; I was sick, and ye visited me; I was in prison, and ye came to me ...Inasmuch as ye did it unto one of the least of my Brethren(sic) even the least, ye did it unto me'" (Matt.25:35-36, 40).[465]

The "statement of purpose" for the creation of the Brethren Service Commission was described as representing "the Church of the Brethren in the area of social action. Its primary function is that of personal rehabilitation and social reconstruction in the name and spirit of Christ."[466] There were four points:

1. To arrest and eliminate, insofar as possible, those forces in human society which contribute to the disintegration of personality and character, and to social stability (I. Thess.5:14-15);

2. To relieve human distress and suffering around the world without regard to barriers of race, creed or nationality. (Gal. 6:10);

3. To represent the church in the area of creative citizenship and Christian testimony on issues of national and intergenerational significance;

4. To develop and organize and apply the spiritual and financial resources of the church to the above areas of service as a concrete and practical expression of the spirit and teaching of Christ as the Brethren understand and interpret them (Rom.12:20-21).

The threat of a larger world war was strongly felt, and Brethren leaders hoped to avoid a repeat of what happened during World War I, when Brethren conscientious objectors had to report to military camps. The national and international conditions were clearly among the dominating issues confronting Brethren church life in the late 1930s and the early 1940s. The Civilian Public Service program had provided the context for what the eminent Brethren historian, Donald F. Durnbaugh, called "The Brethren Service Explosion." The major impetus for the development of the Brethren Service Commission (BSC) during World War II was the Civilian Public Service program. Young men whose conscience and Christian beliefs would not allow them to participate in military activities could work in CPS camps located in Florida, Arkansas, Indiana, Michigan, Oregon, Pennsylvania, Maryland, and other states.

They served as "smoke jumpers", fighting forest fires in national forests, and they worked in conservation and reforestation projects. CPS projects also included work in agricultural units, public health services, mental hospitals, and other projects deemed to be in the national interest. Eventually, about one-fifth of all CPS men were in mental-hospital work. Approximately 6,794 men (1,119 of whom were Brethren) served in CPS camps during World War II. The Church was willing to support those whose conscience would not allow participation in military service, but desired to serve in alternative ways.

Leading up to, during, and after the most destructive war in history, there was an unprecedented demand for relief and rehabilitation work, especially in Europe and Asia. There were also many unmet needs in the United States. As clothing, food, shoes, and supplies poured into the relief center at New Windsor, Maryland, more and more volunteers were needed to process and ship these goods to where they were so desperately needed. In addition, the Brethren agreed to process the relief goods of the Lutheran World Service and of Church World Service. With all of these goods going out from New Windsor, that little village became one of the best-known addresses throughout the world.

B) Heifer Project

The most widely known example of Brethren service to others was the Heifer Project. Dan West, a Brethren farmer, teacher, and activist, had accepted the call to serve in Spain during the Spanish Civil War (1937). While distributing inadequate supplies of food, clothing, and powdered milk to people on both sides of the conflict, he developed the idea of supplying needy people with a cow. Upon returning home, he convinced his rural Indiana neighbors of the practicality of his idea. The first three calves that were donated were named Faith, Hope, and Charity. Eventually, the Heifer Project was born, and early shipments of pregnant heifers went to Mexico, Puerto Rico, and sharecroppers in Mississippi.

In this way, he initiated what has become Heifer International, a multi-million-dollar program that gives not only heifers, but also goats, sheep, alpacas, rabbits, geese, water buffalo, and other animals to persons in poor communities around the world. Each recipient family qualified by showing evidence of being able to house and feed the animal, and agreeing to donate free of charge the first female offspring. The concept of "Passing on the Gift" became a hallmark of Heifer Project, and abundant testimony has been given of the blessing, received by recipients, of being able to become donors. One example was the recent statement of Alves Manyugwo of Mozambique, who said, "My family and I suffered so much. When we received our four goats and learned about passing on the gift, I could not imagine it was I who would help end the suffering of another."

The emphasis has always been to assist people in helping themselves. Fortunately, as more denominations and secular organizations became participants in the Heifer Project, the Brethren were not reluctant to give up possession and control of the organization. It therefore has grown into an internationally known and respected instrument in the fight against poverty and hunger. [467]

C) Volunteer Service

After World War II and CPS, various Brethren leaders recognized that the church needed to develop a positive moral equivalent of war by which to express their Christian faith in action. The church sent M. R. Zigler to Europe in 1945 and 1946-47 to assess the need for aid. At the Annual Conference in Denver, Colorado, in 1948, the youth present were allowed to insert an item on the already approved agenda. Very short, the presenter stood on a box in order to speak into the microphone, but nevertheless, the delegate body unanimously accepted the request that the Church institute and support a program of volunteer service for young people.

Alarmed that the United States Congress was debating the possibility of compulsory conscription, and gratified that the Church had always said "no" to war, Brethren youth were determined that they and the Church should say "yes" to a positive volunteer peace and service program. Youth of both sexes responded fairly equally. While the young women usually served for one year, the young men, most of whom were assigned to projects approved for alternative service, were required to serve two years to fulfill their national draft obligation. Orientation units were scheduled as preparation for volunteer service. In the early years, the orientations were held in New Windsor, Maryland.

After eight weeks of working in material aid and studying various topics, the volunteers were assigned to projects in the United States and overseas. In the United States, they served in inner-city service projects, Native American schools and service projects, women's prison, state hospitals, as normal control patients ("guinea pigs") in medical-research hospitals, rehabilitation centers, service projects in Appalachia, and provided service and ministry to migrants. There were many other projects as well. Since 1948, thousands of Brethren young people had gone into inter-city areas, migrant camps, and many other situations that were completely new and unknown to them. By 2007, over 6,000 youth and adults had served in Brethren Volunteer Service.

D) Work Camps and International Seminars

Though the first work camps were mainly in the United States, Brethren Service also developed and operated work camps and international peace seminars. Beginning with the third unit in June 1949, a small percentage of the BVS volunteers were assigned to projects in Europe

These projects included distributing food and material aid; distributing heifers for Heifer Project, and visitation follow-up contact; directing international work camps and peace seminars; administrating student-exchange programs; staffing education and recreation "houses" in refugee camps, and many other service activities.

American Brethren Service workers, who had come from a sheltered home life, worked, played, sang, and discussed with youth from Holland, Sweden, Ireland, Denmark, Spain, East Germany, Turkey, and other countries. They shoveled rubble, cleaned bricks, mixed mortar, and even laid bricks to rebuild schools, parish houses, and churches. BVSers also worked in Vietnam, Laos, and Cambodia, giving a different picture of Americans than those gained by people fearful of bombs from military jets and strafing by helicopters.

But equally important to the service BVSers performed, they were exposed to different ideas and learned that people from other countries and cultures were also genuine and loving people. In Egypt, parents named their newborn baby "Otis" (a name unknown in their culture) in honor of a Brethren volunteer (Otis Rowe) who worked in their village. By 1980, BVS volunteers had been assigned to projects in fifty-two nations, with projects ranged from caring for children in migrant work camps and inner cities in the United States to relief and development work in Vietnam, Laos, Poland, Iraq, Egypt, and Nigeria.

As an example, Brethren work campers in Mexico were described as "shirtless missionaries with shovels" by a Vera Cruz newspaper, which described their digging a two-and-a-half-mile drainage ditch to help the village avoid malaria. Their work in mucky water, infernal heat, through dense patches of thick jungle, and mosquito-infested swamps was done to address a problem of the village of Paso de Ovejas, where half the population had suffered from malaria the previous year. Other volunteers dug ditches to drain swamps and reclaim land for cultivation in various villages in Mexico. In Xico, volunteers also dug sewer-drainage ditches, sometimes waist deep in muck. Treating needy people with respect while reclaiming land and improving sanitation illustrated the goals of the work-camp program.

The voluntary service experience was truly transformational. Coming from rural backgrounds, they were generally naive to the realities of international life. They learned the native languages and culture, and in most cases, earned the respect and admiration of those whom they served. Returning home from overseas or domestic projects, the volunteers began study in college; others went to graduate school, while still others went into business. Many became leaders in their church, community, and international organizations. Many Brethren youth were searching for the moral equivalent of war and looking for ready opportunities by which to express their Christian faith in action.

E) Other Brethren Service Activities

In 1950, Brethren Service sponsored its first international peace seminar. Held in Vienna, Austria, twenty-seven participants from ten different nations engaged in lively discussions regarding the nature of peace. In addition to living and working with people from different cultures, participating in daily devotions, singing folk songs each evening, and playing games, the participants gained additional insight from twelve guest leaders, who focused on the Christian basis of nonviolence, the causes of wars, and the psychological bases of peace. Leaders with rich and varied backgrounds exchanged experiences and ideas for the future, allowing these peace seminars to become instruments of education and of service. The international participants heard, for the first time, the nonviolent values promoted by the Church of the Brethren. Many other peace seminars were held in subsequent years.

Brethren Service had an active hand in the development and formation of the Christian Rural Overseas Program (CROP). John D. Metzler, Sr., veteran Brethren Service administrator, became the first director of CROP. It sponsored the "Freedom Trains" in the 1940s, which consisted of hundreds of freight cars loaded with American grains and produce, adding more cars as the trains proceeded from the West to the East Coast. CROP became a thriving ecumenical endeavor, which continued strongly into the twenty-first century.

When Brethren relief workers, who had been serving overseas directly after the end of World War II, began returning home, many brought handicrafts produced by refugees and displaced persons they had come to know in refugee camps. They discovered that a ready market existed for these items and decided to develop a program for the sale of handicrafts that would benefit the producer. Refugees and displaced persons languishing in camps could use their skills to produce handicrafts, but they had no way to market

SECTION II. RADICAL REFORMATION PARTICIPATION IN SERVICE

them. In 1949, a small display case with several items was a forerunner to a small gift shop at the Brethren Service Center in New Windsor, Maryland. This eventually led to the formation of the Sales Exchange for Refugee Rehabilitation Vocations (SERRV).

The project grew to include others in weak financial situations as a result of war, natural disaster, and chronic poverty. The idea gradually caught on among many Brethren and members of other churches. Gaining the support of the World Council of Churches enabled the program to attract much wider support, and by 1964, a full-time director was named. Overseas workers related to Church World Service (Methodists, Lutherans, United Church of Christ, and many other groups) contributed to the program by finding sources of supply. Some individuals opened SERRV gift shops in their homes. The Southern Baptist Convention, the nation's largest denomination, began handling SERRV articles and established sixty SERRV outlets in Baptist bookstores. Kreider reports that "By 1981 the full-time staff of 30 people processed sales of $2,528,191 from handicrafts obtained from about 200 producers or suppliers in more than 43 countries" [468]"

A large ecumenical network gave far more craftspeople access to markets and income from their handiwork, providing full-time employment or a part-time supplement to meager income. Artisans who participated in SERRV were most likely among the neediest in their communities, and the least likely to find regular employment. SERRV offered them the chance to maintain their own dignity without being dependent upon handouts.

The high-visibility programs described above were by no means the extent of the activities of Brethren Service. Individuals and congregations also engaged in service projects on the local scene. Whether it was providing meals for a family handicapped by hospitalization, accident, or some other problem; barn-raising for victims of a fire; or assisting friends and neighbors when needed, the Brethren never forgot the importance of coming to the aid of those in need.

Brethren congregations and districts sponsored dozens of work teams (consisting of men and women) to leave their jobs and homes to journey to areas devastated by tornados, hurricanes, floods, or other disasters. Additionally, in some cases, individuals organized work teams to serve in Indiana, Kentucky, West Virginia, Alabama, and (most recently) in Louisiana and Mississippi to clean up and rebuild after Hurricane Katrina.

Along with volunteer programs of sister historic Peace Churches, the Friends and the Mennonites, Brethren Service influenced the formation of other volunteer agencies, particularly the International Voluntary Service (IVS), and Viet Nam Christian Service (VNCS). The influence of Brethren Service on the creation of the Peace Corps, under President John F. Kennedy, however, is less well known. Not only was Brethren input into the creation of the Peace Corps a significant factor, but President Kennedy actually offered the directorship of the Peace Corps to W. Harold Row, executive secretary of Brethren Service.[469] In all of this, caring for aged and orphans, and serving those in need (domestically and overseas) was seen as a normal, if not required, aspect of living a Christian life. Adding to the teaching in Matthew 25 (summarized by the reminder that what one does or does not do for people in need is also being done or not done for the Lord), the Brethren understood the admonition of the second chapter of James, in which we are reminded that, without works, faith is hollow and a sham.

The Church of the Brethren is not a large denomination. However, the Biblical emphasis on service to others was an inspiration to other Christian denominations and secular groups. The Brethren were unselfishly willing to relinquish leadership, direction, control, and ownership of these programs. As these programs became ecumenical, they were able to serve far more people than would have been possible had the Brethren kept ownership and control for themselves.

SECTION III.
The Radical Reformation Ethic of Service

CHAPTER 8.
The Ethic of Serving Others

> *Whereas many within the ecumenical movement have been primarily concerned with the unity of church order and polity, or with the unity of doctrine, the Believers Churches have directed their attention more to the unity of **service—diakonia**.*
>
> —Donald Durnbaugh [470]

The last three chapters offered a review of how the Mennonites, the Society of Friends (Quakers), and Church of the Brethren—recognized as Historic Peace Churches and reflecting aspects of the *Radical Reformation* tradition—were pioneers of the idea of peace practice, especially as it was expressed in voluntary service. These same groups also developed *action* programs derived from the love ethic, which had already operated for centuries in very informal and personal ways. Thus, referring to these groups, Durnbaugh emphatically states: "Probably no characteristic has been so often noted and so appreciated by society at large as the penchant of practicing mutual aid and service."[471] This does not mean other religious groups and organizations were not active in this area, but we cautiously state that the theme of service became a hallmark of the distinctive identity of many Quakers, Brethren, and Mennonites. This chapter presents some basic material on their pioneering work in developing a theology and philosophy of service, which has not been deeply addressed before.

A) I. Mennonite Service Developments.

In 1947, Elmer Ediger stated: "Voluntary Service is not a new idea. It is relatively new as a program organized to utilize a year or less of time young people and others have to contribute to the work of the church."[472] Ediger described voluntary service as "motivated by the Christian teachings that urge us to consecrate ourselves as a living sacrifice in reasonable service, to live so that we do good to all men, particularly those in unusual need, and to live so that we overcome evil with good. Basically, it is an effort toward better discipleship; to do as Jesus would in this world of need and confusion."[473]

In a related article, Ediger proposed the following: "The early Anabaptists like the early Christians were not isolated and withdrawn but were out to live and win for the Kingdom in this world and the next. Today we are endeavoring to regain ground we have lost historically."[474]

He continued: "We can give our positive expressions to the needs of our society through a variety of useful and outreaching vocations, through our participation in the church and larger community, and through our program of missions and service. The Voluntary Service program was launched and developed with the primary objective of increasing the service outreach of our communities."[475]

Ediger argued that Voluntary Service could also be a partner with Mennonite colleges: 1) Voluntary Service gives experiential content to concepts gained in school (college); 2) Voluntary Service is a valuable maturing process; 3) Voluntary Service confronts students with all aspects of group living; 4) Voluntary Service develops an appreciation of service and the church; and finally, 5) Voluntary Service helps to nurture a genuineness of Christian spirit.[476]

Paul Mininger, in his inaugural address as president of Goshen College, on October 17, 1954, defined culture as the humanely created beliefs, practices, and artifacts that do not exist in nature, and argued that these humanly created entities are to be used for a variety of purposes and ends. Since they can be used for selfish or evil ends, as well as for the good of humanity, Mininger asked a critical question: "The practical question for culture then is

SECTION III. THE RADICAL REFORMATION ETHIC OF SERVICE

to what authority is it to submit? What purposes shall culture serve. Whose needs are culture to meet?"[477]

Mininger proposed that the motto "Culture for Service" could be aligned with "biblical theology of service." He proposed that man (sic) "is created by God and that he exists by the will of God his Creator." God commissioned man to use nature with its resources, the nonhuman creation, and exercise control over it under the sovereignty of God. "Man was to create a culture that would glorify God. God's original intention was 'culture in the service of God'." But mankind has misdirected the use of culture "from the glorification of God to the assertion of his own will and the glorification of self."

It becomes his calling to witness to his Creator and Redeemer and bring all of his activities in all areas of life under the lordship of Christ.[478] It is nothing less than agape (redemptive) love seeking and restoring fellowship. It moves man to reach out beyond himself and his egoistical concerns and enter into fellowship with all persons through Christ.[479] Mininger distinguished between the theology of service for Christians and that of the prevailing culture: "In our American society, 'culture for service' is often the struggle for power in the political sphere." Because of this difference, "it frequently becomes necessary for disciples of Christ to withdraw from participation in many cultural activities of their community and to organize their life in a different way in order to be obedient to Christ."[480]

When Orie O. Miller, a leader in promoting and defining the voluntary service movement, was called to serve as the executive secretary of the recently formed Mennonite Central Committee, he decided that service was the form of his calling.[481] In his 1958 report to the Eastern Mennonite Board of Missions and Charities, he wrote:

> "The servant image is the initial of the Christian religion. It is the image which sheds the true light on the mission of Jesus Christ Himself. He took upon Himself the form of a servant. The church fulfills its meaning when it prepares the people of God to be the servants of God. Never let us forget the significance of this fact. The servant image must

> be restored during our time. The church must become afresh a pilgrim church not identifying itself too closely with any culture or any nation." [482]

Calls for an analysis of the scope, nature, and effectiveness of service began to emerge. "Much of the initial impetus for the study of Mennonite service programs lay in the fact that at least two, and possibly three, Mennonite conferences were asking deep questions at the particular time, regarding their own programs." [483] This resulted in "official action accepting a proposal [to study the problem] in September 17, 1962, by the Joint Administrative Committee of the Associated Mennonite Biblical Seminaries." [484] The research was conducted by Wilfred J. Unruh. [485]

Unruh introduced the research project by stating that the Old Testament teaches, "it was steadfast love, kindness, mercy, righteousness and justice that characterized the way that God had acted towards His created people… Compassion is rooted in God, and like all piety, is fundamentally a question of man's relation to God. But our response to God is actualized in our response to our fellows." [486] Unruh maintains that "In announcing the reality of the Kingdom of God as the new framework of human history…life in this new kingdom was characterized by the reality of the redemptive love that God was giving…Men in the kingdom would in turn share with their neighbors this new sense of wonder and love. The purpose of life itself was a redemptive purpose—giving restoration in every relationship." [487]

Unruh proposes that "The mission of the church is to witness to the full reality of God in Jesus Christ and to make known His power and love in the world…The call to truly serve is a call to a disinterested willingness to share and to serve with no obligations demanded."

In the "Philosophy of Voluntary Service" section, Unruh suggests that:

"The phenomenal development of voluntary service in Mennonite circles may be seen as something of a creative revolution. Already in the early years of the 20th century, a deepening sense of conflict was very evident between ideals and the pragmatic evidence of a world increasingly less oriented around these ideals…In its place stood the gaunt frame of deepening

SECTION III. THE RADICAL REFORMATION ETHIC OF SERVICE

pessimism, meaninglessness of life, and the real threat of universal oblivion. The shadow of a nuclear mushroom spread the feeling of futility and the senselessness of life."[488]

In conclusion, Unruh states: "It is this framework of the nature of Christ's own ministry; the reality of the way man feels his ultimate needs in contemporary life; and the resources of power given to the church by the Sprit; that forms the crucial setting of God's call for service. Our search is for the new wineskins to make the ministry of service relevant to man in his pursuit of healing and hope."[489]

Continuing the need to deepen the theological meaning of the voluntary service, Gerald C. Studer was commissioned to present a series of five lectures to the Association of Mennonite Aid Societies in 1965, entitled "Toward a Theology of Servant-hood."[490] Studer conceptualized five principles regarding mutual aid: 1) God's Principle for all Life; 2) an Ordinance of Christ's Church; 3) An Expression of the Holy Spirit; 4) A Secret of Happiness; and 5) the Basis of Judgment.[491]

1). Studer opens his discussion with a citation from anarchist Peter Kropotkin: "We have heard so much lately of the harsh, pitiless struggle for life that it was necessary to oppose to these assertions a wide series of facts showing animal and human life under quite a different aspect"[492] Studer then observed: "In a sense, not only man but all creation is made in the image of God in that mutuality is found to be a basic principle in creation which applies to all life whether within the Godhead, or between God and man, or between man and man, or between man and creation."[493]

2) In "Mutual Aid: Ordinance of Christ Church" Studer pointed to the example of Jesus' feet-washing, which was to become the model for all time. Studer said:

> "The disciples watched Jesus in shocked silence. So Jesus resumed His place at the table and said, 'Do you know what I have done to you? You call me Teacher and Lord; and you are right, for so I am. If I, your Lord, and teacher, have washed your feet, you also ought to wash one another's

feet. Truly, truly, I say to you, a servant is not greater than his master; nor is he who is sent greater than his master; If you know these things, blessed are you if you do them."[494]

Studer maintained that this stance and behavior—servant-hood—is normative for the Christian church by focusing on the Holy Spirit.

3) "Mutual Aid: An expression of the Holy Spirit." "Now had come the real test of their profession of Christ; they must recognize the unmeasured emergency of the present hour and prove the meaning of Christian brotherhood. The Pentecostal baptism took an ancient law of God, even as Jesus said, and fulfilled it."[495] In the brotherhood of the spirit, "what is mine is thine." In this stance, Studer claims that "the New Testament reading of mutual aid is a far cry from the common emphasis in Christendom on 'charity' with the former being unconditional, while the latter is not."

4) In "Mutual Aid: The Secret of Happiness," Studer focused on the Beatitudes in the New Testament that refer to the psychological and spiritual benefits of the life of giving and service, namely, "that it is more blessed to give than to receive." Beginning with the Beatitudes, the theme in the remainder of the New Testament, points to the "blessings" of giving and serving. "Again and again people have testified that the happiest times of their lives have been times when, in spite of the direst conditions of emergency, they have given themselves unstintingly to others."[496]

5) In "Mutual Aid: The Basis of Judgment," the basis for the final consummation of the ages, and the separation of the saints from the non-elect, is illustrated in the last judgment described by Jesus. "When the Son of man comes in his glory, and all the angels with him, then he will sit on his glorious throne. Before him will be gathered all the nations, and he will separate them one from another as a shepherd separates the sheep from the goats." The well-known discourse ends with "Truly, I say THIS to you, as you did it [fed, clothed and gave shelter, and healed people] to one of the least of these my brethren, you did it to me."[497]

SECTION III. THE RADICAL REFORMATION ETHIC OF SERVICE

The work of Jesus' disciples, and the church created after he was crucified, thus rests on the command to serve the needy. Walter Rauschenbusch expresses this concern:

> "For ages the cross of Christ has stood at the center of Christian theology. But many good men who are loud in their insistence on the cross as the only means of salvation have apparently never had any experience of the pain of the cross. They do not bear the marks of the Lord Jesus. Their religion has served to make them respected. Social work, the kind that deals with the causes of misery, is today almost the only form of Christian work that involves the risk of persecution." [498]

Several years later, Peter J. Dyck maintained that Mennonites have long had a latent "philosophy of service, but the theology was[came] first." [499] This theology was based on a rather strict biblicism, and Dyck concurs with J. C. Wenger: "It is the nature of Mennonites to take an attitude of confident trust in Christ and the Holy Scriptures and to render resolute obedience to the Lord as required in His word. The key concept for Mennonites is not philosophical theology but earnest disciples to Christ, even unto death, if need be." [500]

Dyck suggests that the Anabaptist theology of service is based on the following principles: 1) To serve is to confirm God's Abiding Principle of life. Jesus "came not to be served but to serve" (Matt: 20:28). Sub-topics include: to serve is to live, and word and deed are one; 2) Service is concerned with causes and goes to the root of the problem, namely to treat the sources of need, pain, and conflict; and finally 3) Service is Eschatological, hope made visible. In a recent entry in the *Mennonite Encyclopedia*, Dyck added another dimension by stating that the motivation for service often changed or was multifaceted: "One might enter service simply to help the poor but end up realizing one's own poverty and thus take a significant and often first step to authentic self-awareness and spiritual growth." [501]

Dyck was concerned that "service to others" might become "humanitarianism" or stated more plainly, "promoting human welfare without references to God or Jesus Christ." [502] As such, service might become secular and pragmatic. Dyck concluded: "Other Mennonites regard any act of love as a witness to God. All service is of necessity performed by people for people, even when the motivation is to glorify God. To negate the human element in the churches' relief and "development work is to deny that 'love, joy, peace, patience, kindness, goodness, faithfulness, gentleness, and self-control' (Gal. 5:22) need flesh and blood to make them useful and real. When John says that 'the Word became flesh and dwelt among us' (Jn.1:14), he is affirming the humanness of Jesus Christ." [503]

Dyck responds to this concern, and often expressed that motivation to witness and proselytizing could contradict the motivation of "agape love with no strings attached." This concern has been especially significant for the Mennonite Central Committee (MCC) workers and volunteers.

To solve this dilemma, Helmut Harder proposed that "Anabaptists are quick to point out that good deeds are not to be offered as merit before God. Rather the good deeds of the believer are an extension of the gracious work of God in the life of the believer; indeed, they are an extension of the salvific work of God as such. This means that if good works are not in evidence, it is questionable whether the saving work of God has taken root in the person." Harder provides historical evidence based on Menno's statement: "Grace does not make its original entrance with the Fall: it is present already in the act of creation. Inasmuch as the divine act of creation establishes the works of God, grace therefore is integral to works." [504]

Gerald W. Schlabach has suggested that Mennonite motivation to service is based on the example of the Good Samaritan "cup of cold water." Mennonites need Samaritan-like reflexes for responding to human need. Otherwise, our service institutions may grow more sophisticated but lose their soul. In the face of massive global poverty, world hunger, and entrenched systems of injustice, guilt and obligation sometimes drive the would-be disciple to despair rather than service. Individual idealism alone is not sustainable, and service done out of guilt even less so.[505]

SECTION III. THE RADICAL REFORMATION ETHIC OF SERVICE

But "Mennonite theology of service and social responsibility have not kept pace with Mennonite programs. The continuing struggle over how to integrate word and deed is only the first of various areas where we lack church wide consensus."[506] He suggests that Anabaptists' two-kingdom theology has confused us as much as one-kingdom theology has confused other traditions. In the former, we have been caught in an uneasy balance between the building of our own communities and being concerned about God's will for *Shalom* for the whole world. In the latter case, one-kingdom theology tends to under-emphasize the need for the radical change of conversion. "The kingdom toward which we work tends to be merely a reformed version of the present systems of power. One-kingdom theology also tends to underestimate the need for covenanted community."[507]

Schlabach proposes that the "Abrahamic Model" provides a synthesis of the dilemma, though it also is a paradox: At the becoming of a new community, moving beyond the community's self-preservation is what gives the Abrahamic community its creativity and the paradigm its power. The power of this model is that "we may be less likely to confuse specific service institutions with service itself." It will also keep the church's care for itself from becoming neurotic and self-absorbed. "The community loses its reason for being unless it lives for other communities."[508]

Ted Koontz states: "MCC has confronted many complications related to its explicitly Christian identity, particularly in areas where other religions, especially Islam, are dominant. The struggle is to be clear about our identity, open about explaining who we are and what we believe, and yet respectful of and acceptable to another culture and religions. In such contexts, MCC has sometimes been hesitant to speak of Christian faith and invite others to faith."[509]

Ted Koontz critiques the concept of service based on his analysis of MCC's self-definition: "A Christian Resource for Meeting Human Needs."[510] He believes that most Mennonites believe "that 'service' is central to Christian faith and that a program such as MCC's is the vehicle through which they should express their commitment to serve." This "theology stresses the horizontal rather than the vertical relationship. Indeed, in a strict sense the theology here is more ethics (systematic thoughts about right living) than theology (systematic thoughts about God.) ...the accent here is on right human relations and not on worship."[511]

Koontz states that complications can emerge from misunderstanding service. Our patterns of our thinking may contribute to the very sense of dis-empowerment that we seek to overcome. "'Servant-hood' theology can lead to a focus on the centrality of our work." Servant-hood theology that is based on our power will grind us into the dust. Finally, Koontz is concerned that "This theology directs our attention to human action and human need. It causes us to see ourselves and other human beings first and foremost, not God."[512] We need to focus on "God's marvelous resourcefulness, God's blessing" rather than on humans needs. It should make us see that the fundamental point of discipleship is to appropriate and reciprocate God's blessing.

Central to this new way of looking at service is "blessing people rather than only helping them...The deep sense of neediness, scarcity and dependence, which is bred into many of the world's marginalized can most adequately be overcome as they see themselves valued, cared for and blessed."[513] Koontz believes that persons are not themselves the basic 'agents' of sharing but are merely instruments through which God acts. Referring to MCC, he suggests, "Rather than becoming merely a funding agency, blessings are given and received primarily through people. Like the Eucharist, theology begins with God's gift. Discipleship is a response to it. Our life begins as a gift from God's abundance and is lived in the midst of God's provision and goodness, not first and foremost in the context of neediness and scarcity."[514]

The ultimate objective is to understand "the biblical relationship between blessing and servant-hood. The gospel promises that a life of servant-hood is a life of being richly blessed."[515] The ultimate criteria for serving is thus the blessing that the servant experience gives, regardless of whether the needy are fully helped.

Theologian John Howard Yoder proposed a position based on the traditional Anabaptist dualism though with a new emphasis: "Anabaptism, in its attempt to break with the fusion between the authority of the church and

SECTION III. THE RADICAL REFORMATION ETHIC OF SERVICE

the power of structures of governance—Constantinian-ism demonstrated a model of the church as a 'messianic community' of reconciliation and agape love under the exclusive lordship of Christ."[516] Yoder proposed that this cannot be imposed on the larger social order. "It is a revolutionary subordination" as demonstrated in Jesus' own life."[517] Yoder also says, "Jesus' motto of revolutionary subordination, of willing servant-hood in the place of domination, enables the person in a subordinate position in society to accept and live within that status without resentment, at the same time that it calls upon the person in the super-ordinate position to forsake or renounce all domineering use of his status…the claim is not that there is immediately a new world regime which violently replaces the old; but rather the old and the new order exist concurrently on different levels."392 .

Mennonite scholar Lydia Harder interprets Yoder's teaching by suggesting this subordination is characterized by servant-hood, a radical giving up of the need to control the direction in which society is going. For those in super-ordinate positions, this implies a giving up of all domineering uses of their status and power. Following the way of the cross means living the life of servant-hood, self-giving, and even self-abasement in order to demonstrate the reality of the confession that Christ is Lord. Thus, Christians can participate in the character of God's victorious patience with the rebellious powers of his creation.[518]

Yoder's philosophy of the role of the Christian maintains that it is "Far more accurate to say that it is the ethic of Jesus himself that was transmitted and transmuted into the stance of the servant church within society. Since in the resurrection and in Pentecost the kingdom which was imminent has now in part come into our history, the church can now live out, within the structures of society, the newness of the life in that kingdom."[519]

This "revolutionary subordination" is a recent attempt to reconcile the ethics of the Kingdom of God (two-kingdom theology) and the existing socio-political world, which is God-ordained and which Yoder accepts as biblically mandated.[520] Christians must recognize the need for governing institutions, even though they may be corrupt, and that it is in the willing submission through the servant-hood model of Jesus, by which God's rule is ultimately achieved. "The voluntary subjection of the church is understood as a witness to the world." [521]

II. *The Relationship between Missions and Service*

Samuel Escobar was deeply impacted by MCC and proposed that a "rediscovery of mission as God's mission [requires that it be understood as] driven by the Holy Spirit and modeled by Jesus Christ." [522] Observing Mennonites today, he concluded that they should recognize that the Anabaptists ancestors believed "in the relevance and validity of Jesus Christ as a model for life and mission. Life patterned by the model of Jesus was to be a contrast with the predominant values of Christendom at that point." [523]

Mission and service are of one nature. "If actions of service are connected to faith in Jesus Christ, the faithful servants cannot avoid pointing to their Master as the source. They must give testimony of their faith." [524] Escobar maintained that "we cannot afford to separate lifestyle from the truth that nourishes it." Faith in Jesus and obeying him are inseparable. He quotes Jesus in Matt. 7:21-25: "Not everyone who says to me, Lord, Lord, will enter the kingdom of heaven, but only the one who does the will of my father in heaven." He sums up his argument by stating: "As the Father has sent Me, I am sending you. This is the text in which we have not only a mandate for mission but also a model for mission style." [525] That is, healing, comforting, feeding, and liberating.

A close connection between mission and service is also promoted by missions executive Wilbert R. Shenk. He structures his argument regarding missions and service by three distinct stages: "de-provincializing, internationalization, and globalization." [526] Shenk reflects Guy F. Hershberger's statement that Mennonite involvement abroad in the twentieth century was the result of "Mennonites [being] engaged in the recovery 'of the Anabaptists vision of mission and service'." [527] Shenk refers to the social upheavals of World War I and II as part of the awakening to international missions, including the work of the MCC. [528]

Recent contributions to the understanding of service have also been derived from sociological research. One comprehensive sociological/anthropological study utilized score reports from development workers regarding their understanding of motivation to do humanitarian service and what its elements are and have been in the last several decades. An integration of the combined data produced a set of ultimate values, which comprised the "Anabaptist Theology/Ethic." The study concluded that the Anabaptist theology itself was based on a system of values, upon which an ethical system was founded. These fundamental values were justice, sustainability, quality of life, and peace/shalom. [529] The authors maintained that these four ultimate values were inter-related and interdependent. None was independent of the others. For example, no activity or belief was relevant unless it contributed to sustained or affirming life and happiness. Further, quality of life was possible only if there was justice. And finally, peace is clearly not attainable without justice.

Another source for this analysis is a content analysis of leading Anabaptist scholars regarding the essential elements of an Anabaptist's ethic and theology, which produced similar results. It also concluded that there were a set of intermediate or instrumental values "that were necessary for the achievement of the ultimate values. These were people-centeredness, service, integrity, mutuality, authenticity, humility, justice, and peace."[530] There is overlapping and interdependence. For example, justice is an instrumental (a means) value as well as an ultimate goal (the ends). The emphasis on the interrelatedness of these values in the reports of the Mennonite development practitioners and scholars seems striking. [531]

III. Recent movement toward relevancy and responsibility

College President J. Lawrence Burkholder has proposed that, whereas the Mennonite Church was earlier concerned with self-preservation, it has in recent decades desired to become socially relevant.[532] He suggests that the Mennonite church has decided that the road to social relevance is "an alternative approach to the problems of society in the form of world relief, rehabilitation, and social service under the auspices of the church and closely integrated to its missionary program." [533] He believes that the Mennonite tradition "rejects the position of ultimate responsibility for the stream of history and yet seeks to express a position of responsibility by entering into the problems of the world at crucial if not final areas." [534]

Burkholder describes this middle position as "The Guiding Principles of Voluntary Service." The first principal is that "voluntary service is intended to express *agape* love in its purity and in its simplicity in accordance with the synoptic ideal," meaning, personal face-to-to face relations, which are the essential New Testament context. [535] As such, the voluntary service program is "designed to reinstate the simple synoptic situation in which love can flow with the least hindrance from the intermediate (intermediating?) factors of organization and bureaucracy." [536]

The second principle states that voluntary service is offered under the auspices and supervision of the church: "It is the church in action." [537] This means that "a deliberate attempt is made to make a Christian impact with social service all along the way by placing Christian men and women at the points where contact is made with those who benefit by the program." It avoids the danger of secularization by the time social action takes concrete form, because of the direct contact with Christians providing service.

In the third principle, Burkholder proposes that service is a program of lay Christianity: "The appeal of voluntary service is that every member of the church should be confronted with the needs of the world and should give serious consideration to a period of service for the church and world according to his talents and circumstances." [538] This new access to "social responsibility" enables "the introduction of the sacrificial principle into the social structure. It is a kind of functional asceticism which is implicit in the command to seek first the Kingdom of God." [539]

Finally, Burkholder proposes that this alternative voluntary service approach to the needs of society is an extension of the "redemptive community." He proposes that this principle is based on the "conviction that social disorder is ultimately reducible to spiritual disorder (Eph. 6:1'2) and spiritual disorder cannot be corrected genuinely except by full impact of the community of Christ." [540] The emphasis is on redemption, rather than the general idea of the reform of existing structures, which normally leads to disillusionment: "The redemptive approach assumes that peace and justice can be achieved in this world only when men(sic) are reconciled to one another in Christ."[541]

Burkholder describes this ethic of voluntary service as being "An Alternative Approach to the Problems of Society." It is built on the position that *agape* love is the only approach to justice that abjures the use of violence in any form; it is not punitive or retributive. He believes that *agape* love cannot be fully expressed in complex society without violating itself. Voluntary service is a direct channel for enacting agape love with the needs of humanity, and hence working for justice without using violence.[542]

The growing conviction that service is an integral part of the Anabaptist tradition is indicated by recent developments initiated by the Mennonite World Conference. This alliance of Mennonite conferences around the world is formed and committed to nurture and shepherd the various Mennonites communities in over sixty-one countries. A major consultation on "service" was held in San Jose, California on March 7-8, 2006, before the MWC council's annual meeting. The goal of the conference was "to examine how the New Testament deacon role can be adapted to serve the marginalized within the global Anabaptist family in the 21st century."[543]

Among the presentations was one by Ronald Sider, entitled "The Biblical Foundation of Service." In it, he proposed the following: "Service to others is grounded in at least six biblical and theological principles: Service to others is grounded in God's love for us; God's love prompts us to love others; every person is made in the image of God; each person is both body and soul; real service responds to both material and spiritual needs; Jesus' Gospel of the Kingdom means all social relations are being set right, between rich and poor etc.; Christians serve because through the cross of Christ, we are one, so we must serve each other. The cross is a central foundation of service in the church; and finally, we serve each other in the church because we are the one body of Christ.[544]

The assembly consequently "approved a statement of shared convictions to give members round the world a clearer picture of beliefs Anabaptist hold in common."[545] The statement was entitled "Shared Convictions."

It concluded that Anabaptist belief and practice focuses on four major categories (pillars), namely: Fellowship, Worship, Mission and Service." Principle number one states: "God is known to us as Father, Son and Holy Spirit, the Creator who seeks to restore fallen humanity by calling a people to be faithful in fellowship, worship, service and witness."[546] The last principle, number seven, repeats the theme of service again: "We seek to live in the world without conforming to the powers of evil, witnessing to God's grace by serving others, caring for creation, and inviting all people to know Jesus Christ as Savior and Lord."[547]

Historian Sarah Johnson proposes that "The Shared Convictions mark an extremely important point in the history of the Anabaptist movement: (1) Shared Convictions are a global document. They reflect the true nature of the Mennonite and Brethren in Christ church as a global community; (2) the Shared Convictions will play an increasingly large role in shaping the identity of Anabaptist-related churches as they are more and more often asked to define themselves in ecumenical, interfaith, and secular contexts; (3) the Convictions reflect a remarkable unity; (4) Finally, the Shared Convictions are accessible. They are concise yet comprehensive, using simple yet precise language."[548]

It is significant that the first global Anabaptist collective summary of basic beliefs and principles should include the principle of service to others in three of the seven principles. This service attitude may reflect the global perspective of Anabaptists who reside in predominantly underdeveloped countries, where living standards and material needs are more pronounced than they are in the West.

B) The Quaker/Friends Perspective on Service.

This discussion of the Quaker theology and philosophy of service is derived from published writings, but even then, definitive and official treatments are relatively sparse. This is largely because the Quaker denominational process in developing the theology and ethics of service is not nearly as extensive or explicit as the Mennonite or the Brethren.[549] One of the

SECTION III. THE RADICAL REFORMATION ETHIC OF SERVICE

common explanations, as is well known, is that the Society of Friends is not a creedal denomination.

> "Friends did not deny orthodox Christian beliefs; in fact, they took them for granted. Their criticism was directed at the interpretation and use of the creeds as texts of Christian beliefs, not at the beliefs themselves…Thus the Quaker protest against creeds was the danger of their formulation in words, no matter how logical and consistent, that would render these beliefs incapable of expression as personal experience of the Holy Spirit enriched their meaning." [550]

Another reason is that there is considerable variety in Friends theological thinking and action. But there is no question that the amazing service contribution of the Quakers, especially by the widely acclaimed American Friends Service Committee (AFSC) and other service organizations and activities around the world derive from and depend upon an underlying or *implicit theology and ethic*.

Ironically the Quakers, possibly the most universally known for their service activities, especially via the AFSC, should have not provided more public discussion of the reasons, philosophically or theologically, why they have done so much in service to others. It is also probable that the reasons can be traced back to Quaker founder George Fox, who despaired the "professors" and the preachers and discovered "there was none among them all that could speak to my condition." [551] It was instead, as his future wife reported, that George Fox turned away from learned professions and spoke in meeting thus:

> "The Scriptures were the prophets 'words and Christ's and the apostles' words, and what as they spoke they enjoyed and possessed and had it from the Lord. (But) You will say, Christ, saith this, and the apostles say this; but what canst thou say? Art thou a child of Light and hast walked in the Light, and what thou speakest is it inwardly from God?" [552]

What did Fox mean, other than that walking in the Light meant being open to Christ's leading in all of life, whether worship and contemplation or service to humankind? The Christian faith and life were all of one piece, and what is the use in intellectual speculation?

Quaker beliefs and practice have historically been seen pretty much as made of one fabric, and thus theological reasoning was not really the process by which service was derived or vice versa. Thus, Arthur S. Eddington, a leading Quaker intellectual, maintained:

> "In its early days, our Society owed much to a people who called themselves Seekers; they joined us in great numbers and were prominent in the spread of Quakerism. The name has died out, but I think that the spirit of *seeking* is still the prevailing one in our faith, which for that reason is not embodied in any creed or formula... *Finding* has a clamorous voice that proclaims its own importance. It is definite and assured, something that we can take hold of—yet how transitory it proves. The finding of one generation will not serve for the next." [553]

In 1958, the London Yearly Meeting of Friends adapted the following statement:

> "The most important thing is that each one of us should be sensitive to the call of God to ourselves and not spend time in passing judgment on the lives of other. To (some) the most important thing will be to maintain our ancient testimony against "fightings" with outward weapons, for any end, or under any pretence whatever. But perhaps most will be called to the humdrum tasks of serving an employer supremely well, or running a house, bringing up a family, keeping the peace. Our duty is to be sensitive to do what God is asking us to do, and not to dissipate our energies trying to be absolutists in several directions at once." [554]

SECTION III. THE RADICAL REFORMATION ETHIC OF SERVICE

However, the Society of Friends have become party to tensions between the stress on theological "truths" and the stress on "seeking" the Christ in experience. This is indicated in the discussion of service by T. Canby Jones, included below. Alexander Purdy, an accomplished theologian, nevertheless spoke to this rift between "spiritual Quakerism and "service Quakerism" as follows:

> "The ancient words about God's love, about Christ and the cross, about the Holy Spirit and the Church have lost for many their primitive power. They are only sure of a vocation to share humanity's suffering and enlist others in like calling. Are we to rebuke such as these? The love of God in Christ calls for disciplined, selfless service. Our service must have roots deep enough to hold when evil is apparently not overcome by good. It may be that such service will be the pathway to worship and faith, as worship and faith issue in service. The two are one in Christ." [555]

Though few substantive and definitive treatments focusing on the theological meaning and motivation for service in the Quaker tradition are available, they indirectly have a theological implication. One such powerful treatment of service is produced by T. Canby Jones in the journal *Quaker Religious Thought*.[556] His purpose in the treatise is to show how Jesus can bring "reconciliation between 'Christ-centered Quakers' and 'service-minded' Quakers."[557] Though this treatment cannot be assumed to be speaking for all Friends, Jones, with deep experience in Friends experience and life, provides significant understandings to the topic.[558]

Jones presents three approaches to Quaker motivation for service: scriptural, theological, and pragmatic. In the scriptural approach, Jones states there are "many biblical sections dealing with the Servant of the Lord and Christ as servant."[559] But his favorite scripture is this: "But whoever would be great among you must be slave of all. For the Son of man also came not to be served but to serve." This service was in the form of the "suffering servant" (referring to Isaiah 53). "It means we must suffer on behalf of others; we must follow Christ's steps, always seeking to act with redemptive love."

157

Jones believes "it is a curious thing that one of the most striking examples in Scripture of Jesus acting as servant is John Chapter 13, verses 3-15. You will remember that it is the account of Jesus washing the disciple's feet." [560] Jones affirms that "washing his disciple's feet is his final sign of service" (which is expanded upon below). [561]

The concept of *kenosis* (emptying), as stated in Philippians 2:6-11, is (as argued by Jones) the next and major Scriptural basis for service. The statement is as follows: "Though he was in the form of God, did not count equality with God a thing to be grasped, but emptied himself, taking the form of a servant...humbled himself and become obedient unto death, even death on a cross." [562] Jones considers this the essential meaning of the incarnation. "Who then is this who is among us as one who serves, who goes about healing and doing good, who suffers vicariously for others, who empties himself and obeys to the death and thereby is exalted above all? It is Jesus, the Lord's anointed one, acting as a servant." [563]

From a directly theological perspective, Jones suggests that Quakers add another function or "office" of Christ to the traditional three of prophet, priest, and king, introduced by John Calvin. The office of "or function of the eternal Christ—the office of servant." Jones reminds us that George Fox, the early founding Quaker, defined Christ in reference to service as the fourth office. In his well-known phrase, "Jesus Christ is come to teach His people without mediation of sacrament or priests, a living teaching, a guiding presence." Fox seems to suggest a servant role, according to Jones.[564] But Jones is quick to maintain that Jesus came "in his office as servant, and about this Fox and for that matter until our own day almost no one since John Calvin has had anything to significant to say." [565]

The final theological argument focuses on Jesus' rejection of becoming the messiah and establishing the Kingdom of God on earth. Instead, Jesus favored "a Messianism based on the suffering servant of Isaiah. Love, forgiveness, and service replace hatred, revenge, and nationalism as the motif." [566] T. Canby Jones continues: "As servant of Yahweh, Jesus rejected Jewish political Messianism and was therefore despised, and betrayed by a Zealot. He demonstrates the fulfillment of the law and the rule of God by acting

SECTION III. THE RADICAL REFORMATION ETHIC OF SERVICE

as servant in perfect love to God and man. He understood the kingdom of God essentially as a redemptive fellowship where deeds of love culminate in the triumph of his love on the cross."[567]

Jones believes that the Kenotic theory of self-abasement by service does not denigrate the classic omniscience, omnipotence, and omnipresence aspects of God and supports Vincent Taylor's position that the three attributes of God are not discarded, "but remain in our Lord in his servant-hood as latent, potential and undestroyed." After all, the self-abasement of God in becoming a servant is self-imposed and "by the redemptive purpose flowing from it."[568]

Jones concludes the theological approach by stating, "Jesus, the Messiah, in his humiliation and human limitations, in becoming obedient unto death, and in his becoming servant of all, most powerfully demonstrates his exalted lordship, his kingly power, the fact that he is the conquering lamb worthy of all power and riches and wisdom and honor and glory and blessing. He has become first among us and first in the whole creation because he is in truth the servant of all."[569]

The third section of Jones' treatise on service is to deal with "two divergent tendencies, especially in Quakerism: on the one hand are those who accept the Lordship of Jesus as the Christ and have personally experienced his saving grace but are weak in serving humanity through works of mercy. On the other hand, are Friends who focus on man and his needs doing good to mankind on a world-wide scale yet failing to see Jesus as the Servant-Messiah whom every tongue should confess as Lord." Though Jones says no Quaker fits either exactly, the first group tends to be the evangelical type, with "much willingness to honor Christ as prophet, priest, or even king, but few are willing to do what he says and to follow his steps of service, suffering, humiliation and redemptive love."[570]

The second group of Friends are those "who specialize in service and seek to speak only through their lives and deeds." The question for this group is "whether the gospel of work-camps, international student seminars, Quaker United Nations Programs, and Volunteers for International Service Assignments, when not done in the name or power of the Servant who loved us and gave himself for us, is an adequate or sufficient gospel?" Jones does not deny the value of service as such: "Actually great deeds done solely out of human kindness and concern are still great deeds. But if they are not tinged with Galilean compassion or demonstrate the pattern seen on the Mount or reflect the love of God's chosen servant, can they do permanent good or reach the deepest need in the hearts of men?"[571]

Jones appeals to Friends to come together by recognizing that both orientations need each other: "Oh, how Friends need to come together! How they need each other!" How much the 'Christ-centered Quakers' need to **do** and to serve, to act as Jesus the servant did and to follow in his steps. On the other hand, how much the 'humanist' or 'service minded' Friends need to see humanitarian concern fulfilled and climaxed and all humanity reconciled to God and to one another through God's Servant-Messiah from whose love all selfless service springs.[572]

Jones concludes his prophetic call for Friends:

> "Think again of the servant of Yahweh in Isaiah 53, wounded for our transgressions, bearing our sins and our grief, reconciling us to God and to one another. Think, too, of Jesus, the serene Messiah of the Gospel of John, humbling himself and washing the disciples' feet and calling us in like manner to wash the feet of all."[573]

An English Quaker, who has been noted for essays "notable for the quiet lucidity with which they present uncommonly acute insights" regarding Quaker beliefs also provides several important insights.[574] Littleboy maintained that "After all to be a Christian consists not in feeling, but in following; not in ecstasy but in obedience. The human factor that dominates the situation is not the emotions but the *Will*. The purpose of Jesus was undoubtedly that the hearts of his disciples should be untroubled, and their joy be made full." But then Littleboy continues, "Nevertheless Jesus rarely, if ever, made any emotional demand upon those who came to Him. His tests were always practical: 'Follow me.' 'Take up your cross.' 'Go and publish

SECTION III. THE RADICAL REFORMATION ETHIC OF SERVICE

abroad the Kingdom of God.' The proof of love lay not in adoration but in action. 'If you love Me, ye will keep My commandments.'" [575]

Littleboy then zeroes in on the central issue, which seems to be addressed to the Quaker tendency to mystic union with Christ and God:

> "To serve Christ, not to feel Christ, is the mark of His true servants; they become Christians in proportion as they cease to be interested in themselves and become absorbed in their Lord. His divine goodness shone in nothing more brightly than this; that He never allowed the inward conflict to interfere with His service for others. They who so lightly appealed to Him for relief, little knew the burden which rested on His own spirit."[576]

Littleboy concludes by suggesting that the "afflictions of Christ" must, however, be assumed by the Church, since individuals cannot do it by themselves. This seems to imply that some types of service to others demands collective effort.

This is by no means a full exposition of Quaker theology and ethic regarding service, but it provides insights for some of the reasons for the relative lack of producing and publishing of a "theology and ethic of service."

C) The Church of the Brethren Ethic of Service [577]

To discuss the Church of the Brethren motivation and rational for doing good, it's important to look once again to the origins of the Brethren in Schwarzenau in 1708. As mentioned earlier, the early Brethren came to the village of Schwarzenau because the regional Prince allowed religious freedom, which was not allowed in most of the other principalities in Germany at that time. The Treaty of Westphalia (1648) was an agreement that stated that the citizens of any principality were required to have the same religion as the ruling prince, the principle of *cuius regio, eius religio*. It ended thirty years of warfare among the various religious traditions in the Holy Roman Empire.

According to Donald Durnbaugh, the preeminent historian of the Brethren movement, both Anabaptism and Pietism influenced those gathered at Schwarzenau.[578] Pietism was a reaction against the aridity of doctrinal disputes that lead to the Thirty Years War. It called for faith to a heart-felt devotion to God that is openly expressed in love service to one's neighbor. Pietism led to circles of Bible study, along with schools, orphanages and other expressions of service. These beliefs had a powerful effect upon the early Brethren.

Pietism was primarily a movement within the organized Evangelical (Lutheran) Church. However, the more radical Pietists broke with the church. One of the leading radical Pietists was the historian Gottfried Arnold, who wrote two works that were very influential for the Brethren: *Die Erste Liebe,* 1696 (The First Love, i.e., a True Picture of the First Christians in Their Living Faith, and Holy Life), and *Unparteiische Kirchen- und Ketzer-Historie,* Frankfurt-am-Main, 1699-1700 *(An Unbiased History of the Church and Heresy).* The former was an account of the early Christian Church showing how deeply devoted to God they were and how much they loved and cared for their neighbors. The latter was an argument for heresy being central to the true church from the time that Christian creeds were first adopted and enforced. The formal church-controlled believers by condemning them as heretics and frequently executing them. Basically, Arnold's teachings were a mysticism of love coupled with a belief that force or compulsion is not appropriate in religion. When persons are so devoted to God that God's love becomes the primary motive in their lives, then their lives become like the lives of Christians in the early church.

Arnold's influence on the Brethren came through Ernst Christoph Hochmann von Hochenau, a student and disciple of Gottfried Arnold. Hochmann traveled through the Palatinate, the area where Schwarzenau is located, preaching about Arnold's Christian mysticism of love and extolling his listeners to convert before the soon-to-be-expected return of Jesus Christ. Alexander Mack sometimes accompanied Hochmann on these trips. When

SECTION III. THE RADICAL REFORMATION ETHIC OF SERVICE

the year 1700 CE came, and Christ's expected return did not occur, Mack and other radical Pietists were uncertain about how to continue their faith.

They wrote to Hochmann, who was in prison in Heidelberg (having been arrested because of his illegal preaching), to ask him whether they should baptize one another in the manner of the early Christians. Hochmann replied that such an adult, three-fold baptism would be permissible according to the scripture but would be meaningless unless their hearts were filled with the love of Christ. Furthermore, they should consider the likelihood of losing reputation and property, as well as becoming engaged in continual disputes and disagreements that are always found in the organized church. Considering Hochmann's response to be one of support, Mack, his wife, and six others held an open baptism in the Eder River in Schwarzenau.

The adoption of adult baptism shows the influence of Anabaptism upon the early Brethren. Anabaptism emphasized adult decision in matters of faith, consensus among the community of the faithful, and care for one's neighbor. Furthermore, the Anabaptism that influenced the early Brethren included a rejection of violence and a refusal to participate in military activity. It included a love of the enemy, as is described in the Sermon on the Mount (Matthew 5-8), and this love was a part of Arnold's mysticism of love. Donald Durnbaugh considered the Schwarzenau group's decision for open, public, immersion baptism in the Eder River to be a clear indication that Anabaptism was predominant over Pietism in the origin of the Brethren. Indeed, the relationship between Mack and radical Pietist Hochmann was strained by the decision of Mack and those with him.

There has been much discussion about the relationship between Pietism and Anabaptism in the beliefs of the early Brethren. While Donald Durnbaugh considers the decision to have a public baptism evidence that Anabaptism was predominant, others have suggested that the two movements are dialectically related, so that in spite of tensions between the two views, each view influences the other in a living tension, first in one direction and then the other. More recently, German scholar Marcus Meier has reexamined the story of the beginnings of the Brethren and contends that too much has been made of the differences between Pietism and Anabaptism.[579]

In Meier's view, Pietism arose in the seventeenth century under the influence of Anabaptism. Pietism grew up in the communities where Anabaptism was already present. The impulse to have a faith that is more than conformity to doctrinal standard was the context in which Pietism developed. The common people in the Palatinate at that time did not distinguish between the two movements. The considered them to be the same. However, Pietism did bring in a mysticism of love, so that Pietism has two roots: Anabaptism and love-mysticism.

Meier contends that most of the Schwarzenau Brethren had left the Reformed Church and that their doctrinal writings are similar to the Reformed catechism.[580] Furthermore, they were influenced by the controversy between the Amish and the Mennonites, which gave the Brethren an intense devotion to the Bible. They took the non-creedalism drawn from Gottfried Arnold and spoke of it as "no creed except the New Testament." So they interpreted the scriptures in a community setting (*conventicals*), with everyone having a voice as they searched for the "mind of Christ." The scriptures were read simply and directly in the community setting and interpreted through a loving devotion to Christ. This was in accordance with Gottfried Arnold's interpretation of the practice of the early church.

According to Meier, still another influence was important for the Schwazenau Brethren, namely the writing of Jane Leade, an English writer who was a leader of the Philadelphians. Her works were translated into Dutch and German, and they circulated among Pietist circles. She wanted to form a trans-confessional community with love and unity as its highest value, and she believed that this would recover church life as it was among the early Christians. She expected that Christ would return to earth in 1700, and there was heightened religious activity among the radical Pietists as that year approached. When the year came and passed with no evidence of Christ's coming, the Pietists were thrown into a great dilemma about how to proceed. This is when Alexander Mack wrote to Christopher von Hochman asking for his advice about baptism. In the absence of Christ's return, Gottfried Arnold and other radical Pietism returned reluctantly to the State Church. Hochmann, upon his release from prison, ceased his preaching and lived a quiet life in Schwarzenau. The Schwarzenau Brethren followed their

SECTION III. THE RADICAL REFORMATION ETHIC OF SERVICE

Anabaptist and "Leadean" convictions by having an open baptism in the hope of mystically joining the life of the early church, as Gottfried Arnold had shown that the true church had lived through the centuries in the lives of the heretics. They were a visible fellowship of love, bound together with the invisible inter-denominational church of love.

The devotion to love as found in the New Testament and the early church led the Schwarzenau Brethren to "ordinances" of adult baptism, the love feast with feet washing, laying on of hands, anointing with oil, and the holy kiss, as well as turning the other cheek, no oaths, going the second mile, giving a cup of cold water, reconciliation, repeated forgiveness, humility, non-violence, and sharing possessions. These are not unbending obligations so much as freely given expressions of love practiced by the early church and evident in reading the New Testament. They represent the interconnected testimony of the inner word and the outer world.

But there are also summary principles that represent the good to the Brethren. Non-creedalism leads to a separation from the world, especially not giving unqualified obedience to any ruler, governor, president, or religious leader. It leads, as is mentioned above, to mutual discernment of the mind of Christ. For example, a leading member of the Brethren during the American colonial period, and well-known printer, Christopher Sauer displayed over his print shop the phrase "For the glory of God and my neighbor's good." In the Pietistic tradition, Brethren are committed to mutual aid and hospitality toward all, simplicity of life style, reconciliation among all people, and seeking to be of service to others rather than in control of them.

A more recent statement of these values was adopted by the General Board of the Church of the Brethren: "Another Way of Living, Continuing the Work of Jesus Peacefully, Simply, Together." Since the Brethren do not adopt creeds, various versions of this statement have developed in the churches: "Following the Way of Jesus – Simply, Peacefully, Together." Another example is this, "Delighting in God's grace, learning from Jesus, growing in the Spirit, engaging in the world's sorrows and joys, peacefully, simply, together." They all move toward beginning now to live in the anticipated Kingdom of God.

Certain virtues arise from the commitment to a community that embodies the love of Christ. Such virtues include love, truthfulness, joy, integrity, fidelity, kindness, forgiveness, patience, simplicity, peace, perseverance, gentleness, boldness, self-control, gratitude, hospitality, willingness to work, openness to the future, willingness to learn, care for the neighbor, and voluntary service. [581]

To illustrate these virtues, let us consider the story a grandson tells about his grandfather George Miller (1722-98), who was the first preacher in the Big Swatara Congregation, Pennsylvania. His ox was stolen, and he knew who had taken it and where it was. However, it was not George Miller but rather his neighbors who turned in the thief, who was then arrested and placed in the Lancaster, Pennsylvania jail. Concerned the man might be whipped publicly and that he might become ill in the cold jail, George Miller walked twenty miles carrying a bed to the thief in order give him comfort.[582]

The mystical community of love that was strongly a part of the radical Pietistic view of the church did not always rest easily with the visibly manifest Anabaptist community of mutual care for one another and for the neighbor. Jane Leade's belief that the age of a trans-confessional community of love and unity would soon be brought by Christ may also be a part of the Brethren belief. In 1741-42, Count Nikolaus Ludvig von Zinzendorf came to Pennsylvania to bring together the various church bodies. In spite of their inclination to a trans-confessional church, they were suspicious of the endeavor and put off by Zinzendorf's imperious manner. Nevertheless, the visit had the effect of the Brethren beginning to come together in an Annual Meeting.

The issue surfaced again with the advent of Universalism, the affirmation that all people will ultimately be saved. Many radical Pietists, including E.C. Hochman and Alexander Mack, with their belief in a mystical community of love, also believed in Universalism. In his writings, Mack affirmed the doctrine of universal restoration but concluded that it must be held privately. A number of colonial writers, including Benjamin Rush and Morgan Edward, announced that the Dunkers (Schwarzenau Brethren) believe in universal restoration.[583] During the eighteenth and nineteenth centuries, several Brethren congregations left the Brethren to join the Universalists. The issue came up repeatedly at Annual Conference throughout the nineteenth century. It was so controversial that the conference repeatedly counseled the church not to affirm universal restoration publicly. In so doing, they were in agreement with Alexander Mack.

Non-creedalism leads naturally to no force in religion, since Gottfried Arnold had extensively documented the church's use of the creed to force people to accept doctrinal positions. Martin Grove Brumbaugh (1862-1930), elected governor of Pennsylvania in 1914, wrote *A History of the German Baptist Brethren in Europe and America* (1899) and strongly affirmed that no force in religion is a fundamental belief of the Brethren.[584]

With Matthew 25:31-46, Brethren understand that God's Kingdom comes as they feed the hungry, welcome the stranger, clothe the naked, heal the sick, and visit the prisoner. We are to embody God's love in care for the neighbor. And this is to be done without any claim of goodness on our own part. "Why do you call me good? No one is good but God alone" (Mark 10:18). So the Brethren are willing to hand off what they initiate in order that it might grow with the support of others, for Brethren believe in the invisible community of love.

The Brethren belief in an invisible community of love has led them to be active in the ecumenical movement of the twentieth century. Since 1919, the Church of the Brethren has moved toward service for peace and justice. For example, along with Heifer International, the Brethren have been a part the Christian Rural Overseas Program (CROP), Church World Service, Brethren Volunteer Service, International Voluntary Service, and the Peace Corps. When the World Council of Churches adopted the Program to Overcome Violence, in 1998, they invited the Peace Churches to give assistance in seeking cultures of peace. This is not so much a set of doctrine as a way of living. More than protest against war, it is a search for the presence of God's reign on earth, continuing the work of Jesus, peacefully simply, together.

Conclusion

In summary, the emphasis of these early developments in the Radical Reformation churches was reviving the early (Pre-Constantine) church and living in accordance with the example of the life of Jesus with others in community. As noted, the focus was less upon nonviolence as a doctrinal creed and more upon living it in relationships with the neighbor. Therefore, the Radical Reformation primarily emphasized mutual aid and service, which developed from the practical life in community. Less emphasis was placed on the cognitive components of individual action or agency (i.e. having a correct belief in certain dogmas, doctrines, and systematic theologies with the requisite liturgies). Rather, religious devotion was expressed in the voluntarism dimensions of individual agency and to behaviors and actions that promote the good of others.

Nonviolence, or pacifism, was not superseded; it was still considered a constitutive or essential element of the early church, but more directly in terms of the effects of interaction with the neighbor. It is clear that love is not expressed simply as emotion or precept; it expresses itself in ethical action that nurtures and sustains others. In this way, these developments are decisively pro-social. Doing good is a voluntary act of service, charity, and loving your neighbor.

CHAPTER 9.
The Radical Reformation Understanding of Serving as the Path to Justice

We now turn to a synthesis of the major issues in the emerging paradigm of serving as the path to justice, from the perspective of three Radical Reformation/Anabaptist groups. As indicated above, Christian ecumenical churches have been primarily concerned with unity of the church order and polity. But numerous Radical Reformation, Anabaptist, or Peace Churches face a paradox: They reject institutionalism and nationalism, and have emphasized instead the concrete aspects of the Christian enterprise, namely ethical Christianity, ultimately defined as love of neighbor as active human compassion.[585] But because of its public minority status, it turned mainly inward and thus tended to institutionalize service just as the wider Christian church had done in its own spheres [586]

Only in the twentieth century did service become directed outwardly toward responsibility. This dilemma is thus the driving dynamic regarding the role of volunteering for the common good, as service as the path to justice. It is this deliberate outward gaze into the broader social environment that moves from a narrow focus on the concern for purity of motivation for one's own actions, expanding to consider the means and ends of social action in the world that moves along the path to justice. The emphasis on service is a move to truly recognize the needs and dignity of the neighbor.

A) A Brief Historical Review

The "early church" in the decades and centuries following Jesus' death was marked by intense debate about essential doctrines and dogmas of the "new way." For example, the divinity of Jesus was not settled until 325, and the doctrine of the Trinity and role of the Holy Spirit was not agreed upon until 381. [587] Thus, for the first three hundred and fifty years of Christianity, there was a lack of uniformity regarding even the very nature of God. However, the early Christian church was quite unified in their stance towards nonviolence and force: "For the first three to four centuries of Christianity, pacifism was the norm for Christians," although the debates about its meaning and application is ongoing.[588] The goal of the Reformation was not to introduce a new religion but to restore the church to its original authenticity.

While we have chosen to use the term Radical Reformation, we are aware and acknowledge that this includes the three major groups analyzed in this book plus several other denominations and terms (see endnote 585 for details). The Radical Reformers felt the most authentic approach was to focus on the New Testament, and especially the teachings and the life of Jesus. The Radical Reformers felt the most authentic approach way was to focus on the New Testament, and especially the teachings and the life of Jesus. [589] But a coherent and identifiable theology and ethic of the Radical Reformation has evolved rather slowly and unevenly. The theology and ethic that draws upon the teachings and life of Jesus is noticeable, though it was not very consciously expressed, as well as the experience of the early Church as it relates to the practice of voluntary service and mutual aid. It is precisely this growing consciousness that is the focus in the following analysis. On the bases of the witness of service presented in the second section of this book, the evidence convincingly indicates that the Mennonites have been more aggressive in articulating the theological and ethical bases for doing good service, than the Church of the Brethren and Quakers, though they were also notable. [590]

The Radical Reformation terminology was not widely used during the origins of the Reformation. Nor did it exist in organizational or structured ecclesiastical or institutional form. The concept grew partially out of the

SECTION III. THE RADICAL REFORMATION ETHIC OF SERVICE

"Historic Peace Churches" movement, begun in 1935. The Historic Peace Churches defined those religious groups who identified with each other especially as it pertained to pacifism and nonresistance. [591] Their common peace heritage "has become a constructive point of reference ecumenically."[592] A successor, the "Believers Church" idea, emerged around 1955 to define those HPC and other religious groups who also had direct or indirect relations or source in the Reformation." [593]

Durnbaugh states the characteristics of the "Believers' Churches" to include: "scriptural (especially New Testament) authority; discipleship to Christ as Lord; regenerate church membership; covenant of voluntarily-gathered believers; adult baptism, separation form the world, mutual aid and Christian service and a non-organizational (sic) view of church unity." [594] According to Durnbaugh, the list includes the Baptists, Church of the Brethren, Christian Church (Disciples of Christ), Churches of Christ, Churches of God, Friends, Mennonites, Pentecostals, and others, based on having at least having some identification with the Believers' Church. [595]

There was also growing concerns by scholars such as Franklin H. Littell and John H. Yoder that the "Free Church" concept had a message that needed to be shared with the larger Christian community: "[Littell] was a leading participant in [such gatherings] and delineated the significance of the 'left wing' of the Reformation for modern church life." [596] The "Free Church" *perspective*, originally derived from the three main "peace churches" has expanded theoretically to include many other groups who identify with the principles. This perspective broadens the power of the Radical Reformation idea, but whether it will develop into something more inclusive of other denominations remains to be seen [597].

Though Durnbaugh's definition tends to make beliefs an identifying criterion, George Hunston Williams correctly maintained that the Believers' Church "is and was, first of all, not primarily a community of visible explicit behavior, as over against the idea of an invisible church. The stress was far more on obedience, purity, simplicity, discipleship, covenantal accountability, mutual support, mutual discipline, and mutual, though also exclusive, love." [598] In other words, an ethical religion.

> "The visible community is the organ of witness to the surrounding society. As discerning community, it is led by the Holy Spirit to develop criteria of moral judgment in social issues. As forgiven community, she brings to bear the qualities of compassion and love. The democratization of the power structures of society and development of welfare concerns are pioneered and preached by the covenanted community." [599]

There is general consensus that the Radical Reformation orientation maintains that propositions, dogmas, beliefs, and principles cannot be separated from actions, and must also be internally consistent. The emphasis is on discipleship—following Jesus—and less on piety, spirituality, emotions, subjective experience, and propositional expression of faith. [600] Said another way, emphasis is placed on modeling the ethical examples set forward by the life and actions of Jesus and less emphasis upon belief in this or that doctrine. [601]

B) The Radical Reformation and Service

There may be no universal concept or reality called doing good, nor does it operate uniformly in all societies. Who defines what is good? However, a relatively uniform description of voluntary service enterprise, as expressed in the Mennonites, the Church of the Brethren, and the Quakers, is proposed below. [602] The predominant material regarding service, however, will come from the three groups who have already been described above.[603] Durnbaugh, affirms that:

> "Probably no characteristic has been so often noted and so appreciated by society at large as the penchant of Believers' Churchmen [sic] in practicing mutual aid and service. No adequate book can be written on humanitarianism—be it the abolition of slavery, aid to refugees, care of minorities, amelioration of working conditions, improvement of

SECTION III. THE RADICAL REFORMATION ETHIC OF SERVICE

prisons, defense of civil rights—without taking into account of the contributions of these groups."[604]

We need to be mindful, however, that this interpretation of Radical Reformation is also not the only unique expression of the universal concept of good service. Identifying and describing the concept of doing good in the large world or Christian community is beyond the intention of this work. For example, the Roman Catholic Church's participation in *diakonia* is global, including the work of the monastic movement, the Roman Catholic charity organization *Caritas*, which has a strong women's presence, and many other organizations. Other denominations have similar spheres of activity. In other words, good service is found in every denomination, every religion, and every culture.

One of the most significant issues in the specific context of the Radical Reformation was their idea of voluntarism in every aspect of life, not only in the religious sphere. James Luther Adams has maintained that "in modern history, the first crucial affirmation of voluntary-ism as an institutional phenomenon appeared in the demand of the sects for the separation of church and state. The rationale for this voluntarism was worked out theologically by the sectarians of the sixteenth and seventeenth centuries, and more in terms of social and political theory by Thomas Hobbes, and John Locke in the next century."[605]

Adams proposes that this principle gave individuals the basic freedom of choice regarding not only relations and obligations to the state but to the society as well. Adams further states that Hobbes and others strongly objected to this religious freedom, for they thought this would lead to anarchy and chaos. Hobbes and his colleagues were partly right of course, but Adams maintains that with the new freedoms came the pluralistic society and freedom of association, especially for humanitarian reasons, conditions now undoubtedly generally applauded.

This freedom of association resulted in the slow demise of Christendom in Europe and the emergence of denominational religion, coming to fruition in America and slowly dispersing elsewhere. According to Adams, one of the main expressions of Christianity is the concept of voluntarism in religion. A consultation on voluntarism and the Believers' Church, in 1968, proposed that "The doctrine of the Believers' Church has fully articulated the nature of voluntarism: a church voluntarily gathered, of those who voluntarily covenant with God and each other, and who voluntarily support its objectives with their personal resources." A major thrust of the study conference focused on the way "the theological underpinnings of voluntarism provide a major contribution to Christian thought" including a new rational for voluntary associations of all sorts from missions, education, service, and para-church structures, to alliance with the state. [606]

It is now generally agreed that numerous denominations now identified with the Radical Reformation expressed aspects of **voluntarism** not only in the faith components, but also in the form of social and economic life, especially in the world *of mutual aid, compassion, sharing and service*. There can be little doubt that one of the generally accepted and major ethical/social emphases of Radical Reformation was mutual aid and brotherhood—identifying with the needs of others and showing mercy. [607]

Most of the groups that are included in the Believers' Church tradition have been unusually active in mutual aid, as stated in Durnbaugh's chapter entitled "Mutual Aid and Service." [608] He suggests that "The Society of Friends has probably done more in the field of general humanitarian effort proportionately than any other religious body."[609] Other denominations, such as the Baptists, the Church of God, and the Pentecostals, have created a substantial number of relief and service agencies, also far outpacing other denominations proportionately.

Although only a few examples of the voluntarism and altruism in the Believers' Church tradition can be included, the Quakers are illustrative. T. Canby Jones proposed that obedience to Christ is one of the identifications of the Believers' Church.

> "Obedience means walking not where but *as* Jesus walked. He challenged men to believe and enter the kingdom of God. He taught righteousness. He healed the sick. But

SECTION III. THE RADICAL REFORMATION ETHIC OF SERVICE

> walking as Jesus walked means, above all, becoming a servant church. His disciples never understood his mission as Messiah. They still expected him to show a mailed fist and restore the kingdom Israel by force. But he was the Isaianic (sic) servant come to heal, love, persuade, and save by his vicarious Suffering. It is the exalted Messiah of the Gospel of John who humbles himself and washes the disciples' feet. He commands us to do likewise." [610]

The Radical Reformers were leaders in service as mutual aid. Already in the 1530s, Menno Simons, one of the leaders, copiously refers to the importance of compassion for the neighbor, not only in terms of physical possessions but non-material and spiritual as well. Though he strongly rejects the accusation that the Radical Reformers were communist, he incessantly reminds the believers that they are called to share without reservation. Thus, in his "Reply to False Accusations" he states:

> "All those who are born of God, who are gifted with the Spirit of the Lord, who are, according to the Scriptures, called into one body and love in Christ Jesus, are prepared by such love to serve their neighbors, not only with money and goods, but also after the example of their Lord and Head, Jesus Christ, in an evangelical manner, with life and blood. They show mercy and love, as much as they can. No one among them is allowed to beg. They take to heart the need of the saints. They entertain those in distress. They take the stranger into their houses. They comfort the afflicted; assist the needy; feed the hungry; they do not turn their face from the poor; do not despise their own flesh (Isa. 58:7, 8)" [611]

Further, the many passages of Menno Simons, especially where he discusses the responsibility of Christians to "love your neighbor", reveals that his treatment is based directly on the commandments of Christ, from whom the phrase "love of neighbor" originally came. "The whole Scripture speaks of mercifulness and love, and it is the only sign whereby a true Christian may be known. As the Lord says: By this shall all men know that ye are my disciples (that ye are Christians), if ye love one another (John 13:35)."[612]

In any case, the Radical Reformation typology allows us to expand the impact and relevance of the idea of doing good, from which to look at the **service as the path to justice** vision. Although Menno Simons was only one voice in the contribution to the vision of the Believers' Church, he provides a strong summary contribution to its foundations and formation.

C) Mutual Aid versus Service to the World

Radical Reformation tradition was strongly committed to the idea of mutual love, mercy, care, and sharing. But who specifically are included? Donald Durnbaugh proposes that "Those in the Radical Reformation contended that service to the brother and sister was at the heart of Christianity. It was impossible to speak of faith and belief without the practice of Christian (sic) love."[613] Durnbaugh continues by proposing there were several overlapping aspects of mutual aid: brotherly love, material support, admonition and discipline, and concern for those outside the bonds of faith.[614]

Earlier interpreters of Radical Reformation stressed the same theme. J. Winfield Fretz and Harold S. Bender suggested that:

> "The Anabaptists strove to reproduce as nearly as possible the life of the early Christian church and to imitate the life of Christ by attempting to establish a "Kingdom of Heaven" on earth in their own communities. It was in such an atmosphere of freedom and Christian brotherliness that mutual aid could flourish. Mutual aid had its roots intertwined with the very roots of Radical Reformation because their very survival was dependent on it."[615]

SECTION III. THE RADICAL REFORMATION ETHIC OF SERVICE

But there has been a lack of clarity or confusion as to how mutual aid and service to others beyond the Christian fellowship are related. Thus, Durnbaugh observes:

> "The emphasis upon sharing with the brother was sometimes turned against the Believers' Church by critics who concluded that they were narrowly devoted to their own members and thus ignored the rest of the world. George Fox once answered such criticism from a clergyman this way: 'I told him, 'we loved all mankind, as they were God's creation, and as they were children of Adam and Eve by generation; and we loved the brotherhood in the Holy Ghost.' This stopped him." [616]

Durnbaugh proposes an interesting and important sources for the differences and similarities between mutual aid and service: "Mutual aid and relief stem more directly from the Anabaptist Mennonite communal view of the church regarding economic sharing of property and wealth, while voluntary service derives more directly from the concept of Jesus' global and universal ministry, influenced in 20th century America especially by the modern fundamentalism/evangelical movement." [617] In any case, if restricting mutual aid to the congregation is inadequate or too limited, he makes the case for *prosocial service* in general, reaching far beyond the Radical Reformation perspective, even more significant.

The relationship between mutual aid and service was expanded in an article written by Cornelius Krahn, J. Winfield Fretz, and Robert Krieder, entitled "Altruism in Mennonite Life." [618] After they review the origins of altruistic life in Anabaptism, the authors describe how mutual aid expressed itself in Canada, the United States, and Russia in the nineteenth and twentieth centuries. They propose that "the refusal to bear arms in self-defense or for military action, a principle commonly called 'nonresistance', must be viewed in connection with community life and other forms of altruism" [619]

They continue, "the admonition of Paul to 'do good unto all men' has never been completely overshadowed [by the fact that] at times they have lived a rather withdrawn life. This sense of [doing good to all men] is still alive."[620] They model Jesus teaching: "You have learned that they were told. Love your neighbors, hate your enemy. But what I tell you is this: love your enemies and pray for your persecutors, do good to them that hate you, and pray for them which despitefully use you and persecute you." (Matthew, 5:44). [621] This sensitiveness has never been completely lost nor overshadowed by other interests and teachings. However, who the neighbor—who deserves mutual aid—has always been deabted and has been variously understood.

But the main means of illustrating how mutual aid is related to the larger world by service is examining the relief organizations such as the Mennonite Central Committee (MCC), whose motto is "Service in the name of Christ." These mottoes express best the essence as summarized in a statement adopted at the annual meeting, on January 2, 1942, and called the "accepted items of policy in MCC relief." [622] The first point states that the purpose of the program is to "relieve need regardless of the recipients' race, class or political sympathies, and consistently administered in a Christian manner and as an evangelical witness to Christian love." [623] It concludes by proposing that the source of this service motivation is "rooted in biblicism", and that "a Christian is simply a steward of his time and possessions for the work of the Kingdom." [624]

If mutual aid were limited to members only, it would dramatically limit the compassion or altruistic mode. Or, as Jesus said, do not the tax collectors do the same? As discussed earlier, loving only those who are part of our family or community misses the universal aspect of Jesus' message. Though some members of the Radical Reformation would disagree, there seems no objective conflict between the practice of mutual aid and altruistic service. Quite the contrary, mutual aid (service on the local or ethnic level) and prosocial service are merely differing faces of the same issue: love.

It seems reasonable to suggest that the Radical Reformation stressed a communal economic life whereby material wealth was considered a gift from God for the benefit of the congregation first, and then to the larger human population. The "Protestant Ethic" (discussed further below) is therefore not fully operative for the Radical Reformation community alone. The amassing of wealth for personal benefit was restricted. The Sermon of the Mount proclaimed by Jesus was the "naive" model applying to all mankind: "If a man asks you for your shawl, give him your coat as well." [625]

D) The Radical Reformation Service Symbol: Foot Washing

Possibly the most powerful image of a theology of service, especially in the Anabaptist Church, is the practice of foot washing, which Jesus instituted, even though it is recorded only in John's Gospel. [626] Guy F. Hershberger cites Mackay regarding foot washing:

> "This image is found in the foot-washing scene in the thirteenth chapter of John, a scene in which Christ sums up in Himself what was most distinctive of Israel, of manhood, and of Deity. Israel had been called of God to a ministry of service to all peoples. In his public ministry Christ pours out His life for His people. He symbolizes the meaning of it all by girding Himself with a towel and stooping to wash His servant's feet. Water and towel portray the victory of the God-man in life; a cross was His triumph in death." [627]

For those unfamiliar with the practice of foot washing—washing the feet of a fellow member of the religious community—it may seem odd and awkward. Though practiced in the early Christian church, it practically disappeared in the Roman Catholic Church (though it was maintained in some of the monastic orders) and Reformation traditions. In these traditions, it was understood more as a sacrament, thus it lost its personal and practical meaning for the lay person. In a recent treatment, Mathew Pinson "regards foot washing as an *ordinance*" and strongly maintains that it was one of the strongest obligations Jesus laid on his disciples: "You ought to do it." [628] Significantly however, the practice has been re-instituted and maintained to this day by some of the members of the Radical Reformation/Anabaptist tradition Church. [629]

The foot-washing ceremony service has historically been very extensively practiced by several of the Radical Reformation church groups, especially the Mennonite, Quaker, and Brethren traditions. In regard to the Church of the Brethren (COB), Carl Bowman suggests that "Feet-washing was associated with love and sacrifice, service and humility and purification and cleaning. In general feet-washing's symbolism of service has gained ground during the twentieth century." [630] This is illustrated by the Basin and Towel symbol, which is extensively used in COB communications. Donald Durnbaugh makes one of the most direct theological relationships between service and feet-washing: "Some [Believers' Churches] have seen a link between the evidence of concern for mankind and the practice of foot washing. Kneeling in imitation of Christ to wash the feet of the brother in lowly service seems to condition men (sic) to be ready to serve the needs of the world in the same prosaic and practical fashion."[631]

T. Canby Jones, a leading Quaker theologian, has maintained that foot-washing is a sign of the Radical Reformation, and provides a concrete interpretation:

> "I think it very significant that at least three of the traditions represented among us here today (Believers' Church conference) still practice foot washing as an ordinance. What a sign for the servant church! But our Lord's command that we wash one another's feet did not mean that we should go into the universal foot-bathing business, complete with automatic coin-operated machines, but that we should serve man in all his needs-physical, economic, and spiritual-with both grace and joy." [632]

But Jones also provides one of the strongest arguments for foot-washing as a mandate as well as sign for all followers of Christ. He states:

> "One of the most striking examples in Scripture of Jesus acting as servant is the account of Jesus' washing the disciples' feet (John, 13:3-15). Jesus washing his disciples' feet is his final sign. In it the serene and exalted son of

SECTION III. THE RADICAL REFORMATION ETHIC OF SERVICE

> God pictured in John's Gospel humbles himself and girds himself as a slave and washes their dirty feet. In a larger sense, Jesus' washing his disciples' feet and his command that we wash one another's feet means selfless, humble service at its widest."[633]

Jones reaches back to quote Jonathan Edwards: "Washing the feet of guests was the office of servants and one of their meanest offices, and therefore was fitly chosen by our Savior to represent that great abasement which he was to be the subject of in the form of a servant, in becoming obedient unto death."[634] Nowhere is the reversal of the customary status relations more evident than Jesus washing the feet of his followers.

Guy F. Hershberger proposes that the foot washing was one of Jesus' most powerful teachings regarding the Christian's mission. He accordingly cites theologian John A. Mackay, approvingly: "Members of [the Christian community] are under the obligation to take seriously their Christian calling, and to follow in the steps of Him who said 'He came not to be ministered unto, but to minister.' For the formation of their Christian spirit and the guidance of their Christian service lay men and women must keep constantly before them the essential image of the Christian religion."[635] The emerging ambivalence among the Radical Reformation denominations, regarding the foot-washing institution and image, may well be the lack of clarity about whether love, compassion, mutual aid, and service illustrated in the foot-washing ceremony and teachings are therefore restricted to members of the "household of faith."[636]

The meaning of foot-washing is difficult to contextualize in contemporary practice. In the Radical Reformation, foot-washing is clearly a very intimate practice, so how can it be seen as a mandate for universal application? "Mutual assistance to those outside the household of faith" was rarely called mutual aid but began to be interpreted as "relief and service."[637] Accordingly, in an article on "Relief Work," Guy F. Hershberger presents the historical development of sharing of material goods and other assistance both to the community and to others, and defines the latter as relief and service work without alluding to the concept of mutual aid.[638] Whether or not the actual practice of foot-washing itself is universal or local, the meaning of loving and serving others is still very evident.

Even though it is of paramount symbolic importance, foot-washing as a practice is declining. In a recent article on foot-washing, theologian Jim Brenneman reviews the practice in Anabaptists groups and states that "Mennonites and other Anabaptist groups have been washing feet as a religious ritual since the earliest days of the Radical Reformation."[639] Then Brenneman asks, "Why was foot-washing so important to the Anabaptist-Mennonite tradition?"[640] He proposes that it symbolized "several ideals at the heart of the tradition" including "yieldedness *(Gelassenheit)* to God's will (and) abandonment of self."[641] In contrast to its symbolism alone, he enlists John Howard Yoder, who proposes that a sacrament "should be seen as 'an act with everyday social significance rather than a purely symbolic meaning.'" Quoting Yoder, "Bread eaten together is economic sharing, not merely symbolically, but in actual fact it extends to a wider circle of economic solidarity."[642]

Brenneman proposes that Radical Reformers and others do not have a formal theology of foot-washing, including the concreteness of service, because "…[it] was, after all, the very embodied nature of the foot-washing ritual that made it so easy for many contemporary Mennonites to disregard it."[643] He proposes that "Mennonites such as Yoder were very appreciative of the symbolic value of foot-washing when promoted as a lesson (only) in service and humility." In other words, feet washing is a *symbol* of G*elassenheit* (humility) and service but also an *act that has daily reality*. Yoder proposes that, though washing feet may not be existentially needed, it is highly charged with commitment to *go and serve* the world.[644]

E) The Social Relevance of Service

Foot washing has two foci: the intimate relationship symbolizing unconditional submission to the committed fellowship, and the more literal service to the other as unconditional service to the world. Obviously, the symbol and reality cannot be mutually exclusive. It is clear that foot-washing symbolizes

SECTION III. THE RADICAL REFORMATION ETHIC OF SERVICE

and defines the theology of service. It is personal involvement. It is concrete, active, and egalitarian. It removes and denies all social status differences. It is also a symbolic statement of rejection of individual egos, desires, status, and goals to the welfare of the neighbor. It is global in its inclusiveness. Finally, it symbolically provides a needed service (offering oneself for any need), deeply emotional and relational, which implies action and the idea of justice. At the same time, foot washing also involves the challenge to the sociological concept of status.

In the common usage and in the social sciences, status refers to the honor or prestige attached to one's position in society or in a social group. [645] As such, status relations are defined as rank-ordered pairings of individuals in some social situation. Research suggests that high-status people tend to experience pride, satisfaction, and happiness from interaction, while low-status individuals often report feelings of fear, resentment, and anger. [646] Status is purely a social phenomenon, rooted in the social reality of interpersonal relations. Status is unique in that it relies exclusively on the appraisal of others; one cannot simply grant status to oneself. We can speak of "status symbols", which are tactics and artifacts employed in the attempt to persuade others to grant status.

And it may be a testament to the value of having positive status conferred that some of us go to such great lengths in the hopes of accumulating it. Thorstein Veblen referred to many of these efforts as "conspicuous consumption", wherein resources are spent lavishly for the purpose of displaying income or wealth in the hopes of convincing others to confer status. [647] The term is commonly used to describe the use of expendable income that is not based specifically in the intrinsic utility of goods but rather are used to show status. [648]

Status is not exclusively nor necessarily tied to economic achievements. For example, high levels of social status can be granted to those with relatively low incomes, such as community and religious leaders, teachers, etc. And those with massive accumulations of wealth can be granted low status (Max Weber gave the example of the stingy boss). Sociologist Max Weber viewed status as one of the main components of social stratification, that is, differentiation and ranking between individuals and groups in a society. Status differentiation allows for some to be labeled and treated as inferior and thus rejected or exploited.

It is here that loving our neighbors as ourselves, exemplified by foot washing, can dissolve the socially constructed categories of social status. Jesus captures the irony of the reversal of status distinctions when the messiah appears as a servant, washing others' feet, not as a king. Foot washing is at the heart, symbolically and concretely, of the radical revolution Jesus is bringing. Foot washing represents both the moral framework for humility and service and an interpersonal ethic for relating to others. This is a truly radical dimension in the teaching and life of Jesus: Jesus' refusal to acknowledge traditionally accepted status categories.

F) The Conflict between Faith and Works

The Christian tradition has been deeply involved in a conflict over the nature of salvation and redemption, especially since the Reformation. The question has been "How is salvation achieved?" Do humans have any role to play or is it totally an act of God's goodness? Does God act unilaterally? Is salvation predetermined? Do humans play any role? This has also been generally referred to as the "faith versus works" conflict, which was already being argued and interpreted by the Apostle James, especially Chapter 2:14ff. In this context, "works" is literally defined as service.[649] The conflict began in the early church and emerging Christianity. Walter Rauschenbusch, arguably the most eloquent early defender of "social Christianity," states that "Christianity set out with a great social ideal. The live substance of the Christian religion was the hope of seeing a divine social order established on earth." He defined this as the Kingdom of God.[650]

Rauschenbusch documents some of the leading early Christian spokespersons regarding the "social promises" of Christianity, but he believes "the chief causes for the eclipse of the social hope was the ascendancy of the organized institutional life of Christianity—the Church."[651] The return to a more traditional Christianity was the main dynamic of the

SECTION III. THE RADICAL REFORMATION ETHIC OF SERVICE

Reformation, especially its Lutheran stream, which under Martin Luther's leadership emphasized the "faith alone" (*sola fide*). The Reformed tradition partly identified with this orientation, adding a predestination dimension, which enhanced the position that humans can in no way influence their eternal fate, even though they are instruments in carrying out God's plan for creation. Thus, any attempt to relate salvation to human effort or "works" was heresy and cannot secure righteousness.[652]

This faith and works controversy received great energy from the liberal and conservative interpretations of the Judaic-Christian Bible. The former is popularly defined as liberalism, modernism, or the "social gospel," and the latter as orthodoxy, conservatism or fundamentalism.[653] The liberalism-conservatism debate exposes a colossal divide and involves how the Kingdom of God is to be expressed or realized on earth. The conservative wing of Christianity understands the Christian gospel as consisting of accepting in faith a series of Christian principles, with the basic issue being "have you been saved from everlasting punishment?"[654] This focuses on the fate of the individual rather than the issue of ethics—of "doing good to the neighbor." Doing good to the neighbor is thus more of a by-product than an essential requirement for salvation and redemption in this orientation, and the Kingdom of God is interpreted personally, metaphorically, or apocalyptically.[655]

The liberal Christian tradition, as expressed by Walter Rauschenbusch, believes "the Kingdom of God must slough off apocalypticism if it is to become the religious property of the modern world. Jesus flatly contradicted such expectations and laid down the law of service as the fundamental law of his kingdom. He himself had not come to be served, but to serve to the death, and all greatness in the Kingdom would have to rest on the same basis."[656] Similarly, the Radical Reformation tradition holds that obedience to Christ is expressed in discipleship and involves praying and work for the kingdom of God "coming to earth as it is in heaven." Interestingly, Rauschenbusch refers to the persecuted sects, such as the Waldensians, Lollards, Taborites, and Anabaptists as "first stirrings of Christian democracy, expressions of lay religion and working-class ethics. They heralded the religious awakening of the common people and their cry for the Reign of God on earth."[657]

Unfortunately, Rauschenbusch did not have the benefit of more recent concepts of the "Radical Reformation" [658] and the concept of the Radical Reformation,[659] both of which have been extensively analyzed in recent years. It is now generally understood that the Radical Reformation has taken a "third way" regarding the division between the liberal and conservative wings of Christianity. It has rejected the authority of institutionalized religious structures, and the rationalist and nationalist orthodoxy of fundamentalism, focusing rather on following Jesus' commands to "follow me" and join God's work on earth as it is in heaven, further emphasizing the ethical dimensions of Christian faith. [660]

The problem of "faith versus works" has hounded the Radical Reforamtion membership for many years. The reasons for the fundamentalist and evangelical inroads are complex, with some scholars maintaining that it is a form of accommodation to mainstream conservative Christianity. [661] There are signs that its inroads are decreasing. Many congregations have been involved in conflicts, have experienced loss of membership, or have drifted from the Radical Reformation perspectives. Traditional commitments to service, as discussed above, have been affected, because the emphasis on personal salvation tends to downplay the work of participating in the Kingdom of God, as Jesus admonished his followers to do. [662] The apparent mutual exclusion of "service versus proclamation" has plagued the Radical Reformation in the last half century. [663]

It seems illogical and inconceivable that a split between sharing of the faith and service should emerge in the Radical Reforamtion. The explanation appears in what has already been alluded to above, specifically the influence of modern conservative Christianity, especially its fundamentalist and evangelical elements. Extensive literature has emerged documenting how conservative Christianity has not retained much of "true evangelical faith" as Menno Simons defined it. One major survey of conservative Christianity states bluntly: "Christian conservatives are Christian capitalists." [664] The philosophy of Capitalism is not noted for its emphasis on voluntarily serving others; rather, it is recognized as an economic system that is based on the principle of self-interest, which supposedly serves the interest of all." This fundamental contradiction was treated more extensively in Chapter 4.

SECTION III. THE RADICAL REFORMATION ETHIC OF SERVICE

Conclusion

Although the Radical Reformation and terms such as the Free Church, Believer's Church, and Anabaptism, among others, are academic and theological constructs, it is very helpful in identifying a number of realities that have strongly affected the Western world, *namely service to all mankind*. At a conference on "The Concept of the Believers' Church, in 1968, the concluding address was entitled "A People in the World: Contemporary Relevance." In the section "*Servanthood*," Louis P. Meyer concludes: "The church is to become available among men. The members of the body of Christ in the world today must subordinate their plan of life to that of others; they must be among those of need. The church is assigned her place among people who need to be served. If the church tries to go about her work outside the sphere of service, she withers and chokes on self-concern." [665]

It is probably correct to conclude that the Christian Church's fundamental cohesive bond and witness **is serving the world,** which is as relevant today as it was yesterday or decades back. Anabaptism as one facet of the Radical Reformation concept described above, is struggling with all these issues. The challenge remains.

The importance of service and justice is presented in chapters one through four along with the relationship between service and justice. Briefly, we have concentrated on serving others as a way to promote the common good and defined service and justice in procedural and distributive forms as ways of doing good to others and ourselves. We presented perspectives from several disciplines, since service and justice are inexorably related, The concept of justice deals with one of the most fundamental realities in human history. In other words, this is not the last word on the subject but rather a beginning. In fact, we could have used other words, like democracy; for example, public policy specialists affirm our general thesis by declaring that:

Government shouldn't be run like a business; it should be run like a democracy...Administrators are realizing that they have much to gain by *listening* to the public rather than *telling*, and by *serving* rather than *steering*. [666]

The primary insight is that prosocial responsiveness to the concerns of others is central to creating and sustaining the common good and central to ongoing survival and evolution toward ultimate peace.

In the second section the insights of service and procedural and distributive justice are illustrated by the examples drawn from the three minority religious groups. How they dealt with this major topic provides materials on how love of neighbor emerged and became central theological and ethical focuses and vocations.

The final section focuses on how service is related to procedural and distributive justice, in other words, the ethics of loving the neighbor. It discusses some theological and ethical challenges when justice becomes the central focus. These three groups -- Quakers, Brethren, and Mennonites -- are by no means the only Christian groups that have labored to employ serving as the path to justice. In addition, many other religious groups around the world and throughout history share in the fundamental axiom described as the Golden Rule -- **do unto others as you would have others do unto you.**

The following points summarize the assumptions and principles which we attempted to address:

- Serving others is the source of human survival — the image of mother serving the child is universally true.

- Serving others is the expression and source of justice because it is based on accepting the fundamental equality and value of every human being.

- Justice is love in action. Said another way, it is a verb and is concrete and specific to particular people and in particular contexts.

- There can be no peace or peacemaking without the implementation of justice. Without justice, peace is suppressed oppression.

- Individual and societal competition, including capitalism and sports, can be very destructive if not controlled.

SECTION III. THE RADICAL REFORMATION ETHIC OF SERVICE

- All world religions include the love of neighbor as a fundamental teaching. Those religions and members that ignore this principle are antisocial.

The path to justice requires the prosocial attitudes and acts of serving others. Where do we serve? We serve where we find injustice. We hope others will contemplate, clarify, correct, and expand on what we have sketched above.

APPENDIX 1:
Reflections on Volunteering in Vietnam, Earl Martin.[667]

I am pedaling my bike down Phan Thanh Giang, heading downtown. As I turn the corner, I see down the street an abandoned American tank. I am but a hundred meters from the tank when the machine suddenly begins to explode. Multiple blasts like the detonation of grenades. I ditch my bike and take flimsy shelter at a street-side fruit stall. From my crouched position, I watch as a young lad runs screaming from the tank ... in flames! Then another. And another. The explosions seem to have stopped for the moment, so I run and kneel down beside one boy and roll him on the street to quench the flames. While others attend the other boys, I gather this boy into my arms, wave down a passing pick-up trunk, and we race off to the nearby hospital. As we ride in the back, I am aware that this boy's molten skin is adhering to my shirt. I pray desperately for his life.

By morning, I learned this young lad of golden skin—who had been playing with the shiny phosphorus grenades in the abandoned tank—was dead.

Not many years prior, I had been that innocent, curious lad. What I knew of the world was only what managed to seep through the filters of my sheltered farm community. I was still in that stage of "having no culture, if you have only one culture." I was barely aware of the notion of culture.

What I now suspect is that many of my compatriots in the United States—despite all the gadgets like Internet, cell phones, and 24/7 news coverage—are not a lot more attuned to other cultures than I had been in my rural community in Lancaster County, Pennsylvania. What "saved" me—and wounded me, in its own way—was curiosity. How did the rest of the world live? What did young people in China really care about? What really lay behind the armed conflict in the Congo? How would I respond, as a supposed pacifist, in a setting of warfare, if I or my loved ones would be threatened?

And so, after two years of junior college, I volunteered to go. Where to? Anywhere needed. Why? To serve, yes. To help, yes. But even then, it was equally about learning. Curiosity. Nurturing that yearning to know about other people. To touch the "elephant" of our world in new places.

So, there I was, in Vietnam as a conscientious objector, sitting on a bamboo bed in the mud and thatch refugee cottage of Ba Loan. She explained that, when she lived six kilometers to the west on their simple rice farm, the aerial bombings and nightly shelling became so intense that they had to tunnel underground to live in a bunker. So many of the farmers were part of the National Liberation Front, or the Viet Cong, that the U.S. had deemed this area a "free fire zone," meaning, fire on whatever moved. Ba Loan explained that when she cooked underground, they had to pipe the smoke away fifty meters. That way, if the ever-present spotter plane called in a jet strike on your smoke, you might be able to survive the bomb blast.

My transformation came in listening. Sitting and listening. Of course, as service workers, our team and I distributed food, clothing, and medical care. We set up vocational training programs for the dislocated rural youth. We devised programs to clean up some of the unexploded munitions left lying in the farmers' fields. But our real work was listening.

Listening to the weeping mother as we witnessed her child fall victim to a random bullet falling from the sky. Listening to the pure joy of a neighbor couple as they said their vows in marriage. Listen to the American GI lament how his unit was "just shooting up the whole countryside."

It is this kind of listening that eventually transforms you into a life-long soldier for peace. A life-long disciple for a new humanity, which invites you to share stories with children in the school classroom back home, or to testify in the Congressional hearing room or in the halls of the Pentagon or the op-ed pages of the *New York Times,* or with the neighbor over the backyard fence. Most of all, this kind of learning through service invites you to a life of walking with your Muslim neighbor with empathy, of seeking alternatives for our broken criminal justice system, or finding common ground with an obstreperous co-worker.

When we serve, we seek to transform a difficult situation. But in the process, it is we who are also transformed.

APPENDIX 2:
A Critique of Effective Voluntary Justice, Urbane Peachey

Service, the Path to Justice explains and helps conserve the twentieth century service legacy of Mennonites and related peace groups. Service reflects and expresses a disposition of character and faith, of heart and mind, and a proactive way of being present in human need. Service is compassionate engagement "where cross the crowded ways of life" and has its own justification. Although the legacy is informed and inspired by the great themes of love and compassion, peace, justice and mercy, taught in Scripture and embraced by faith, that is not where and how the legacy was formed. It was hammered out against the anvil of twentieth century wars, oppression, injustice, inequality, and impoverishment. It was not shaped in a study conference, but rather "Above the noise of selfish strife, (where) we hear the voice of the Son of Man" (i.e. the supremely human one).

What I want to ask in the postscript to this volume is this: "In what ways does the worldly cauldron in which we served the common good, equip us for other things?" I spent twenty-six years of my life in MCC in close collaboration with others, recruiting and orienting new people for service, administering emergency relief and development program in Palestine, Jordan, Egypt, and Lebanon. I supported and promoted works and witness for peace for eleven years in the MCC Peace Section and Mennonite World Conference. I am a devotee of the servant posture for the church in the world.

But I am uneasy, because I believe that MCC decision makers across the U.S. and Canada focused too narrowly on service for peace. Surely more attention could have been given to the question, "What could we have done to address the causes of the human need we came to address?" What caused the conflicts in which we wanted to be peacemakers? What caused the poverty, the poor education, and racial discrimination in those communities where we sent voluntary service workers? Why did three million Koreans and perhaps three million Vietnamese die in each of those wars? And who is responsible for the devastation of villages and societies in those wars? The same questions beg for attention in the several Iraq wars and the war in Afghanistan. There is not much to add to the meaning of serving human need. We are called to do more than venerate the past. The issue begging for our attention is how can we address the powers and the systems that cause human suffering or fail to address human suffering when it occurs? And the parallel question is this: How does the service legacy, which we treasure, equip us to serve the present age?

The serving vocation takes us outside of ourselves into the interior or the ethos of another people—their histories and their cultures, their language and their religion. In identifying with those we serve, we learn about their hopes and aspirations, their suffering and their capabilities. In the servant posture, we are given a trusted front seat to the obstacles they face in the pursuit of their "common good." We have been to the interior of human need. While we engage in compassion, charity, and service, we should help our supporting network understand the systemic causes of hunger, war, and poverty and equip the saints to be faithful advocates for the common good.

One of my major projects in the Peace Section was the compilation of Mennonite Statements on Peace and Social Concerns, 1900-1978. This includes official statements and documents of major Mennonite denominations or conferences and Mennonite Central Committee for their own internal practice, and very importantly, the compilation includes statements and letters addressed to national and state governments. What is quickly self-evident is that Mennonites did and do address public policy when our self-interests are at stake, such as appeals made for recognition as conscientious objectors. Many eloquent statements were made to congressional committees for our own concerns, and there were eloquent and courageous voices for peace against militarism, along with appeals for COs. But not much energy went into defense of the interests and the well-being of others. I say this with caution, because we obviously can't do everything. One example illustrates:

In the 1970s, 30,000 people disappeared in the military state system of Argentina. There were similar circumstances in other Latin America military state systems. One of those disappeared persons (*desaparecidos*) was Patricia (Patti) Erb, daughter of Mennonite missionaries in Argentina and a sociology student who worked in a slum barrio as part of her university studies. The Mission Board rightly pulled out all the stops on her behalf, with appeals to the State Department and other policymakers. She was released after 15 days. There were 29,999 others who were not released and disappeared forever. Should we not ask if we should have done more on their behalf? **That is what we should call advocacy for the common good, not only service for the common good.**

Keith Graber Miller describes the events in his *Wise as Serpents, Innocent as Doves: American Mennonites Engage Washington* (1):

> "Erb was abducted from her parents' home in September 1976 and imprisoned and tortured for fifteen days, after which was expelled from the country. Erb says that the last day she was tortured, the man torturing her told her he had been taught to torture in the Panama Canal Zone by U. S. officials in the army's School of the Americas. The man became angry when he was told to stop torturing Erb because she probably would be freed. 'I don't understand,' he told Erb. 'After they teach us how to do it, they get mad at us and tell us to stop.'"

After Erb returned from Argentina, the MCC Washington office, through then Director Delton Franz, arranged for forty appointments with Washington policy makers to share her experience and appeal for U.S. military training to Argentina to be terminated. Graber Miller's book is an eloquent statement of MCC's Washington office lowkey advocacy on behalf of those affected adversely by war, poverty, oppression, and U.S. military actions. This is large long-term vocation, but unfortunately, the MCC board failed to translate the skillful and creative experience of the Washington office into the theology and practice of church institutions and congregations. Many were interested and supportive, but I recall years when MCC board members cautioned staff members against taking positions controversial in the churches.

Robert Kreider is quoted by Graber Miller: "Dare the peaceable Mennonites become the outspoken Mennonites?...One senses in MCC a progressive unfolding of awareness of the deep-rooted causative factors in social evils which cannot be touched with temporary first aid. There is a huge vacuum in our theology, and our public witness. Mennonites, like other groups, focused or focus on piety and prayer, charity and personal ethics. Even though church colleges and seminaries teach courses in Christian ethics and peace and conflict studies, biblical perspective for public policy witness can be found in only selected congregations. There is a strong historical stream of Catholic and Protestant Christian social ethics and "social teaching" but it does not get translated into congregational life and practice in most of their congregations.

The Social Teaching of the Churches is strongly illustrated in the Pacem in Terris Encyclical of Pope John XXIII on "Establishing Universal Peace in Truth, Justice, Charity and Liberty." I only offer a sample from a much longer part of the Encyclical from paragraph 54: "The attainment of the common good is the sole reason for the existence of civil authorities…." Section 58 reads in part, **"The common good must take into account of all those social conditions which favor the full development of human personality." On justice, the Encyclical reads, "Relations between States must be regulated by justice." (3)**

The biblical call for public policy witness, however accomplished, is strong and pervasive. Consider these representative words drawn from larger passages: "Is this not the fast that I choose, to loosen the bonds of injustice, to undo the thongs of the yoke, to let the oppressed go free and to break every yoke? Is it not to ... share your bread with the hungry and to bring the homeless poor into your house...? Isa. 58:6¬8 (NRSV). Amos 5 reads, "I take no delight in your solemn assemblies...Take away from me the noise of your songs.... But let justice roll down like waters and righteousness like an ever rolling stream."

The spirit of the second Testament is well stated in Mary's Magnificat and by Jesus in the Synagogue in Luke 4:18: "The Spirit of the Lord is upon me, because he has anointed me to proclaim release to the captives and recovery of sight to the blind, to let the oppressed go free, to proclaim the year of the Lord's favor." The promise of Isaiah 58:8¬14 is that if the hungry are fed, and if the needs of the people are satisfied, "Then your light shall break forth like the dawn, and your healing shall spring up quickly..." v. 8, "and we will ride on the heights of the earth." v.14

Martin Luther King's Riverside address is the best summary:

> "A true revolution of values will soon cause us to question the fairness and justice of many of our past and present policies. On the one hand we are called to play the Good Samaritan on life's roadside, but that will be only an initial act. One day we must come to see that the whole Jericho Road must be transformed so that men and women will not be constantly beaten and robbed as they make their journey on life's highway. True compassion is more than flinging a coin to a beggar. It comes to see that an edifice which produces beggars needs restructuring." (4)

1. Keith Graber Miller, *Wise as Serpents, Innocent as Doves: American Mennonites Engage Washington*. (Chicago: University of Tennessee Press, 1996) p. 146. 2. Ibid.

3. *Pacem in Terris, Encyclical of Pope John XXIII*, "On Establishing Universal Peace In Truth, Justice, Charity and Liberty", April 11, 1963. Available on the Internet in its entirety.

4. Washington, James M., Editor, *Martin Luther King Jr., I Have a Dream: Writings & Speeches That Changed the World.* (New York: Harper Collins Publishers, 1992 (p. 148)

APPENDIX 3:
A Brief Review of Service Organizations in the Twentieth Century.

The references to and sources of service as central to societal functioning and health, as has been analyzed in this work, are massive. An early discussion of humanitarian service was ironically published by Herald Press in 1943.[668] Entitled *International Relief in Action*, author and researcher Hertha Kraus describes service according to twelve classifications, from "temporary emergency services" to "population transfers and group resettlements." There are other sources too numerous to discuss here.

But more recent sources are easily accessed by "Surfing" the internet. Regarding doing good, i.e. service, the mere listing of organizations promoting voluntary service is voluminous and staggers the imagination. One of the most inclusive listings of volunteer service is a national organization consisting of agencies organizing voluntary service, "*The National Voluntary Service Organizations Network*" (www.nvoad.org/voad-newtork) and has many sub-categories. One such sub-category is the *"National Voluntary Organizations Active in Disaster."* *Mennonite Disaster Service*, a very extensive, well-known and successful organization is a member of this organization and illustrates the permeation of specialized types of service among the many religious organizations.[669]

Another organization among many is *Volunteers of America*, "founded in 1896, to 'volunteer' one's time in service to others [and] was a full-time commitment…Today each year *Volunteers of America* touches the lives of more than two million people in over four hundred communities in forty-six states and the District of Columbia.[670]

There is a remarkably extensive listing of organizations involved in voluntary service, focused on opportunities for persons of various age, educational, status, interest, and other variables, available on the internet Federal Organizations, such as the Peace Corps, and Vista, which are well known and need no introduction here.[671]

The concrete activities in voluntary service in the Believers Churches groups are similarly accessible via the internet. Among them, the American Friends Service Committee is the most impressive, which indicates how central to Quaker faith the service motif is.[672] There are AFSC offices in thirty-four locations in the United Sates, and fifteen in foreign countries. Of course, this does not list local centers from which the service work is conducted. AAFSC offers annual reports including financial statements, totaling millions of dollars, but unfortunately does not provide the numbers of individuals who have or are serving. Neither do other organizations, which is probably because such information would add a huge amount of labor, which can be better utilized in more productive work.

The Brethren Church's service website is not fully developed yet, possibly because of the massive survey of Brethren Service published in *A Cup of Cold Water: The Story of Brethren Service*.[673] This volume provides the history of Brethren voluntary service, the various types of service in the many locations, and the copious listings of persons who served in the many specific programs, times, and places. It is possibly unsurpassed in its coverage and cannot be easily condensed into an internet website. Melvin Gingerich's *Service for Peace* is a similar genre but focuses mainly on civilian public service during World War II. It is equally extensive in specific items.

The Mennonite Central Committee, which emerged in response to a humanitarian calamity in 1920, has evolved into a multifaceted program, including social and material assistance and service, including international development.[674] The listings include both permanently employed persons as well as volunteers in a variety of time spans, similar to most other relief and service agencies.

ENDNOTES

1   The sociological term "prosocial" defines the conceptualization that includes and combines sociological, theological, and philosophical orientations of the love ethic.

2   Menno Simons. *The Complete Writings of Menno Simons* (Scottdale, PA. Herald Press, 1956) 558.

3   By Mennonite bishop Benjamin Hershey (1875), in J Craig Haas, *Readings from Mennonite Writings* (Intercourse, PA. Good Books, 1992,) 224.

4   Broder, David. "A Bipartisan bill Worth Celebrating", *Washington Post*, April 5, 2009

5   "Radical Reformation/Anabaptism" includes actual denominations, and is a theoretical construct to allow for a broader and more constructive framework for our analysis. It is defined below.

6   Leon Kass. *The Beginning of Wisdom* (Chicago: University of Chicago Press, 2003), 3.

7   Jeremy Rifkin. *The Empathic Civilization: The Race to Global Consciousness in a World in Crisis* (New York: Penguin, 2009), 183.

8   Stephen Carter. *Civility: Manners, Morals and the Etiquette of Democracy* (New York: Harper Perennial, 1998).

9   Thomas Oord. *The Altruism Reader* (Philadelphia: Templeton Foundation Press, 2007).

10   E. O. Wilson. *The Creation: An Appeal to Save Life on Earth* (New York: Norton, 2006); and, Robert Axelrod. *The Evolution of Cooperation* (New York: Basic Books, 1984).

11   Stated in terms of power, Robert Bellah: "In our description of leadership in egalitarian societies as well as of the incipiently hierarchical, we have come across another disposition that seems as basic as the disposition to dominate: the disposition to take care of, to 'hold' using the analogy of a nursing mother holding her child, that is, the disposition to nurture." *Religion in Human Evolution* (Cambridge: Harvard University Press, 2011): 191. This philosophical/ethical proposition, widely accepted, obviously cannot be fully proven by empirical research. Idealistic values can only serve as a compass by which humans try to guide behavior.

12   The interrelationships and distinctions of these three entities are explicated in chapter 9 and includes the three major groups analyzed in this book plus several other denominations. The **"Historic Peace Churches"** was generally used as most appropriate to include those groups when war and peace making based on Jesus teachings were central in the discussion. The **"Believers' Church"** has been the term when the theology of salvation and personal faith challenged mainline Christianity's institutionalism. **Anabaptism's** focus on following Jesus, i.e. discipleships was the "foundation" (Menno Simons) and has probably promoted most of the elements defining **"Radical Reformation."** [1] The **"Free Church"** focuses on the historical dynamics of the **"Radical Reformation"** in which these groups revolted from the "Corpus Christiana" or the "magisterial state-church" and demanded total freedom from state alliance or control. In this chapter we use these several terms somewhat interchangeably, depending on the focus and context . We propose **"Radical Reformation"** and **"Anabaptism"** closest to creating mutual self- identity of the groups studied here. The least acceptable terms are "Sectarian Churches", and "Sects," which were derogatory, used by the persecuting "Magisterial state churches." and are not relevant here A fine brief description of the Radical Reformation can be found in **Wikipedia. https:// en.wikipedia.org/wiki/File:P_christianity.svg**

13   Mohandas K. Gandhi. *An Autobiography: The Story of My Experiments with Truth*, trans. Mahadev Desai (Boston: Beacon Press, 1993), 158, 175.

14   Karen Armstrong. *The Great Transformation: The Beginning of Our Religious Tradition* (New York: Alfred A. Knopf, 2006), 379.

15   The term prosocial was coined in the 1980s. For further research, see Nancy Eisenberg, Richard A. Fabes, and Tracy L. Spinrad. "Pro-social Development." *Handbook of Child Psychology* (New York: John Wiley and Sons, 2006); Louis Penner, John Dovidio, Jane Piliavin, and David Schroeder. "Pro-social Behavior: Multilevel Perspectives", *Annual Review of Psychology. (2005)*, 56, 365-392; and Monica Bartlett and David DeSteno. "Gratitude and Pro-social Behavior Helping When It Costs You." *Psychological Science* 17, no. 4 (2006), 319-325.

16   John is a personal friend of one author and asked that his identity be concealed.

17   For a detailed discussion of this case, see Stephen Smith and Terry Beitzel, editors, *One Hundred Years of Service in Community: A Gould Farm Reader* (Lanham, MD: University Press of America, 2013).

18   Sara Algoe. Jonathan Haidt, and Shelly L. Gable. "Beyond reciprocity: Gratitude and Relationships in Everyday Life." *Emotion (Washington, DC)* 8, no. 3 (2008), 425.

19   Robert Allinson. "The Confucian Golden Rule: A Negative Formulation" *Journal of Chinese Philosophy*, Vol 12 (1985), 305-315.

20   See, for example, Richard Reilly. "Compassion as Justice" *Buddhist-Christian Studies*, Vol 26 (2006): 13-31.

21   See Chapter Nine for more exploration and analysis of this issue.

22   Many scholars and philosophers maintain that the world religions have contributed to some of the most violent anti-social acts in human history. The fact that war has not been eradicated indicates that human intentions and institutions cannot, or least have not yet. However, if religion is defined as a product of culture, as social scientists do, then the accusation is blunted or even moot.

23   For a contemporary account and critique, see Rob Jenkins, *Peacebuilding: From Concept to Commission* (London: Routledge, 2013)

24   See "Miller House Stories", adapted from Alta Schrock, *Joel B. Miller Family History* (Scottdale, PA: Mennonite Publishing House, 1960).

25   For a more nuanced and theoretical account, see Terry Beitzel. "Living with Ambiguity, Risk and Uncertainty: Ethics and Agency in a Nonkilling Society" in *Nonkilling Futures* (Honolulu: University of Hawaii, 2012), 55-96.

26   "Nicomachian Ethics," *The Works of Aristotle II* (Chicago, Encyclopedia Britannica: 1952) 419.

27   "Nicomachian Ethics," Book V, *The Basic Works of Aristotle*, edited by Richard McKeon (New York: Random House, 1941), 1002.

28   This is a complex debate in social and political theory, has been addressed by numerous scholars, and is beyond the scope of space available here. Some refer to this as a debate between *communitarians* and *liberals*.

29   Amitai Etzioni. *The New Golden Rule: Community and Morality in a Democratic Society* (New York: Basic Books, 1996): XV. See also, Gerald Dworkin. *The Theory and Practice of Autonomy* (Cambridge: Cambridge University Press, 1988).

30   Among numerous examples, see Eviatar Zerubavel and Eliot R. Smith. "Transcending Cognitive Individualism." *Social Psychology Quarterly* 73.4 (2010): 321-325; Randall Collins, *The Sociology of Philosophies: A Global Theory of Intellectual Change* (Cambridge: Harvard Belknap Press, 2000); and, Eviatar Zerubavel. *Social mindscapes: An Invitation to Cognitive Sociology* (Cambridge: Harvard University Press, 1999). Our view contrasts with those who attempt to place ethics primarily within an ideology of evolutionary naturalism, such as the sociobiology of E. O. Wilson in *Sociobiology: The New Synthesis* (Cambridge: Harvard University Press, 1975).

31   For a useful summary from a former student of John Rawls, see Michael Sandel. *Liberalism and the Limits of Justice* (Cambridge: Cambridge University Press, 1998).

32   For examples, see Lenn Goodman, *Love Thy Neighbor as Thyself* (Oxford: Oxford University Press, 2008).

33   Douglas Fry. *The Human Potential for Peace: An Anthropological Challenge to Assumptions about War and Violence* (Oxford: Oxford University Press, 2006), 2.

34   This "gap" implies an obvious analogy to the Christian Faith with terms such as sin, the fall, salvation, and redemption, but this analysis also references the scientific world view.

35   Rodney Stark proposes that Christian communities were a stronghold of mutual aid, which resulted in a survival rate far greater than the general population.

36   Thus, when the term service is used, it encompasses all the elements included in this definition. Leon Kass's important work maintains that the Noahide law, which forbids killing, is the fundamental but NEGATIVE law of human life, namely the equal status of every human being. "Civil society is instituted, first of all, to protect and preserve human life." *The Beginning of Wisdom*, (Chicago: University of Chicago Press, 2003), 181. This negative foundation however must be superseded by its positive face "doing unto others as you would have them do to you." (Matthew 7:12)

37   See Bellah Chapter 4, "From Tribal to Archaic Religion: Meaning and Power" for a global survey of the balancing of domination and egalitarianism. It is possible that the "fairy tale world" is precisely the false fiction, or anti-realism that people continue to hold, knowing that the "fairy tale" egalitarian democratic world does not exist, but long for it anyhow.

38   Gideon Lewis-Kraus. Review of Adam Phillips, *Going Sane*, (Harper-Collins, 2005) *New York Times Book Review*, p. 26

39   The romanticizing of war in fiction as well as scholarly writing remains incomprehensible in the light of its horrific consequences.

40   (News York: Doubleday, 2003): 29.

41   The irony that "doing good" is almost always couched in "evil" contexts provides a major basis for the thesis of the book.

42   Some examples include: "Do not do to others what you would not like yourself. Then there will be no resentment against you, either in the family or in the state" Confucianism (Analects 12:2); "Hurt not others in ways that you yourself would find hurtful." Buddhism (Udana-Varga 5,1); "This is the sum of duty; do naught onto others what you would not have them do unto you." Hinduism (Mahabharata 5,1517); "No one of you is a believer until he desires for his brother that which he desires for himself." Islam (Sunnah); and, "That nature alone is good which refrains from doing another whatsoever is not good for itself." Zoroastrianism (Dadisten-I-dinik, 94,5).

43   Albrecht Dihle. *Die Goldene Regel* (Gottingen: Vandenhoek and Ruprecht, 1962).

44   Randall Collins goes so far as to state that conflict is normal when more than one person associates. See Randall Collins. *Four Sociological Traditions* (Oxford: Oxford University Press, 1994). See also Robert Bellah, op.cit

ENDNOTES

45 Jeffrey Wattles. "Levels of Meaning in the Golden Rule" *The Journal of Religious Ethics*, 2001, 106-129.

46 Keith D. Stanglin. "The historical connection between the golden rule and the second greatest love command." *Journal of Religious Ethics* 33.2 (2005), 357-371.

47 See Celia Deutsch. *Lady Wisdom, Jesus, and the Sages: Metaphor and Social Context in Matthew's Gospel*. (Trinity Press International: 1996); and Gene Outka and John P. Reeder. *Prospects for a Common Morality*. (Princeton, Princeton University Press, 1993).

48 See Jeffrey Wattles. "Levels of Meaning in the Golden Rule", 107-113.

49 Immanuel Kant. Preface to the *Metaphysical Elements of Ethics*, trans. T. K. Abbott, in *Kant's Theory of Ethics*, 6th ed. (London: Longmans, Green & Co, 1909), 304.

50 Marcus Singer, "The Golden Rule" *Philosophy* Vol 38, no. 146 (Oct. 1963), 293-314, 313.

51 Paul Ricoeur. "Exegetical and Theological Perplexities." *New Testament Studies* 36, no. 03 (1990), 392-397, 394.

52 Paul Ricoeur, "The Golden Rule" 1990.

53 For an early theory of social conflict from the individual's perspective and a theory that has traveled far in conflict studies, see Leon Festinger. *A theory of Cognitive Dissonance* (New York: Harper and Row, 1957).

54 Dean Pruitt and Sung Hee Kim. *Social Conflict: Escalation, Stalemate, and Settlement* (New York: McGraw Hill 3rd edition, 2004), 40-41.

55 Paul Ricoeur. "The Golden Rule" 397.

56 Ibid. Pruitt and Kim, 6.

57 See, for example, *Building Peace: Sustainable Reconciliation in Divided Societies* (Washington, DC: United States Institute of Peace, 1998)

58 Carl Rogers. *A Way of Being* (Boston: Houghton Mifflin, 1980), 151.

59 Carl Rogers. "Rogers, Kohut, and Erickson: A Personal Perspective on Some Similarities and Differences," *Person-Centered Review*, I (1986), pp 125-40, 130.

60 Geoff Goodman. "Feeling Our way into Empathy: Carl Rogers, Heinz Kohut, and Jesus" *Journal of Religion and Health*. 30, 3 (1991), 191-206, 200.

61 Erik Erickson. "The Galilean Sayings and the Sense of I," *Yale Review* 70, 321-362, 358.

62 Heinz Kohut. *The Search for the Self: Selected Writings of Heinz Kohut:1950-1978*, edited by P. Ornstein (New York: International Universities Press, 1978).

63 John Noss, *Man's Religion* (New York: Macmillan, 1968) 191.

64 Ibid, 191.

65 Kristin Goss. "Altruism" in *Encyclopedia of Community: From the Village to the Virtual World*. V. 1, 36-7.

66 John Noss, Man's Religion, 382. Note that "doing good" and "serving" are used interchangeably.

67 "Duty," The *Great Ideas: A Syntopican of Greet Books of the Western World* (Chicago, Encyclopedia Britannica, 1952), 358.

68 Ibid., 359.

69 Ibid., 359. We shall return to the idea of the relation of love and justice in chapter 9

70 Kristin Gross, "Altruism", 37.

71 "Although the law regarding prohibition of killing is mainly negative, that is punishment, the Noahide law at the same time implicitly conveys a lofty moral message: radical equality regarding the sacred value of human life." Leon R. Kass, op.cit, 183.

72 Ibid., 467.

73 Agape love will be defined more fully below.

74 See Gregory A. Boyd. *The Myth of a Christian Nation* (Grand Rapids: Zondervan, 2005). Boyd's maxim is based on Christ's intent to establish a kingdom: "It would not be a 'power over" kingdom'; it would be 'power under' kingdom. It would be a kingdom where greatness is defined by serving and sacrificing for others." 28. "Our unique calling is simply to replicate Christ's sacrificial love in service to the world." 65.

75 It should be noted that we have adapted the term "service" in our analysis of "doing good." Ironically, the word service has become the standard term for "doing good." But what Jesus meant with the term "service" will be clarified as it is understood by the Believers' Church.

76 C.J. Cadoux. *The Early Church and the World* (Edinburgh: T. and T. Clark,1925), 364.

77 Cadoux, 27-34. We cannot enter the debate as to whether the early Christian Church uniformly rejected war, but we believe the predominant position was rejection of war. See the *Mennonite Quarterly Review*, (October ,2001) for a very extensive and spirited debate on the issue. The consensus seems to come down on the pacifist side.

78 Here one of the many uses of the word "service" emerges. Early Christians assumed that military service was anti-social service.

79 Ibid., 361-362.

80   Ibid., 403.

81   Ibid., 363 Underlining by present authors.

82   362.

83   (New York: Fellowship Publications, 1928).

84   The conflation of religion and state is still apropos today. See Gregory A. Boyd, *The Myth of a Christian* Ibid., 403.

Ibid., 363 Underlining by present authors. 362. (New York: Fellowship Publications, 1928). The conflation of religion and state is still apropos today. See Gregory A. Boyd, *The Myth of a Christian Nation*. op.cit.

85   Ibid., 232.

86   See Kenneth Scott Latourette. *A History of Christianity* (New York: Harper and Brothers, 1953) for an extensive survey.

87   Although many of these movements seemed to be mainly religious, many had social and economic motivations as well. Latourette provides a survey of the laxity of morals, exploitation, and corruption in the Christian Church. See Chapter 28, "Western Europe: Decline and Vitality".

88   *DHI*, Peter N. Stearns. "Protests", 670. He continues, "Religion was the only formal system of ideas that hand any hold on the common people, and a protest ideology before 1789 (was) a common man's interpretation of Christianity's social message." 670. Stearn's bibliography exemplifies the magnitude of protest through history.

89   A related approach is the massive utopian tradition. According to experts, the utopian tradition is based on Christianity's social message." 670. Stearn's bibliography exemplifies the magnitude of protest through history.

A related approach is the massive utopian tradition. According to experts, the utopian tradition is based on responses to the existential reality by proposing a more just and perfect world. One of the best historical treatments is Frank Manuel, *Utopian Thought in the Western World* (Oxford. Basil Blackwell, 1979).

90   Leo Driedge. *Mennonite Identity in Conflict* (New York: Edwin Mellon Press, 1988). See also, Gordon Kaufman. *Nonresistance and Responsibility and Other Mennonite Essays* (Newton, KS: Faith and Life Press, 1979); Mark Allman. *Who Would Jesus Kill: War, Peace and the Christian Tradition* (Winona, MN: Anselm Academic, 2008) and Ervin R, Stutzman. *From Nonresistance to Justice*. (Scottdale: Herald Press, 2011). This latter book makes major contribution to the movement toward social responsibility.

91   Radical Reformation is more extensively described in chapter 9

92   See C. Norman Kraus. *The Community of the Spirit: How the Church is in the World* (Scottdale, PA: Herald Press, 1984) for a theological discussion of the mission of the church. p. 81ff

93   "Mennonite," *ME*. V 556. op.cit.

94   Theron Schlabach. "To Focus a Mennonite Vision" Kingdom, *Cross and Community*, Edited by J. R. Burkholder and C. W. Redekop (Scottdale: Herald Press, 1976), 15-50, 16.

95   "Outside Influences on Mennonite Thought" *Mennonite Educational and Cultural Problems Proceedings*, 1953.

96   Harold S. Bender. "To the Youth of the Mennonite Church" *MQR* 1: ii.

97   Guy F. Hershberger. *War, Peace, and Nonresistance* (Scottdale: Herald Press, [1944, 1953), 374

98   Millard Lind. "Reflections on Biblical Hermeneutics" in Burkholder and Redekop, 91-102

99   Norman Kraus. "Toward a Theology for the Disciple Community" Ibid.: 103-117, 106

100 See, for example, Jack Donnelly. *Universal Human Rights in Theory and Practice* (Ithaca, NY: Cornell University Press, 2002).

101 Glenn Paige. *Nonkilling Global Political Science* (Honolulu: Center for Global Nonkilling [2002] 2009).

102 Howard Zinn. "Nonviolent Direct Action" in *Nonkilling History: Shaping Policy with Lessons from the Past*, edited by Antony Adolf (Honolulu: Center for Global Non-killing, 2010), 292-3. See also 287-93, 288.

103 Pitirim Sorokin. *On the Practice of Sociology*, edited by Barry V. Johnston (Chicago: University of Chicago Press, 1998), 42.

104 For an extensive discussion of the Believers' Church, see Donald F. Durnbaugh. *The Believers' Church*, (Scottdale: Herald Press, 1968).

105 For example, Western Christianity is now informed in many ways by the individualistic self-seeking society best described as market capitalism individualism, guiding utilitarianism assumptions, where the predominant guiding philosophy is "self interest in the long run works for the benefit of most people, if not all people." This issue is analyzed in Chapter 9.

106 *Aristotle II.* "Nicomachian Ethics", (Chicago: Encyclopedia Britannica, 1952), 340.

107 The variety of definitions of service and its use is almost incomprehensible. The word is practically synonymous with economics (providing services); with governance (government service/military service!) religion, (servant, ceremony etc.), domestic (table setting) etc. The

word service has as many uses and connotations as many words in the English language, and may have a similar status in other languages.

108   Webster's *New Collegiate Dictionary* (Springfield: Merriam,1973) has thirty-five entries treating the word "service." p.1059-1060. Ironically, more philosophically oriented writings, such as the *Dictionary of the History of Ideas* (New York: Charles Scribners Sons, 1974), do not have an entry for the words/concepts of service, charity, giving, reciprocity. It also missing in the *Great Books of the Western World* (Chicago: *Encyclopedia Britannica*, 1952).

109   *Webster's Encyclopedic Unabridged Dictionary of the English Language*. New York: Gramercy Books, 1993).

110   It will become obvious how the term service thus can so easily be confused and misused.

111   "Killing people" could be indirectly implied but not stated.

112   The senior author, on a tour of the Great Wall in 2006, was informed by the guide there were literally thousands of "slaves" buried in the wall itself, it being too cumbersome to bury them elsewhere.

113   This literature is cited in other sections of this book. These incompatibilities, interdependencies, and conflicts between the US military, the Peace Corps, and the Mennonite Pax program is illustrated in Calvin Redekop, *The Pax Story* (Telford, PA: Cascadia, 2001).

114   Richard Danzig and Peter Szanton, ix. An influential Quaker maintains that James was referring especially to work or service camps when he coined the term "an army enlisting against nature." He did not mean our natural environment. See Thomas E. Jones. *Light on the Horizon: The Pilgrimage of Tom Jones* (Richmond. IN.: Friends United Press, 1973), 136.

115   See Alasdair MacIntyr. *After Virtue: A Study in Moral Theory* (South Bend, IN: University of Notre Dame Press, 1984).

116   Dietrich Bonhoeffer. *Ethics*, trans. Neville Horton Smith (New York: Touchstone, 1995).

117   Quoted in Rabbi Zelig Pliskin. *Love Your Neighbor: You and Your Fellow Man in Light of the Torah* (Brooklyn: Aish Ha Torah, 1977), 229-230. "Loving the neighbor" warns that is possible to love family and friends in such a way that makes it difficult to love others.

118   When the super-ordinate/subordinate relationship is thoroughly instituted, it can be said that the distinction between voluntary and involuntary service disappears, at least philosophically. Were the natives serving the INCAS of Peru doing it voluntarily or involuntarily?

119   Charlton Lewis and Charles Short. *A Latin Dictionary* (Oxford: Clarendon Press, 1879).

120   For an overview, see James Perry and Mark Imperial. "A Decade of Service-Related Research: A Map of the Field", *Nonprofit and Voluntary Sector Quarterly*, 30, 2001, 462-479.

121   For more details about the scholarship of volunteerism from different perspectives, see Louis Penner, "Dispositional and Organizational Influences on Sustained Volunteerism: An Interactive Perspective", *Journal of Social Issues*, 58, 3, 2002, 447-467; John Wilson and Thomas Janoski. "The Contribution of Religion to Volunteer Work", *Sociology of Religion*, 56, 2 (1995), 137-152; and David Smith. "Altruism, Volunteers, and Volunteerism", *NonProfit and Voluntary Sector*, 10 (1) 1981, 21-36.

122   Ibid.

123   Again, unless the inequality structure is so ingrained that there is no conscious or sub-conscious resistance. Kurt H. Wolff, ed. *The Sociology of Georg Simmel* (Glencoe: Free Press, 1950). This is a classic and provocative analysis of class and power, and their relation to service.

124   Sociologist Ralf Dahrendorf divided society not between classes but between those who lead and those who follow. The main distinction is between those who give commands and those who obey commands. See *The Modern Social Conflict: The Politics of Liberty* (New York: Transactions Publishers, 2007).

125   There are almost infinite sources for the idea of work and labor. We purposefully restrict our analysis to "service" because "work" and "labor" veer into economic analysis, which tends to ignore the role of values when labor or work is involved. However, Marx made it the central basis of his analysis, which explains its major impact.

126   Thus, in this book, "service" will align only in some ways with the "service sector", which is all remunerated and is strictly an economic term. See, for example, David C. Korten. *When Corporations Rule the World* (San Francisco. Kumarian Press, 2001), which describes the movement from a market to a service economy and how the poor are the losers. In the United States, service comprises five of thirteen main occupational groups, and at present claims 31.6 percent of all employed. (http:www.bls.gov/opub/m/r/1984/03/)

127   The ethical dimensions in these spheres are, of course, very problematical and are discussed below. For an ethical approach on how service is "exploited", see Kevin Phillips. *The Politics of Rich and Poor* (Random House, 1990), especially chapter six.

128   In fact, the concepts of differentiation and interdependencies of species have been developed in the biological world as well, as (for example) the ant societies.

129   Robert Nesbitt. *The Unit Ideas of Sociology*, (New York: Basic Books, 1966), 88. But the question of how service, as an ethical issue, is not addressed.

130   A major theory in sociology/anthropology that pertains to the idea of service is exchange theory. "Exchange processes are the result of motives among people to realize their needs." Jonathan H. Turner. *The Structure of Sociological Theory*. (Homewood, Il: Dorsey Press,1982), 201.

131   Charles Horton Cooley. *Human Nature and the Social Order*, (Glencoe. IL: The Free Press,1956), 37. The evolutionary process assumes that this process could emerge "from the beginning" but this process has not yet been satisfactorily explained.

132   In this table, Voluntary Service could easily be present in all three types of objective behavior on the continuum. That is, a person could voluntarily be involved in anti-social actions. But it is the motivational dimension, **and its consequences,** that pro-social service can only be expressed on the compassion, cooperation, and possibly egotism levels, based on the duty of love. In other words, only in the pro-social dimension of behavior can the duty of love be fulfilled, including voluntary service.

133   The biological and psychological motivation for service is analyzed further in Chapter 4.

134   The remuneration is not limited to wages/salaries/benefits alone, but the entire career conundrum obtaining in any culture or society.

135   This is the sector normally defined as work or labor, freely given, but based on some contractual understanding or reward. Thus, this service is normally what is meant by labor.

136   Public service and State and Federal programs refer to the public sector service discussed above.

137   *Thomas Aquinas, Summa Theologica*, Pt. II, (Chicago: *Encyclopedia Brittanica*, 1952), 511

138   Simmel, op. cit, 392.

139   Simmel develops an extensive theory on the idea of social reciprocity, and proposes that the very possibility of society depends upon the idea of obligation, which serving and gift giving produces. The biological, genetic, and psychological motivations of altruism and service are discussed in Chapter 9.

140   The "group nature" that is the sociological dimensions of the voluntary service, as implied here, is a crucial variable, which forms the framework within which the Believers Church case is analyzed.

141   August Comte apparently was the first to use the term "altruism" around the year 1850 (Goss, op.cit.,36).

142   Karen Christensen and David Levinson, eds. (Thousand Oaks, CA. Sage Publications)

143   The individual motivations for altruistic service have some basis in evolutionary genetics, but even here the measurements are weak.

144   Don Yost ."More than Money", *Goshen College Bulletin*, Spring, 2014, 25-24-25.

145   Warren Buffett, one of the wealthiest Americans, is often cited as paying less taxes than his secretaries! According to one source, the US ranks thirty-sixth in life expectancy. http://en.wikipedia.org/wiki/List-of accessed 5/4/2011

146   "The state and human governance" has been one of the most contested and discussed issues in human history. Since our focus is doing good, we restrict its role on its affects on "doing good" as here defined.

147   Robert C. Lieberman. "Why the Rich are Getting Richer." *Foreign Affairs*, Jan./ Feb. 2011, 154-156.

148   The relationship between governmental policy and the capitalist free market ideology is incredibly complex and is explored more fully in Chapter 9.

149   See, for example, Jack Donnelly. *Universal Human Rights in Theory & Practice* (2nd edition) (Ithaca & London: Cornell University Press, 2003); David Forsythe. *Human Rights in International Relation* (Cambridge: Cambridge University Press, 2000); Michael Ignatieff, *Human Rights as Politics and Idolatry* (Princeton & Oxford: Princeton University Press, 2001); Ellen Frankel Paul, Fred Miller, and Jeffrey Paul. editors, *Natural Law and Modern Moral Philosophy*, (Cambridge: Cambridge University Press, 2001); and J. Steiner, and Philip Alston, *International Human Rights in Context: Law, Politics, Moral* (Oxford: Clarendon Press, 1996).

150   For a further discussion of the range of problems associated with the nexus of problems around defining and assigning accountability, see Andrew Kuper. *Democracy Beyond Borders: Justice and Representation in Global Institutions* (Oxford: Oxford University Press, 2004).

151   Onora O'Neill. *Towards Justice and Virtue: A Constructive Account of Practical Reasoning* (Cambridge: Cambridge University Press, 1996).

152   Thomas Pogge. "Human Rights and Human Responsibilities" In *Global responsibilities: Who must deliver on human Rights?* ed. Andrew Kuper (New York: Routledge Press, 2005), 3-35.

153   This is the approach to social order presented by Adam Smith: Allow complete freedom to atomistic individuals and social order will emerge spontaneously. The critique of this position is that Smith turns a vice — individual narcissism — into a virtue.

154   One popular solution to this dilemma, derived from Adam Smith and enshrined in classical market liberalism, is that individuals should be free to pursue their own self-interests and nothing more.

155   The first of these approaches is exemplified by Robert Nozick, *Anarchy, State, and Utopia* (New York: Basic Books, 1974) and the second by Henry Shue. *Basic Rights* (Princeton: Princeton University Press, 1996).

156   Discussed more fully in chapter 10. See Leo Driedger and Don Kraybill. *Mennonite Peacemaking: From Quietism to Activism*, (Scottdale: Herald Press, 1994) and Ervin Stutszman.

From Nonresistance to Justice, (Scottdale: Herald Press, 2011). John Howard Yoder, in *The Politics of Jesus* (1972) argues that the ethics of Jesus is a relevant social strategy for the traditional socio-political tactics. Increasingly, many Mennonites are not content to maintain a negative attitude toward war, but (especially in North America) want to be engaged in a corresponding positive act. In the broader context, concerns about warfare and direct and structural violence have stimulated the development of peace studies and conflict transformation programs at many Mennonite colleges and universities, as is true of the other Believers Church colleges.

157 For a more comprehensive general discussion, see David Cortwright. *Peace: A History of Movements and Ideas* (Cambridge: Cambridge University Press, 2008).

158 John Howard Yoder. (1997) "The Original Revolution" in *For the Nations: Essays Public and Evangelical*, (Grand Rapids, MI. Eerdmans Publishing:1997), 165-198.

159 Yoder. "The Original Revolution", 171.

160 Yoder. Ibid., 172.

161 See Michael Walzer. *Just and Unjust Wars* (New York: Basic Books, 1977), 22.

162 Ibid., 23.

163 Ibid., 329. It is most interesting that, though Walzer in his classic analysis of war makes it very clear that war is basically a moral issue, he does not discuss why human beings throughout history have continued to support the "moral absurdity" called war.

164 We will expand on the issue of justice and service in chapters 8 and 9.

165 This major issue is in reference to resentment, alienation, and estrangement, and has been most famously analyzed by Karl Marx and his disciples: "The problem of alienation concerns the relations of the individual with society." Adam Schaff. *Marxism and the Human Individual*, (New York: McGraw Hill, 1870), 105

166 The "Good Samaritan" is a most universal story of the myriad ways in which human beings become disadvantaged in the struggle for existence. Every human being has his/her own experience of this fact.

167 Oliver Richmond. *The Transformation of Peace* (New York: Palgrave Macmillan, 2005), 2.

168 Why the attempts to be more egalitarian has failed is generally ascribed to the reality that no society can be egalitarian unless the individuals are so inclined. In other words, both the individual and collective must be equally invested in doing good service. How should a community deal with the "free-rider problem" when a few members reap the benefits but refuse to bear the costs of living in a community? For a recent review of utopianism, see Ruth Levitas. *The Concept of Utopia* (Syracuse: Syracuse University Press, 1990).

169   Bernard Berelson and Gary S. Steiner. *Human Behavior: An Inventory of Scientific Findings* (New York: Harcourt, Brace and World, 1964), 665. The authors conclude with T.S Eliot's famous dictum "Go, go, go, said the bird, human kind cannot bear very much reality.", 665.

170   Ibid., 666. Anthropologists have done a lot of work in cross-cultural analysis, but the outcomes are mixed. A comparison of pro-social behavior among other cultures has clear limits.

171   *Oxford Dictionary of Quotations*, (Oxford: Oxford University Press,1979), 536.

172   The full story is found in Genesis 29. There is no common understanding of service and volunteerism, because there are so many cultures and sub-cultures from which to analyze them. We obviously limit ourselves to the western /Christian perspective

173   For example, see: *The Roots of American Economic Growth 1607-1861* (New York: Harper and Row, 1965); Thomas C. Cochran and William Miller. *The Age of Enterprise: A Social History of Industrial America*, (New York: Harper and Row, 1961); Jacques Ellul. *The Technological Society* (New York: Random House, 1967); and Robert L. Heilbronner. *The Worldly Philosophers: The Lives, Times and Ideas of the Great Economic Thinkers*, (New York: Simon and Schuster, 1953).

174   For a recent instructive and fascinating relationship between the technology of printing, societal evolution, and religion and its effects on the publication of the King James Version of the Bible, see Adam Nicolson. *God's Secretaries* (New York: Harper Collins, 2004**)**

175   Max Weber's studies were directly concerned with the sources of Capitalism, beginning already in the Renaissance but coming to fruition especially in the Reformation. See Weber's *The Theory of Social and Economic Organization*, (Glencoe: The Free Press, 1947), and his famous work *The Protestant Ethic and the Spirit of Capitalism* (New York: Charles Scribners Sons, 1958). The emergence of science and technology are fundamental factors in this revolution as also cited in Ellul.

176   There are many sources that describe the general conditions and situations, but the classic still remains R.H. Tawney. *Religion and the Rise of Capitalism* (New York: Harcourt, Brace, 1926). He states, "The facts of class status and inequality were rationalized in the Middle Ages by a functional theory of society, as the facts of competition were rationalized in the eighteenth by the theory of economic harmonies.", 17 The analysis of the role of capitalism and its justification (rationalization) is discussed more fully in Chapter 11.

177   For a scathing analysis of capitalism, see Thomas Piketty. *Capital in the Twentieth Century* (Cambridge, Harvard U. Press, 2014). The United States prides itself as the leading free-market capitalist nation, but its standing in the parameters of health, morbidity education, nutrition, and social services are appalling. *The United States World Population Prospects Report for 2005-2010* places the United States thirty-sixth in life expectancy, the statistic

which most widely reflects the overall health and well-being of a nation. http://en.wikipedia.org/wikiLists of countries, Accessed May 22, 2011.

178   This will be dealt more philosophically in Chapter 9

179   "Doing good includes the entirety of human/material existence. Although we will not focus on the environment, it is ultimately included in any kind of "peaceable kingdom."

180   Bruce Grelle and David A. Krueger. *Christianity and Capitalism: Perspectives on Religion, Liberalism and the Economy* (Chicago: CSSR, 1986), ix. The Christian tradition has often couched the problem in the form of "sin" and disobedience to God's will. But this is a vast oversimplification, because so-called Christian nations, denominations, and individuals have often expressed very brutal and cruel "service" of the neighbor. One such example is slavery. Even the godly Quakers developed an extensive slave industry. That religions are themselves at least partially social constructions is assumed by almost all scholars. For a Believers Church perspective, see Henry Rempel. *A High Price for Abundant Living*, (Scottdale: Herald Press, 2003)

181   There is a massive body of studies that deal with this topic; among the early classics is Ernst Troeltsch's *The Social Teachings of the Christian Churches*, (New York: Harper and Brothers, 1960) but from a specifically Believers Church point of view, see James Halteman. *The Clashing Worlds of Economics and Faith*, (Scottdale:Herald Press,1995); see also Henry Rempel. op.cit. Both have very helpful bibliographies.

182   The Hutterite tradition is of course one of the most dramatic positions, but other Anabaptist groups have also taken a strong position on faith and economics. See Calvin Redekop, Victor Krahn, and Samuel J. Steiner. *Anabaptist/Mennonite Faith and Economics*, (Lanhan: University Press of America, 1994).

183   William V. DeAntonio. "Voluntary Associations", *Encyclopedia of Sociology*, 199-227.

184   Quoted in Harriet Claude Kipps, ed. *Volunteerism* (NY: R.R. Bowker, 1991), xi.

185   Quoted in Robin Williams. *American Society: A Sociological Interpretation*, (New York: Alfred Knopf, 1955), 466.

186   Ibid., 466

187   Though de Tocqueville does not directly ascribe the motivation to the religious factor, it is well known that many American citizens were part of the strongly Protestant Calvinist, non-conformist and Roman Catholic traditions.

188   Pitrim Sorokin. *Altruistic Love*, (Boston: Beacon Hill Press, 1950), 9. This research consisted of a sample of a thousand people identified as "good neighbors" by a selected group of persons who were asked to nominate good neighbors. Sorokin's definition of "freely" given is at the foundation of mutual aid, but also of voluntary service.

189   Ibid., 4. Already in the 1930s and 1940s, Sorokin saw the developing cultural emphasis on egotism, selfishness, greed, aggression, racial violence, and sexual exploitation in the US. He led an almost single-handed crusade to encourage social science, to study and analyze pro-social values and actions. He was not very successful.

190   Ibid., 47. This statistic is increasingly supported in continuing research.

191   Cornelius Krahn, J. Winfield Fretz, and Robert Kreider. "Altruism in Mennonite Life," in P.A. Sorokin, ed. *Forms and Techniques of Altruistic and Spiritual Growth* (Boston: Beacon Press, 1971), 328.

192   One of the most universally applauded illustrations of American compassion is the Marshal Plan, sponsored by the United States to help Europe recover from the ravages of World War II.

193   Robin Williams. *American Society: A Sociological Interpretation* (New York: Alfred Knopf, 1955), 398-399

194   Ibid., 467.

195   Ibid., 533

196   Ibid., 470

197   W. Lloyd Warner, *The Living and the Dead* (New Haven: Yale University Press, 1959), 243.

198   Ibid., 242.

199   Ibid., 247. Warner emphatically suggests that associational behavior expresses and reinforces basic religious symbols and beliefs. Another more recent volume that reports on concern for the neighbor from a Christian perspective is Robert Wuthnow's *Acts of Compassion*, (Princeton: Princeton University Press, 1991).

200   Bellah, Robert, et. al. *Habits of the Heart* (New York" Harper and Row: 1985), "American cultural traditions define personality, achievement, and the purpose of human life in ways that leave the individual suspended in glorious, but terrifying, isolation.", 6.

201   Ibid., 172.

202   Ibid., 194.

203   Ibid, 247.

204   Ibid., 246-247. The goal of balancing individualism with "sympathy" for others, which Bellah promotes, is closely aligned with the general thesis of this book, namely that society can only survive if this positive balance exists.

205 Ibid., 167.

206 Richard Danzig and Peter Szanton. op. cit. (Lexington: D.C. Heath, 1986).

207 Ibid., viv

208 E. J Dionne, E.J. "What We Lost." *Washington Post*, November 21, 2013, 1

209 "Warrior for peace and against poverty", *Washington Post* (January 19,2011), A.1. Shriver died January 18, 2011. Ironically, the anti-government stance of many contemporary conservative churches does not share this positive view of government.

210 Ibid., A p. 8

211 Richard Danzig and Peter Szanton, 180. The authors present a wide overview of types of service, including a chapter on voluntary service in America.

212 Economic News Release. *Volunteering in the United States*, 2010, p 1, http:www.bls.gov/news.release/volun.nr0.htm

213 Obviously, the question arises, as to how this North American reality compares with other societies and cultures. Thus, for example, is voluntary service different in a "command" (i.e. a socialistic or totalitarian) society? What of a traditional African society? Is voluntary service a specifically Western capitalistic concept? This question cannot be addressed here.

214 Farmington Hills, MI. Gale Publishing, 2008.

215 "Dualism", *Encyclopedia of Religion and Religions*, (New York, Meridian Library,1958), 131. In January 2001, President Elect Bush referred to the "Axis of Evil" in his inaugural address, based on his position as a good Evangelical Christian. However, in reality, the line cannot be that neatly concentrated and limited to two spheres.

216 (Philadelphia"Westminster Press, 1978), 192.

217 This possibility opens a very complex question, namely the role that Christianity has played in the development of the value systems of the West. As is well known, ethically positive social virtues and actions do not sell books and movies, as Hollywood continues to remind us. See Henry Rempel, op. cit. Chapter 3, "Sacred Values and the Worship of Abundance."

218 By Hertha Kraus. (Herald Press, Scottdale: 1944). This detailed book about the variety of relief services that were provided around the globe is an impressive indication of the commitment to "do good" through voluntary religious, secular, and public organizations and agencies.

219 Ibid., For a history of mutual aid in the Anabaptist tradition, see Donald Durnbaugh. *Every Need Supplied: Mutual Aid and Christian Community in the Free Churches. 1525-1675.*

(Philadelphia: Temple University Press, 1974). See also "Mutual Aid and Service" in Donald Durnbaugh. *The Believers Church* (Scottdale, Herald Press: 1968), pp.264-282. For a history of Mennonite Disaster Service, see Lowell Detweiler, ed., *The Hammer Rings Hope* (Scottdale: Herald Press, 2000).

220   A considerable number of conservative, fundamentalist, and evangelical groups do not consider providing social welfare "doing good" as part of the Christian faith. Michael Lienisch states the new Christian Right maintains "that equality is undesirable, being both unbiblical and unrealistic...in ancient Israel not only was it forbidden to grant special favors to the rich and powerful...it was also forbidden to give the poor special treatment...Just as equality and justice are inimical, so are equality and equity." *Redeeming America: Piety and Politics in the New Christian Right* (Chapel Hill: University of North Carolina Press, 1993), 119.

221   There is of course variation between Christian groups—fundamentalist and evangelical groups do not have much theological conviction on "social" solutions to the ultimate issues, which is the redemption of the soul.

222   See p 4 ff. Ironically, it is admitted in many Christian groups that it is external pressures such as military draft or lack of governmental responses that has often motivated them to act.

223   "Peace Churches" are defined in chapter 9.

224   Harold Josephson. *Biographical Dictionary of Modern Peace Leaders* (Westport, CN: Greenwood Press, 1985), 150.

225   Ibid., 150. See also 142.

226   In February 20, 1918, "A letter [was] sent to Mennonites and Church of the Brethren asking them to co-operate in Friends relief work [in France]: Mary Hoxie Jones. *Swords into Plowshares: An account of the American Friends Service Committee.*(Westport Conn: Greenwood Press,1971), 321. A very useful chronology of Quaker developing voluntary service activities is included, pp 319-361. Thus, in early 1918, the newly formed Mennonite Relief Agency, at the request of the AFSC, sent young men to serve under it. For an extensive report on the AFSC reconstruction program in post-World War I Europe and Russia, see Rufus M. Jones. *A Service of Love in Wartime* (New York: 1920); see also Calvin Redekop. *The Pax Story*, op. cit 28.

227   John D. Unruh. *In the Name of Christ* (Scottdale: Herald Press, 1952), 294.

228   Kenneth Kreider notes that Ziegler "organized 'One Hundred Dunkers for Peace' as a 'moral equivalent to war'." 7. Ibid.

229   Danzig and Szanton, 7.

230   Kraus, Hertha. op. cit. This book, now almost forgotten, co-sponsored by the Church of the Brethren, the Quaker, and the Mennonite service organizations, describes the massive service activities of scores of organizations during the World War I and II decades.

231 Charles C. Moskos. *The New Conscientious Objection: From Sacred to Secular Resistance* (New York: Oxford University Press, 1993).

232 See J. Kenneth Kreider. also Redekop (*The Pax Story*) for brief accounts and further bibliography.

233 For a brief and history of the Peace Corps, see J. Kenneth Kreider. op. cit. and Redekop. *The Pax Story*, op. cit.

234 Yoder, Redekop, and Jantzi, 19.

235 Ibid., 40.

236 Ibid., 20.

237 Ibid., chapter 6, see especially Raymond Martin. "My Journey from the Cornfields to the World Bank", p.156 ff.

238 It is not possible to explore this topic here. For an attempt to spell out this problem from an Anabaptist perspective, see Yoder, Redekop, and Jantzi, especially part I and chapter 9.

239 See Ibid, 283ff.

240 In fact, a young person serving in the Peace Corps can be as idealistic and compassionate (or more so) as the most "pious" NGO volunteer.

241 For example, see Lowell Detweiler. *The Hammer Rings Hope*, (Scottdale: Herald Press, 20--), which describes the Mennonite Disaster Service work. See also "Disaster Services". *ME, V* 237-238. Also, the recent depth analysis by Brenda D. Phillips. *Mennonite Disaster Service* (Lanham: Lexington Books, 2014)

242 This type of service has often been criticized as merely responding to human suffering, but not attending to the causes of misery and pain. Still, assisting humans in need is clearly an undeniable moral good.

243 For a recent survey, see the recently published, massive and comprehensive *Encyclopedia of Religion and Nature*. (London: Thoemmes Continuum, 2005)

244 See Calvin Redekop. ed., *Creation and Environment: An Anabaptist Perspective on a Sustainable World*, (Baltimore: Johns Hopkins University Press, 2000). An extensive bibliography is included.

245 Ibid., 217.

246 This issue is finding increasing attention. See, for example, Thomas Berry. *The Dream of the Earth* (San Francisco: Sierra Club Books, 1988). "All human professions, institutions, and activities must be integral with the earth as the primary self nourishing, self-governing

and self-fulfilling community. To integrate our human activities within this context is our way into the future." 88. See also Kleindienst, op cit.

247   "Good and Evil" in Mortimer J. Adler, ed. *The Great Ideas: A Syntopicon of the Great Books of the Western World* (Chicago: Encyclopedia Britannica, 1952), 605. (contains a bibliography, 605-635)

248   From lecture notes by Calvin Redekop in 1958.

249   Ibid., 47.

250   Danzig and Szanton, 17.

251   This quote from Jesus has been notoriously misused. It is not a justification for a conservative acceptance of the poor, but rather a fact with the implication that it is our duty to serve in compassion.

252   See footnote 64. The inequalities are basically the result of anti-social tendencies, which will be explored further below.

253   A recent approach to the problem is Wendell Berry's proposition that all human issues can best be solved by dispensing with the "rhetoric of abstractions (such as the state), rather dealing with personal and local issues, which are the most effective political activities ever invented. (Richard Klinedienst, "Rethinking Politics as Statecraft: Wendell Berry Among the Anabaptists", *Mennonite Quarterly Review*, Vol 83, No. 4, 517-538.

254   The United states ranks among the lowest in health care, education, and has one of the greatest gaps in income between the rich and the poor in the world. "Approximately 35 million Americans were living in poverty in 2009. According to the Associated Press, experts believe that 2009 saw the largest single year increase in the U.S poverty rate since the U.S. government began calculating poverty figures back in 1959. The U.S. poverty rate is now the third worst among the developed nations tracked by the Organization of Economic Cooperation and Development: http://www.lewrockwell.com/rep/15t-shocking-povearty-stats.html. So much for the compassion of the market Capitalist ethics.

255   Our vote for the best example of this is Mennonite Disaster Service.

256   Brenda Phillips. *Mennonite Disaster Service*, (Lanham: Lexington, Books 2114), 21.

257   It is widely assumed the original "evangelical" Christian tradition was deeply concerned about the social well being of all peoples. Christianity is generally defined as a salvation religion (God forgives humans for their rebellious nature and alienation), but the variety of interpretations of the process of repairing the broken relationships existing in the world includes social justice. Some more conservative evangelical traditions, however, pay less attention to helping the "less fortunate" on a physical, economic, and social level.

258   The importance of justice is expanded in chapters 9.

259 Yoder, *The Original Revolution*, 172.

260 Injustice describes and causes the gap between the ideal and the real, service corrects injustices, which produces peace. The authors propose that working for peace as such, without concern for injustice that cause conflict, is confusing cause and effect.

261 John Howard Yoder. *The Politics of Jesus* (Grand Rapids, MI: William Eerdmans, 1972), 190.

262 Ibid., 213.

263 The term "Radical Reformation" is the "umbrella concept" used in this book for the religious movement that challenged the "established Churches" of pre-Reformation Christianity. The best brief description and bibliography is the *Wikipedia* article "Radical Reformation". The most authoritative analysis is George H Williams, *The Radical Reformation.*, 3rd ed. (Truman State University Press, 2000) For a similar, more contemporary and secular account of responding to human needs with social justice since the enlightenment, see Brian Barry. *The Principles of Social Justice* (Cambridge: Cambridge University Press, 1999).

264 Yoder gives the following example: "The conscientious objector who refuses to do what his government asks him to do, but still remains under the sovereignty of that government and accepts the penalties which it imposes, or the Christian who refuses to worship Caesar but still permits Caesar to put him to death, is being subordinate even though he is not obeying." See *The Politics of Jesus*, 212.

265 See Phillips, op. cit, for examples of the religious groups involved in disaster service. P 22 passim The argument of this volume is based on a "Believers Church" theological foundation, which emerges by inference, not by explicit statement.

266 (Bloomington, IN: Indiana University Press, 1994).

267 *Can Science Save Us?* (New York: Longmans, Green and Co.1947), 8. We are not at all confident that science will provide the final paradigm by which "progress" will be achieved.

268 A father of an adolescent girl recently remarked in a public meeting, "Teenagers are really mean to each other."

269 There is no sharp separation of these two behaviors, as evidenced in war soldiers involved in killing are given means for saving their comrades, risking their own lives.

270 Fry. *The* medals for *Human Potential for Peace*, op.cit, 1.

271 Fry, Ibid., 248.

272 David Hinde, "Forward", in Fry. *The Human Potential for Peace*, xi-xii.

273 William Ury. *Getting to Peace: Transforming Conflict at Home, at Work, and in the World* (New York: Viking Press, 1999),199.

274 Leon Kass. *The Beginning of Wisdom*. Op. cit. Kass maintains that the Jewish tradition, through its "Noahide law", provided one of history's most fundamental precepts for the pro-social position ever devised. 174. Kass also maintains that the Jewish law was one of, if not the most, important "legal" contributions in human history.172ff

275 Pitirim Sorokin, who spent a lifetime in comparative studies of human societies, suggests that "Eternal struggle *is* a universal and everlasting law. Such a struggle goes on among atoms, organisms, human beings, societies."

276 Aristotle. "Nicomachean Ethics", *Great Books: Aristotle. II* (Chicago, Encyclopedia Britannica, 1952), 339

277 The reality that Greece and Rome were based on slavery for the majority of people is clearly a blatant contradiction to the sublime ideas of good noted above.

278 A major sociological theory called the "conflict school" has become dominant. "No single social process in sociological theorizing has received as much conceptual attention as conflict. There are, no doubt, good reasons for this emphasis." Jonathan J. Turner. *The Structure of Sociological Theory* (Homewood, Il: Dorsey Press, 1982), Op. cit. 175.

279 Thomas Hobbes, *The Leviathan* (Chicago: Great Books, 1952), 76-77. Often described as the father of social psychology, Hobbes dealt extensively with the nature of human nature by distinguishing it from animals, including such ideas as appetite, desire, and love.

280 "Of Man" in *Leviathan* 61 passim. It is interesting that Hobbes even discusses these differences under the heading "Of the Interior Beginnings of Voluntary Motions", 61.

281 Clearly, the hope of disposing of war cannot be achieved by this perspective.

282 Ibid., 76.

283 Ibid., 76.

284 Ibid., 86.

285 Ibid., 84.

286 Ibid., 87.

287 Ibid., 87. (our italics)

288 John Locke, *Concerning the True Original Extent and End of Civil Government*, (Chicago: Great Books, 1952), 42.

289 Ibid., 55. Most social theorists propose that the family was the most primordial form of social structure, followed by sib-ships and clan. For a recent Believers Church perspective, see Paul Peachey. *Leaving and Cleaving: The Human Significance of the Conjugal Union* (Lanham: University Press of America, 2001) especially Chapter 2, "The Making of the Human."

290 Ibid., 25.

291 "Moral Sense" *DHI*, III, 234.

292 "Of Ethics" *Critique of Practical Reason* (Chicago: Encyclopedia Britannica. 1952), 376.

293 http://www.econlib.org/library/Enc/bios/Becker.html, accessed 9-15-14, http://www.newyorker.com/news/john-cassidy/gary-becker-and-the-economics-revolution-that-wasnt, accessed. 9-1-14

294 "Natural Law and Natural Rights," in Philip Wiener, ed., *Dictionary of the History of Ideas* (New York: Charles Scribners's Sons, 1973), 14.

295 Sorokin. 433ff.

296 Hobbes. 87. Hobbes suggests that the "golden rule" is the best way to understand how this could come about, but he does not give us a clue where the motivation is to come from. A classic example of what is good for the individual destroying the good of the community is Garret Hardin's "The Tragedy of the Commons." *Science*. Vol. 162(Dec. 13, 1968), pp. 1243-48.

297 Sorokin. 313. For the social theoreticians, this orientation is, of course, reflected in the relatively recent "conflict school" noted above, in which "social equilibrium" refers to the balance between constructive and destructive forces. See Jonathan Turner (especially Chapter 6), "The Conflict Heritage", 117ff. op. cit.

298 According to Max Weber and Joachim Wach, prophecy is a special dimension of most religions, which functions to actualize these concerns and teachings with behaviorist ethics pertaining to the conflict school. See *From Max Weber: Essays in Sociology* (New York: Oxford University Press, 1946), especially *The Social Psychology of the World Religions* 267-301; and Joachim Wach, *Sociology of Religion* (Chicago: University of Chicago Press, 1944), especially "The Prophet", 346-351.

299 This issue will be treated below in the section on natural science.

300 The lack of focusing on voluntary service may be because it seems to be a value-laden issue mainly organized by religious groups,

301 From a philosophical perspective, this dilemma will probably never be answered, but of course, most religions, including Christianity, present cosmologies that explain the origin of evil.

302 Calvin Redekop. *Strangers Become Neighbors* (Scottdale, PA: Herald Press 1980), 60.

303   See Kass, cited above. Again, the source for this motivation is not explained.

304   The brutality and violence expressed between Christians and Muslims in the Middle East staggers the imagination. For a recent survey, see Bernard Lewis. *From Babel to Dragomans: Interpreting the Middle East*, (New York: Oxford University Press, 2004).

305   For a significant analysis of Christianity and War, see J. Samuel Preus, *Explaining Religion, Criticism and Theory from Bodin to Freud* (New Haven, Ct: Yale University Press, 1987)

306   Human nature is a very ambiguous and contested idea. There is little agreement that there is such a thing, and if so, what it actually is. We propose the most general conclusion is that it is everything that humans do and are capable of doing.

307   This thesis, that only a surplus economy, or a "slave economy", can provide the occasion for reflection, is illustrated by the well-known aphorism: "Only the wealthy have the luxury of mental illness and hence need and can afford psychiatrists."

308   A recent example of the genetic causes of anti-social behavior is Richard Dawkins. *The Selfish Gene* (New York: Oxford University Press, 1989). For an extensive review of evolution and genes in altruistic behavior, see Samir Okasha. "Biological Altruism" in *Stanford Encyclopedia of Philosophy*. *http://plato.stanford.edu/entries/altruism-biological*, accessed May 15,14

309   Okasha. op. cit, 21.

310   Laurence Miller. "Motivation", *Encyclopedia of Ethics*, 577.

311   This why religion has a "leg up. It always starts with an objective authority beyond the observer.

312   A scholarly debate rages regarding the nature of human behavior (however it is defined). Is it predominantly or basically "fighting with red tooth and claw" or a cooperative and altruistic response to the antagonistic. Or is it the other way around? Pinker, for example, tends to believe it was the physical and cultural environment that came first.

313   W.C. Allee. "Animal Sociology", *Encyclopedia Britannica*, (1966). Vol. 20:916. We propose that this body of knowledge forms the empirical basis for the conditions described in the thesis in Chapter 1.

314   E. Gil Clary. "Altruism and Helping Behavior," in V.S. Ramachandran. *Encyclopedia of Human Behavior,* Volume 1, page 93.

315   "Altruism," *Encyclopedia of Sociology*, 115.

316   Samir Okasha. po. Cit.16

317   Roger Masters, quoted in Don Ortner, *How Humans Adapt: A Bio-cultural Odyssey* (Washington, D.C.: Smithsonian Institution,1983), 151-152. (Underlining mine) In any case, we do not need to take a definitive position on this question here, because the scientific enterprise has given us support to the premise that humanity expresses **both** anti- and pro-social behavior, based on the "reduction" process of evolution itself!

318   http://www.warresisters.org/pages/piechart.htm (viewed May 2011).

319   See Eugene Jarecki, 2008, and Chalmers Johnson, 2008, op.cit.

320   Richard Rubenstein. *Reasons to Kill: Why Americans Choose War,* (New York: Bloomsbury Press, 2010), 171.

321   Henry Rempel. Ibid., 41. Rempel's position is a major expansion of the position regarding capitalism taken in this book. op. cit.

322   Ibid., 261

323   We expand this topic in chapter 9, (pp. 170ff). Proponents of the Capitalistic ideology self-righteously condemn communism for its brutality and imposing its views on the population. But Capitalism's "indoctrination "of the "masses" through mass persuasion, advertising, and high-pressure marketing are surprisingly similar and even more effective. One fascinating example of this process is provided by Richard M. Pfeffer. *Working for Capitalism,* (New York: Columbia University Press, 1979). Pfeffer states, "Workers hold themselves responsible for their feelings of absence [incompetence] at work and blame themselves for not making more of themselves. They blame themselves for being in the position of having to take orders. Class is a personal responsibility, despite the fact that he never had a chance." 307.

324   Adam Smith. *The Wealth of Nations* (Chicago: Great Books, 1952), 194. Although, he also admitted that there are some "altruistic" tendencies which cover weaknesses in the selfish drive, and that social restrictions are necessary to restrain unlimited selfish drives. See footnote 50.

325   One of the most ideological, representative, and celebrated defenders of the free-market capitalism is Friedrich van Hayek, who wrote *The Road to Serfdom* (Chicago: University of Chicago Press, 1994). However, many thinkers have rejected his beatification of individualism. For example, Alfred Keynes advised Hayek "to take up the restoration of right moral thinking (so that) you would not feel quite so much like Don Quixote." (Yergin and Stanislaw, 143-144). A more scathing and derisive judgment can hardly be imagined.

326   Ayn Rand is a "true believer and disciple" of Hayek's extremism. See her *Capitalism: The Unknown Ideal* (New York: Signet Books, 1967). On the other hand, many more "communally oriented" thinkers have opined the exact opposite, namely that it is precisely the unbridled expression of self interest which is the worm in the capitalist apple and in any unregulated society. See William Greider. op.cit., 12 passim.

327 William Greider. op. cit 12. The contemporary irrational salaries of CEOs, not to mention their unethical behavior, is an example of an economic system out of control working only for the rich and powerful.

328 McCoy Charles Allan. *Contemporary Isms. A Political Economy Perspective* (New York: Franklin Watts, 1982), 118-122. See also Chapter 4. "Liberalism: The Case of the United States.", 155-208. For a Mennonite analysis of modern capitalism, see Henry Rempel, cited above.

329 Laurence Dickey. "Historicizing the 'Adam Smith Problem'", *Journal of Modern History*, 58, Sept. 1986, 579-609

330 McCoy, 121. Note that Smith does not refer to the moral aspects of fairness etc, but merely refers to the need for state regulations to restrict unlawful actions in the realization of profits. He says "No society can surely be flourishing and happy, of which the far greater part are poor and miserable," but doesn't take that idea further. The *Wealth of Nations* (Chicago: Encyclopedia Britannica. 1952). See, for example, "The Wages of Labor", 33.

331 See Hazel Henderson. *The Politics of the Solar Age* (Garden City: Doubleday, 1981), Chapter 8. "Three Hundred Years of Snake Oil."

332 Karl Marx and Frederich Engels. "The Communist Manifesto", 19, in Lewis S. Feuer, *Marx and Engels* (Garden City, NY: Anchor Books, Doubleday and Co: 1959).

333 An objective approach to the various Marxist applications, such as Cuba, had laudable goals and achievements. But the means were often, if not always, very inhumane and even brutal.

334 Daniel Yergin and Joseph Stanislaw. *The Commanding Heights: The Battle Between Government and the Marketplace that is Remaking the Modern World*, (New York: Simon and Schuster, 1998), 390.

335 And when the political system is not vigilant, the capitalist forces aggrandize their power.

336 The dynamics that produce differences in the population in relation to "competing" in the free-market system are many, but among the basic reasons are personal, physical, psychological, and mental dis-abilities, and inherited wealth and social status, which "stack the deck—basically the distinction between liberalism, which believes there is a need for a "social" conscience, and conservatives believing in the Darwinian market survival of the fittest."

337 For recent powerful critiques of capitalism, see the widely acclaimed books by Thomas Pikkety. *Capitalism in the Twentieth Century,* (Cambridge: Belknap/Harvard University Press, 2014), and David Harvey. *Seventeen Contradictions and the End of Capitalism* (Cambridge: Oxford University Press, 2014)

338 The first and classic book that proclaimed this reality is by Donald Meadows et. al. *The Limits to Growth*, (New York: Universe Books, 1972). It was viciously scorned and rejected but

has proven to be basic. The latest rejection of capitalism in the new "post-growth" paradigm is comprehensively analyzed in *Sacred Economics*, by Charles Eisenstein (Berkely; Evolver Editions, 2011)

339 Daniel Yergin and Joseph Stanislaw. op.cit 398. Adam Smith implies a moral-foundational necessity of economics by stating, "No society can surely be flourishing and happy, of which the far greater part of the members are poor and miserable", 33. *An Inquiry into the Nature and Causes of the Wealth of Nations* (Chicago: Encyclopedia Britannica, 1952). See also the reference to Smith's later position in Chapter 3.

340 "Karl Polani predicted in the *Great Transformation* that a system of allocation emphasizing only market transactions would simply dislocate the social, human, and environmental components of society and that it would require continual government intervention and ever-larger income transfers to keep it going." Hazel Henderson, op. cit, 250. For a trenchant critique of the "unlimited growth" and "free-market capitalism" ideologies, see especially Chapter 7, "Economists as Apologists."

341 Alvin Gouldner. *The Dialectic of Ideology and Technology* (New York: Seabury. The Press, 1976), 26. This analysis is a valuable source of ideology and paradigm. Gouldner suggests paradigm is the concrete, while the ideology is the abstract dimension of belief systems. See p. 220.ff. One of the best studies of how the capitalist ideology has "captured" the blue-collar American population to support it is presented by Thomas Frank in *What's the Matter with Kansas? How the Conservatives Won the Heart of America* (New York: Henry Holt and Company: 2004).

342 "Ethics", *Mennonite Encyclopedia*, IV, 1079.

343 There are voluminous attempts to define Anabaptism, and to suggest even one source would seriously curtail the definition. For a summary of what many other scholars have proposed, see Calvin Redekop. "The Community of Scholars and the Essence of Anabaptism", *Mennonite Quarterly Review*, (October, 1993), 429-450.

344 "The Confessional Heritage in its New Mold: What is Mennonite Self-Understanding Today?" Calvin Wall Redekop and Samuel J. Steiner. *Mennonite Identity: Historical and Contemporary Perspectives*, (Lanham: University Press of America, 1988), 5.

345 For a general overview and bibliography, see Walter Klaassen, "Anabaptism" *ME. V*, 23-25.

346 The various Mennonite groups are better termed "conferences" than denominations, since the variations are mainly ethnic differences. This also applies more specifically to the organized voluntary service programs, sponsored by a para-church organization such as Mennonite Central Committee (MCC). See, for example, Brenda Phillips. *Mennonite Disaster Service*, (Lanham: Lexington Books, 2014).

347 Lowell Detweiler. *The Hammer Rings Hope* (Scottdale: Herald Press, 2000), 98. See also Brenda Phillips. *Mennonite Disaster Service, op.cit.* for an extensive analysis of MDS. Anabaptism's communitarian and even utopian ideas regarding economics has resulted in their being defined as communists. Peter Jamers Klassen. The *Economics of Anabaptism. 1525-1560,* (The Hague": Mouton & Co. 1964) p.24 ff. See also Brenda Phillips, 14.

348 Probably the first voluntary service in America was launched by the American Friends Service Committee, which received the Nobel Peace Prize in 1947. See "Voluntary Service" by H.A. Penner for a fine overview and history of the spread of voluntary service in North America, *ME, V,* 917-918.

349 Wilfred Unruh. "An Evaluation of Mennonite Service Programs," *Proceedings of Mennonite Education and Cultural Problems,* XVI., 1967, 147. See also his *A Study of Mennonite Service Programs* (Elkhart, IN: Institute of Mennonite Studies, 1965). This volume is the most extensive history and analysis of voluntary service including foreign services (Pax) to date.

350 Paul Toews. *Mennonites in American Society,* 1930-1970 (Scottdale: Herald Press, 1996), 120. The A.F.S.C. had operated work camps in the US as early as 1935.

351 Ibid., 120. Toews states that Otto B. Reimer of Reedley, California advocated a similar project in California, but nothing seems to have materialized. 121. As indicated above, a number of General Conference Mennonite young people had been active in A.F.S.C., including Elmer Ediger, and Robert Kreider and Edna Ramseyer in the mid to late 30s. Voluntary service camps had already been conducted before 1938 in some Mennonite communities, but information is not available.

352 For a parallel description of the Church of the Brethren voluntary service program, see J. Kenneth Kreider. *A Cup of Cold Water,* op.cit. The Church of the Brethren voluntary service record is truly phenomenal and may have exceeded the Mennonite record, on a per-capita membership basis.

353 "Voluntary Service," *Mennonite Encyclopedia.* IV, 848. Bender ignores the General Conference actions since he refers only what was then known as the "Old Mennonite Church."

354 Ibid., 848-849

355 Ibid., 849.

356 Ibid., 849. For the most extensive review of CPS, see Melvin Gingerich. *Service for Peace: a history of Mennonite Civilian Public Service* (Akron, PA. Mennonite Central Committtee:1949); see also "Civilian Public Service" *ME,* I, 604-611.

357 W. Unruh. A-131.

358 Penner. "Voluntary Service", *ME,* V, 917.

359 Ibid., A-171.

360 Wilfred Unruh's "A Study..." cited above is the most comprehensive source for the entire voluntary service development. See footnote 8. There is no comprehensive statistical compilation of the entire voluntary service operations in the twentieth century among Mennonites, of which the writers are aware. The program was immense in terms of persons, projects, and consequences for the recipients and communities.

361 "The Voluntary Service Program", *Proceedings of the Mennonite Educational and Cultural Problems,* VI, 1947, 31. This must be an error, for no records were found of a unit operating in 1943. This must refer to a "Training School" held at Goshen College in the summer of 1943, which prepared women to serve in mental hospitals. See Paul Toews. *Mennonites in American Society. 1930-1970* (Scottdale: Herald Press, 1996), 168.

362 It is not clear whether Bender's reference was the "Mennonite Church" or the entire Mennonite society. Bender was deeply involved in the MCC sponsored CPS program (dean of education) and the Peace Section created in 1942, so it is reasonable that he communicated the voluntary service concepts back and forth between the MCC and MRSC, so that the parallel timing is no accident. See Al Keim, 296-299.

363 Report of MCC secretary to MCC Annual Meeting, Dec. 28-29, 1945, 6.

364 Rachel Goosen. "Women in Alternative Service", *MQR*, 66:4 (October, 1992), 525. Goosen reports further: "In 1945, MCC established summer service units for women at Poughkeepsie, New York, Cleveland, Ohio, Wernersville, Pennsylvania, and Akron, Pennsylvania." 525.

365 Harold Penner. "Voluntary Service," *ME*, 5, 917. For a brief survey of voluntary service in North America, see chapter 16: "Voluntary Service" in John D. Unruh. *In the Name of Christ* (Scottdale: Herald Press, 1952). Interestingly. Unruh does not mention women in the entire chapter, nor does he mention women in the chapter on Civilian Public Service.

366 Albert N. Keim. *The CPS Story: An Illustrated History of Civilian Public Service,* (Intercourse, Pa: Good Books, 1990), 41.

367 Melvin Gingerich. *Service for Peace* (Akron, Pa.: Mennonite Central Committee, 1949), 85. This huge volume is the most complete record of the CPS service program during World War II.

368 Edward Yoder and Don Smucker. *The Christian and Conscription* (Akron, Pa: Mennonite Central Committee, 1945), 98. The issue of dissatisfaction with the "irrelevance" of CPS service has been recently analyzed by Perry Bush in "The Mennonite Leadership and the Line of Least Resistance", in his book *Two Kingdoms, Two Loyalties Mennonite Pacifism in Modern America* (Baltimore: Johns Hopkins Press, 1998). Bush speaks about the "embarrassment" emanating from "bull sessions in CPS barracks late at night and from the embarrassment of hardworking farmers who, try as they might, could not quite will full approval as good citizens from their neighbors." p. 89.

369 Jennifer Blosser, available at WVPT,

370 The questionnaire contains five questions on the nature of the work project, with only one dealing with the satisfaction or significance of the work. It is not clear whether the CPS men were aware of the ambiguous nature of their concern with "important work." (478-488).

371 Edward Yoder and Don Smucker. op. cit. *The Christian and Conscription,* 56-57.

372 Ibid., 402.

373 Ibid., 406.

374 *A Study of Mennonite Service Programs,* (Elkhart: Institute of Mennonite Studies, 1967), 85. Also cited in C.J. Dyck. *Witness and Service in North America* (Scottdale: Herald Press, 1980), 95.

375 Unruh, in Dyck, 96.

376 Ibid., 97-98. Paraphrased by authors.

377 Ibid., 98. We have not changed gender language in order to indicate the prevailing usages at the time.

378 Ibid., 98-99.

379 "Voluntary Service", *ME,* IV: 849.

380 C. J Dyck. *Witness and Service in North America,* (Scottdale, PA: Herald Press, 1980), 97-98.

381 Ibid., 102.

382 Toews. op. cit., 242. Although the I-W men were not volunteers in the strict sense, the intent was clear: Service situations are opportunities for witness.

383 John D. Unruh. *In the Name of Christ,* 307.

384 "Voluntary Service", by Glen Esh and Gordon Dyck, in *MCC Annual Report,* 1955, 5.

385 "Our Colleges and the Voluntary Service Program in the Present Crisis." *Proceedings...* VIII, 1951, 55.

386 Ibid., 55.

387 Volume 5, 917ff.

388 *Mennonite Directory,* (Scottdale: Herald Press, 2001). The smaller Mennonite groups, such as the Mennonite Brethren and the Beachy Amish also have their own voluntary service programs.

389 Kauffman, Howard, and Leo Driedger. *Mennonite Mosaic: Identity and Modernization*, (Scottdale PA.: Herald Press, 1991), 177.

390 See Chapter 4, in Calvin Redekop. *Strangers Become Neighbors* (Scottdale: Herald Press, 1980). See also J. Winfield Fretz. *Pilgrims in Paraguay*, (Scottdale: Herald Press, 1953). See also, Edgar Stoesz. *Like a Mustard Seed Mennonites in Paraguay,* (Scottdale: Herald Press, 2008)

391 John D. Unruh, 203

392 Gerhard Ratzlaff. *Ein Leib-viele Glieder: Die mennonitischen Gemeinden in Paraguay* (Asuncion: Paraguay: Gemeindekomittee, 2001), 248.

393 For this remarkable story, see Gerhard Ratzlaff. *Die Ruta Transchaco: Wie Zie entstand* (Asuncion: NP, 1998). PAX was an alternative service program for military service.

394 Neufeld, Alfred. "Paraguay: The Diaconal and Social Experience." *Conrad Grebel Review*, Winter, 2009, 22.

395 John D. Unruh. *In the Name of Christ*, 300. The CMAC was composed of Mennonite and Brethren in Christ colleges in the United States. See chapter 16, "Voluntary Service", for a brief history of voluntary service in North America and in Europe. See also Redekop. *European Mennonite Voluntary Service*, (Telford.PA: Cascadia Publishing House, 2011).

396 ME, 300;

397 Ibid., 301; See also "Council of Mennonite and Affiliated Colleges", *ME*, I, 722-723,

398 Ibid., 301.

399 Emily Brunk. *Espelkamp,* (Frankfurt MCC: Schneider Verlag: 1952)

400 Ibid., 32. Of the ninety volunteers, eighty were Mennonite, thirteen Protestants, one Catholic, and one Church of England. (See Calvin Redekop 2011)

401 Pierre Ceresole (1879-1945) was a remarkable visionary for the cause of justice and peace. Among other things, he was the founder of Civil Service International, and a main force in the formation of the International Fellowship of Reconciliation, and in 1924, he was the force behind the first work camp for peace in Ormonts, Switzerland.

402 See Redekop, 2011, for more extensive information. During the short time that the European MVS program operated, from 1950 to 1971, a total of two hundred and forty-one work camps had been implemented in at least fifteen different countries and 4,338 volunteers had given at least three weeks of service in these projects (See Appendix A for a tabulation of the number of camps, dates, and location.) See also *MVS Newsletters*, 1950 ff.

403 Ibid., 77ff, 91ff

404   Unruh. op.cit. 280.

405   See Redekop. *The Pax Story*, 70 passim.

406   The authors believe MDS is one of the most promising and significant illustrations of the love ethic today.

407   Conrad L. Kanagy. *Road Signs of the Journey: Profile of Mennonite Church USA*. (Scottdale: Herald Press, 2007), 83.

408   Ibid., 83.

409   Penner, "Voluntary Service", *ME*, *V* 918.

410   Ibid., 918.

411   *Christian Faith and Practice* (London: London Yearly Meeting: 1960), pg 597 is our emphasis. It is interesting that Littleboy would use service as a term to define Quaker essentials.

412   Ibid.

413   Gerald Jonas. *On Doing Good* (New York: Charles Scribner's Sons:1971), 5-6. The title of this book is partially derived from Jonas' book.

414   *Letter to all Friends from Friends Foreign Mission Association and Council for International Service, 1936. Christian faith and practice in the experience of the Society of Friends* (London Yearly Meeting of Friends, 1960), 660.

415   The receipt of the Nobel Peace prize in 1947 points to the recognition of this global achievement and commitment. The presentation address stated: "The Quakers have shown us that it is possible to carry into action something that is deeply rooted in the minds of many people—a sympathy with others; a desire to help to others." D. Elton Trueblood, *The People Called Quakers* (New York: Harper and Row, 1966), 257.

416   Ibid., 257.

417   Underlining by present authors.

418   Ibid., 258.

419   Ibid., 258.

420   It was specifically referred to in the 1947 Nobel Peace Prize ceremonies. Persons associated with FAU include a veritable who's who of international personalities. See A. Tegala Davies. *Friends Ambulance Unit* (London: George Allen & Unwin, 1947)

421   Mary Hoxie Jones. *Swords into Ploughshares* (Westport: Greenwood Press, Publishers, 1937), 43.

422 Jones, op.cit., vii.

423 Ibid., viii

424 Jonas, Gerald. *On Doing Good*, (New York: Charles Scribner and Sons, 1971), 90-91

425 Jones, op. cit., 4

426 Ibid., 4. No reason is given for the change.

427 The acronym AFSC is also often cited as A.F.S.C., depending on the source.

428 Jones, 8. This comment is rather curious, since Quaker institutions are widely known for their openness to integrate non-Quakers with ease and grace.

429 Ibid., 16.

430 Ibid., 17.

431 Ibid., 18.

432 Ibid., 19.

433 Ibid., 46.

434 Ibid., 133. Focusing more on prosocial theories as definitely more efficient and effective.

435 Ibid., 134.

436 Ibid., 128-171. Jones's account provides only the bare outline of the scope and variety of the activities. It is clear that an accounting of all the specific activities and services provided under the auspices of AFSC would demand an almost unimaginable amount of documentation and research.

437 For example, the Austrian work resulted in the formation of the "Friends Center", which became the locus for a Quaker Monthly Meeting. (150).

438 http://afsc.org/afsc-history, accessed 3-11-05.

439 Jones, 172.

440 Ibid., 172.

441 George Fox. *The Journal of George Fox*, cited in Jones (145)

442 Jones, 172-173,

443 Ibid., 173. This strong commitment to root out the causes of war has resulted in the Quakers being accused of a naïve understanding of human nature and society.

444 Ibid., 178

445 Ibid., 178-181.

446 AFSC Annual Report, 2014.

447 Ibid.

448 Wilmer Cooper. *A Living Faith,* (Richmond: Friends United Press, 1990), 137. See Chapter 10 endnotes for extensive bibliography of Quaker sources recording the witness and service of AFSC.

449 E.B. Castle. *Approach to Quakerism,* (London: Bannisdale, 1961), 173-4.

450 The Wikipedia article on the Quakers is a useful source for a review of Quaker service activities.

451 The complete roster of organizations and projects directly committed to service broadly defined includes dozens of programs and projects around the globe. An up-to-date listing and description can be found at http:www.quakerinfo.org

452 Ibid., A useful overview of the development of Quaker service is found in Trueblood, op. cit. beginning on page 257. He believes "The best aspect of the Service Committee work has been the way in which programs are initiated with the expectation that they will eventually be taken over by others." 259.

453 *Christian Faith and Practice*, 199. Prepared by the Commission on Faith and Order, Yearly Meeting, 1917, 199.

454 Ibid., 205.

455 Ibid., 205.

456 Joseph Gittler. "Friends in the Twentieth Century", early version, later published in *Research in Human Conflict,* (Stamford, CT. JAL Press, 2000), 1.

457 Ibid., 1.

458 See Cooper. Appendix A, p. 165

459 Trueblood. 286.

460 *Christian Faith*, 8-9.

461 This chapter was written by J. Kenneth Kreider, author of the definitive book, *The Story of the Brethren Service.* (Elgin: Brethren Press, 2001). Some additional specific citations have been added by Don Miller

ENDNOTES

462 The membership of the Church of the Brethren was asked to contribute a total of $250,000 for Armenian relief. Although this was a huge sum in 1919, the Brethren responded with enthusiasm. By February 1921, members of the Church of the Brethren had contributed $267,265 to Armenian and Syrian relief.

463 *The Brethren Encyclopedia*, Vol. 1, p. 55.

464 Kreider, 9.

465 Ibid, 15.

466 Ibid, 11.

467 Now known as Heifer International, the headquarters is located in Little Rock, Arkansas. In fiscal year 2006, Heifer used its income of over $95 million to sponsor seven hundred and twenty-six projects in fifty-seven countries and a number of American states. Since the modest, if not small, beginning by Dan West and the Brethren, Heifer Project has helped over 7 million families in more than a hundred and twenty-five countries. Kreider, 146-7.

468 Kreider, 100.

469 Returning from the White House that evening, Row told his brother than he had to decline the president's offer, because he realized that political realities would prevent him from guiding the new federal program the way he thought it should operate.

470 Donald Durnbaugh. *The Believers Church's*, (Scottdale: Herald Press, 1968), 302.

471 Ibid., 264. Space prohibits including other related denominations.

472 "The Voluntary Service Program", *Proceedings of the Conference on Mennonite and Educational and Cultural Problems*, VI, 31-40 1947, VI, 31.

473 Ediger. Ibid., 31. This statement points to the religious source of volunteerism in contrast to American history in Chapter 3.

474 "Our Colleges and the Voluntary Service Program in the Present Crisis", *Proceedings*. 1951, 54. The "crisis" Ediger refers to is the Korean War and the possibility of another global war.

475 Ibid., 54.

476 Ibid., 56-57.

477 Mininger. "Culture for Service", *Mennonite Quarterly Review*, 39: (January 1955), 6.

478 Ibid., 7.

479 Ibid., 9.

480 Ibid., 9.

481 Paul Erb, his biographer, stated that the church needed "men to organize, balance, direct, and finance, so that the church could accomplish the task God gave it to do." *Orie O. Miller, The Story of a Man and an Era,* (Scottdale: Herald Press, 1969), 27

482 Ibid., 27. It can be safely said that no Mennonite church administrator did more to promote the service motif. His theology of service, though brief, points to the central theme of this book.

483 Ibid., 1.

484 Ibid., 2.

485 *A Survey of Mennonite Service Programs,* (Elkhart: Associated Mennonite Biblical Seminaries, 1965)

486 Ibid., A-2.

487 Ibid., A-4-5.

488 Ibid., A-17.

489 Ibid., A-15.

490 In H. Ralph Hernley. ed. *The Compassionate Community,* (Scottdale: Association of Mennonite Aid Societies, 1970). This conflation of mutual aid and service without any distinction illustrates the assumption that service was a fundamental aspect of mutual aid, and vice versa.

491 Ibid., 227.

492 Ibid., 229.

493 Ibid., 230.

494 Ibid., 245. We develop and expand the significance of feet-washing below.

495 Ibid., 257.

496 Ibid., 270.

497 Ibid., 280.

498 Ibid., 286.

499 Peter J. Dyck. "A Theology of Service," *Mennonite Quarterly Review*. 44:262-280. (July, 1970), 31. He has recently summarized the historical development of the concept of service in the *Global Anabaptist Mennonite Encyclopedia Online*. "http:www.gameo.org/encyclopedia/contents/S4823ME.html" (1989).

500 Ibid., 262.

501 V, 813.

502 Peter Dyck. "Humanitarianism." *ME*, V, 400.

503 Ibid., 400.

504 "Salvation", *Mennonite Encyclopedia*, V. 785. At first reading, this sounds suspiciously like Max Weber's *The Protestant Ethic and the Spirit of Capitalism*, but Harder seems to believes Menno's position is exactly the opposite.

505 Gerald W. Schlabach. "The Blessing of Abraham's Children: A Theology of Service," *Mission Focus,* 19:4, (December, 1991), 53. This concept points to the thesis of this book, but he does not develop it.

506 Ibid., 53.

507 Ibid., 54. Schlabach states: "Two kingdom theology is an inherently rigid model" because it ignores the world while concentration on building its own.

508 Ibid., 55.

509 Ted Koontz. "Commitments and Complications of Doing Good", *Mennonite Quarterly Review,* LXX, #1 (January 1996), 70. Koontz probably means MCC volunteers when he refers to MCC in this section.

510 "Commitments and Complications in Doing Good", Robert Kreider, and Ronald Mathies. *Unity and Diversity,* MCC, (Akron, PA:, 1975, 1996).

511 Koontz. 99.

512 Ibid., 101.

513 Ibid., 101.

514 Ibid., 103.

515 Ibid., 104. The intrinsic rewards of doing good as a motivation for doing good is discussed below.

516 Lydia Harder, in Benjamin Redekop and Calvin Redekop, *Power, Authority and the Anabaptist Tradition* (Baltimore: The Johns Hopkins University Press, 2001), 88

517 John Howard Yoder. *The Politics of Jesus*, (Grand Rapid: MI, Eerdmans, 1972, 1994), 162ff.

518 Harder. 88.

519 Ibid., 192.

520 Yoder states "The subordination that is called for recognizes whatever power exists, it does not affirm [however] a divine act or institution or ordination of a particular government." 200. Craig Boyd, cited above, credits Yoder with this insight for his own position, as cited above. This also supports the thesis of this book.

521 Ibid., 190. The concept of servant-hood is a general interpretation of the Anabaptist understanding of "humanitarian service". Mennonites usually marshal Jesus' teachings, among them: "But Jesus called them to him and said, 'You know that the rulers of the Gentiles lord it over them, and their great men exercise authority over them. It shall not be so among you; but whoever would be great among you must be your servant, and whoever would be first among you must be your slave; even as the Son of man came not to be served but to serve, and to give his life as a ransom for many.'" (Matt. 20:25-28 RSV).

522 In March of 1995, a conference was held to evaluate MCC's philosophy and its implementation to 'celebrate, reflect and recommit' to MCC service 'in the name of Christ'." Samuel Escobar, a seminary professor at Eastern Seminary who was deeply indebted to MCC, titled his presentation "Mission as Service for the 21st Century."

523 145.

524 146.

525 146.

526 Wilbert R. Shenk. "Mission and Service and the Globalization of North American Mennonites", (*MQR*, LXX, #1, January 1996), 7-22, 7.

527 Ibid., 16. Thus, for example, he states, "there is no doubt that mission and service efforts have been used to extend the reign of God around the world in response to the original globalization." (P. 22) No reference to how service fits with missions.

528 It is as though the term "missions and service" is a traditionalized term for "outreach" but that service is really a handmaiden to missions.

529 Calvin Redekop. "The Community of Scholars and the Essence of Anabaptism." *MQR*, 67. Fall, 1993.

530 Richard Yoder, Calvin Redekop, and Vernon Jantzi. *Development to a Different Drummer: Anabaptist-Mennonite Experiences and Perspectives*, (Intercourse, PA: Good Books, 2004), 224 ff.

531 Ibid., 239ff.

532 *The Problem of Social Responsibility from the Perspective of the Mennonite Church*, (Elkhart, IN: Institute of Mennonite Studies, 1989)

533 Ibid., 176.

534 Ibid., 176. Burkholder's emphasis.

535 Ibid., 179.

536 Ibid., 181.

537 Ibid., 182.

538 Ibid., 183.

539 Ibid., 184.

540 Ibid., 185.

541 Ibid., 185

542 This approach to the idea of justice is treated more fully in Chapter 9.

543 Pakisa Tshimika. "Service Consultation", *Courier*, Quarter 4, 2004 September 23, 2005.

544 *Courier, 2006*; 3. p. 2-3.

545 Ibid., *Courier*, 2006, 1 and 2. p. 9.

546 *Courier*, 2006, 1/2, 9.

547 Ibid., 9.

548 The "'Shared Convictions' of Mennonite World Conference", *Conrad Grebel Review*, Winter, 2009, 48.

549 On the other hand, there is a huge store of material regarding the actual work performed by Quakers.

550 E.B. Castle. *Approach to Quakersism*, (London: Bannisdale Press,1961), 88.

551 George Fox. Cited in *Christian Faith and Practice*, op. cit., 5.

552 Margaret Fell. Cited in *Christian Faith…*20.

553 *Christian Faith and Practice in the experience of the Society of Friends*, (London: London Yearly Meeting of Friends, 1960), 124. (Italicizing by authors)

554 Ibid., 595.

555 Ibid., 591.

556 Interestingly, only one article in the journal's history, beginning in 1958, deals with the topic of service.

557 "The concept of Christ as Servant as Motivation to Quaker Service", *Quaker Religious Thought*, 5. #1, 1963, 23.

558 The senior author's friendship with T. Canby Jones convinced him that he speaks with considerable knowledge regarding Quaker beliefs and practice.

559 Ibid., 23.

560 Ibid., 27.

561 Ibid., 28.

562 Ibid., 29.

563 Ibid., 30.

564 Ibid., 31.

565 Ibid., 31.

566 Ibid., 32.

567 Ibid., 33.

568 Ibid., 35.

569 Ibid., 37.

570 Ibid., 37.

571 Ibid., 38.

572 Ibid., 39.

573 Ibid., 39.

574 Jessamyn West. *The Quaker Reader* (New York: The Viking Press, 1962), 472.

575 Ibid., 477.

576 Ibid., 477-478.

577 This slightly edited section was written by Donald Miller.

578 *Fruit of the Vine* (Elgin, IL: Brethren Press, 1997).

579 *Die Schwarzenauer Neutaufer*, (*Gottingen:* The New Baptist of Schwarzenau, 2008).

580 Alexander Mack. *Rights and Ordinances of the House of God*, 1715.

581 *Brethren Encyclopedia*, 1983, pp. 456-58.

582 *Brethren Encyclopedia, pp. 458.*

583 *Brethren Encyclopedia*, Vol. 2, p. 1292.

584 This non-creedal ethos of the Church of the Brethren reflects the relative paucity of the literature.

585 To repeat footnote 12. The term **"Radical Reformation"** includes the three major groups analyzed in this book plus several other denominations. The **"Historic Peace Churches"** was generally used as most appropriate to include those groups when war and peace making based on Jesus' teachings were central in the discussion. The **"Believers Church"** has been the term when the theology of salvation and personal faith challenged mainline Christianity institutionalism. **Anabaptism's** focus on following Jesus, i.e. discipleships, was the "foundation" (Menno Simons) and has probably promoted most of the elements defining '**Radical Reformation.** " The **"Free Church"** focuses on the historical dynamics of the **"Radical Reformation"** in which these groups revolted from the "Corpus Christiana" or the "magisterial state-church" and demanded total freedom from state alliance or control. In this chapter, we use these several terms somewhat interchangeably, depending on the focus and context. We propose **"Radical Reformation"** and **"Anabaptism"** are closest to creating mutual self-identity of the groups studied here. The least acceptable terms are "Sectarian Churches", and "Sects," which were derogatory, used by the persecuting "Magisterial state churches", and are not relevant here. A fine brief description of the Radical Reformation can be found in Wikipedia. **https://en.wikipedia.org/wiki/File:P_christianity.svg**

586 We propose that the "Historic Peace Churches" as a group have maintained love of neighbor and enemy, as central to the gospel. Obviously all Christian groups expressed these traits, possibly not as thoroughly. https://en.wikipedia.org/wiki/File:P_christianity.svg

587 See Kenneth Scott LaTourette. *A History of Christianity*, (News York: Harper and Brothers, 1953), Chapter VI "Christianity Takes Shape in Organization and Doctrine." Pp.112-192.

588 Mark Allman. *Who Would Jesus Kill: War, Peace and the Christian Tradition* (Winona, MN: Anselm Academic, 2008), 77. Recently there have been voices challenging this position. See *MQR*, 85; # 4 October, 2011.

589 See Robert Friedman, for a superb overview of the "Radical Reformation movement". The New Testament was supreme authority, and following Jesus was the means.

590 The Brethren (all groups) and Quakers were less creedal and more committed in doing good. Thus, doing good proceeded theological investigation, reflecting the idea of "Praxis," which idea is now becoming more respectable in social science. For example, the Church of the Brethren, described in Kreider's *A Cup of Cold Water*, contains little theological material and Don Miller indicates below that the Church of the Brethren has not produced an extensive theological foundation for their tremendous achievements in service.

591 "Historic Peace Churches", *ME*, V, 373. See also "Historic Peace Churches, *ME*, Vol. IV, 1092,

592 Ibid., 373.

593 Don Durnbaugh. "Believers Church", *ME*, V 63.

594 Ibid., 63.

595 Ibid., 63.

596 Ibid., 64.

597 For a brief discussion of the Free Church concept, See Calvin Redekop. "The Requirements for a Free Church" in *The Free Church and Seductive Culture*, (Scottdale: Herald Press, 1970) Ch. 7.

598 George Hunston Williams. "A People in Community", in James Leo Garret, Jr. *The Concept of the Believers Church*, (Scottdale: Herald Press,1969), 140.

599 "Report of the finding committee", in Leo Garrett, op. cit. 321.

600 There has been a continuing ambiguity and ambivalence regarding the stress on the objective (discipleship) emphasis and the more subjective "evangelical" and pietistic posture dominant in American Christianity, and which proving very attractive to many latter-day Mennonites. On this tension, see for example Arnold Snyder. "Anabaptist Spirituality and Economics", in Calvin Redekop, Victor A. Krahn, and Samuel J. Steiner. *Anabaptist Faith and Economics* (Lanham, MD: University Press of America, 1994).

601 We have not utilized the concept of the "Free Church" in relationship to the Believers church, even though members of the Believers Church are often included in this rubric. Durnbaugh gives the best clear explanation: "The truth is that 'Free Church' is one of those concepts which mean virtually all things to all people." *The Believers Church*, p.4. See also Calvin Redekop. *The Free Churches and Seductive Culture*. (Scottdale, Herald Press, 1970).

602 For example, the Church of the Brethren, emerging in the context of the Anabaptist movement and south German pietism, has grown relatively parallel to the Mennonite tradition, differing more in muted theological beliefs than overt practices.

603 18 The *Believers Church* is a derivative of that principle and is defined by George H. Williams, as "the gathered church of committed believers living in the fellowship of mutual correction, support, and abiding hope." Donald Durnbaugh. *The Believers Church,* (Scottdale: Herald Press,1968), 33. Durnbaugh adds, "The Believers Church, therefore, is the covenanted and disciplined community of those walking in the way of Jesus Christ. Where two or three such are gathered, willing also to be scattered in the work of their Lord, there is the believing people." p. 33.

604 Donald Durnbaugh. *The Believers' Church,* 264.

605 James Luther Adams. "The Historical Origins of Voluntaryism" in J. Ronald Engel, *Voluntary Associations* (Chicago: Exploration Press, 1966), 176, This issue was discussed in the introduction. The refusal to accept political-state interference in religion is probably the most significant contribution of the Radical Reformation paradigm.

606 Ibid., 196. This development has normally been termed the "Post-Constantine Reformation" in which the state and religious societies are totally separated. (see Heering, op. cit.)

607 The Roman Catholic Church has expressed similar principles in different ways, and more recently, many sectors of the RMC are adopting Free Church/Believers Church principles.

608 Durnbaugh. *The Believers' Church,* 264ff,

609 Ibid., 273.

610 T. Canby Jones. "A Believing People: Contemporary Relevance", in Leo Garret, op. cit, 85-6. The relevance of foot-washing is discussed below.

611 Menno Simons. *The Complete Writings of Menno Simons,* (Scottdale: Herald Press, 1956), 558.

612 Ibid., 558.

613 Donald Durnbaugh. *Every Need Supplied,* (Philadelphia: Temple University Press, 1974), 7.

614 Ibid., 9. Durnbaugh thus suggests the character of the Believers' Church is defined by five traits: discipleship, apostolicity, mission and evangelism, church and state, mutual aid and service, and sectarian and ecumenical. *The Believer s' Church,* viii.

615 J. Winfield Fretz and Harold S. Bender. "Mutual Aid", *ME,* III, 796.

616 Donald Durnbaugh. *Every Need Supplied,* 14.

617 Ibid., 4.

618 Sorokin, Pitirim. *Forms and Techniques of Altruistic and Spiritual Growth.* (Boston: Beacon House, 1971)

619 Ibid., p. 319.

620 Cornelius Krahn, J. Winfield Fretz, and Robert S. Kreider. "Altruism in Mennonite Life" in Pitirim Sorokin, op.cit, 312.

621 Ibid., 312.

622 Ibid., 325.

623 Ibid., 325.

624 Ibid., 328.

625 See Peter James Klassen, op.cit.; see also Calvin Redekop, Stephen Ainlay, Robert Siemens. *Mennonite Entrepreneurs,* (Baltimore: John Hopkins University Press, 1995), especially "The Weberian Interpretation," pp. 199-208.

626 We cannot engage in the exegesis of this "problem" here. Regarding the term, "There is no uniformity in the writing of the term 'foot-washing.' Five other terms often used are: foot washing, foot-washing, feet-washing, feet washing, and feet-washing." Harold S. Bender, *ME*, II, 351. We shall use the term "foot-washing", but also use the terms as they are used by authors in the text.

627 Guy F. Hershberger. *The Way of the Cross in Human Relations* (Scottdale: Herald Press, 1958), 47.

628 J. Mathew Pinson. *The Washing of the Saints Feet* (Nashville, TN: Randall House Publications, 2007), 28, 41-42. Pinson maintains that foot washing (sic) symbolizes sanctification, while communion symbolizes justification. He does not discuss foot washing as a symbol of service.

629 H. S. Bender. "Foot-washing," *ME*, II, 348.

630 Carl Bowman. *Brethren Society* (Baltimore: Johns Hopkins University Press, 1995), 368-369.

631 Durnbaugh. *The Believers' Church*, 265. (Underlining ours) H. S. Bender's very extensive analysis of foot-washing is referred to only in passing. Interestingly, *Confession of Faith in Mennonite Perspective*, (Scottdale: Herald Press, 1995) states "We believe that Jesus Christ calls us to serve one another in love as he did [in foot washing]. In this act, Jesus showed humility and servant-hood." p.53. The earlier Mennonite confessions do not refer to service as a theme in the ordinance.

632 T. Canby Jones. Op. cit. 86. The three denominations referred to are the Church of the Brethren, the Friends, and the Mennonites.

633 T. Canby Jones. "The Concept of Christ as Servant as Motivation to Quaker Service", *Quaker Religious Thought. Vol V. #2, Autumn, 1963. 28.* This is one of a very few major treatises on service by a Quaker, and the only treatment in the Journal.

634 29.

635 op.cit. 47.

636 This reflects the same issue discussed above regarding mutual aid and service.

637 Durnbaugh. *The Believers Church*, 1968, 265.

638 Cited in Calvin Redekop, Vic Krahn, and Henry Regehr. "Service in the Anabaptist/Mennonite Tradition." Unpublished paper, 1989, in author's files, 3.

639 Brenneman, Bob. "Yoder and the (Body) politics of Foot-washing." *MQR*, Jan. 2009, 9.

640 Ibid., 11.

641 Ibid., 22.

642 Ibid., 22.

643 Ibid., 27.

644 Ibid., 27.

645 Status can be inferred in two ways. Ascribed status refers to status as a result from birth, such as whether or not one is a member of a monarchy, and achieved status refers to acquisitions as a result of ability, knowledge, skills, etc.

646 See Shane Thye. "A Status Value Theory of Power in Exchange Relations" in *American Sociological Review* (65): 407-32; and, Joseph Berger and Morris Zelditch, Jr.. eds, *Status, Rewards, and Influence* (San Francisco: Jossey-Bass, 1985).

647 Thorstein Veblen. *Theory of the Leisure Class: An Economic Study in the Evolution of Institutions* (New York: Macmillan, [1899] 1994).

648 For example, types of cars are often marketed and purchased according to status criteria (such as Cadillac) and not intrinsic utility function (such as Chevrolet). See Thomas Stanley and William Danko. *The Millionaire Next Door* (New York: Simon and Shuster, 1998).

649 There can hardly be any argument that service would not be classified as "works" by Martin Luther!

650 Rauschenbusch, Walter. *Christianity and the Social Order* (New York: MacMillan Company,1919) 69.

651 Ibid., 76.

652 This, of course, is a highly simplified definition. The Reformed concern with the Kingdom of God on earth is very complex, and the Lutheran "sola fide" emphasis is only one strand.

653 William Hordern. *A Layman's Guide to Protestant Theology* (New York: MacMillan, 1955). See Chapter three, "Fundamentalism or Conservative Christianity: The Defense of Orthodoxy" for one of the most succinct descriptions of conservative Christianity, especially fundamentalism. He proposes that fundamentalism is a highly rational interpretation of salvation, hence downplaying the "social" aspect to Christianity. p 73ff.

654 Hordern. 69.

655 Ibid., 69ff. The central role of pre-millennialism affirms the focus on the hereafter. But it has not kept many conservative Christians from having been active in socially and ethical reform.

656 Rauschenbusch, 60. In other contexts, Rauschenbusch includes the Baptists, Quakers, Church of the Brethren, and Mennonites as belonging to this general category of Anabaptists, what has since been denominated as the Believers' Church.

657 Rauschenbusch. 83.

658 See Robert Friedman "Radical Reformation" in *ME*, 4, 242-244. The article contains citations for early sources.

659 "Believers' Church," by Donald Durnbaugh, *ME*, 5, 63-64. The article contains useful bibliographical notes.

660 This has been most effectively developed by Stuart Murray in *Naked Anabaptist*, (Scottdale, Pa: Herald Press, 2010)

661 See, for example, Paul Toews. "Fundamentalism." *ME*. V. 318-320. "Fundamentalism was a way of responding to the groups changed relationship to the dominant culture." 319.

662 See, for example, Calvin Redekop. *Leaving Anabaptism: From Evangelical Mennonite Brethren to Fellowship of Bible Churches*, (Telford, PA: Pandora Press, 1998). Even though MCC was earlier considered a good organization, it finally severed all relationships with MCC, since it was considered a "works gospel" program.

663 See Dyck, Peter J. (1989), "Service", *Global Anabaptist Mennonite Encyclopedia Online*. Op.cit. 2009. http://www.gameo.org/encycloperdia/contents.S4823ME.html, 2 . In fact,

some earlier Mennonite conferences have withdrawn from Mennonite Central Committee, accusing of it of merely "doing service" without proclaiming the gospel of repentance.

664   Michael Lienesh. *Redeeming America* (Chapel Hill: University of North Carolina Press, 1993), 107.

665   James Leo Garret, Jr. *The Concept of the Believers' Church*, (Scottdale: Herald Press, 1969), 294.

666   Janet Denhardt and Robert Denhardt, *The New Public Service: Serving Not Steering*, (New York: Routledge, 2015): 1.

667   Earl Martin spent five years in Vietnam as an MCC Pax volunteer. He is the author of *Reaching the Other Side: The Journal of an American who stayed to witness Vietnam's postwar transition*, (New York: Crown Publishers,1978)

668   (Scottdale: Herald Press, 1944). It is ironic, since Mennonite ecclesiology has generally avoided ecumenical identification, relationships, and cooperation.

669   Brenda D. Phillips. Mennonite Disaster Service (Lanham: Lexington Books), 2014,

670   http://www.voa.org/volunteer?gclid=CIaWiYm75MQCFQMT7AodsysA_A

671   It is well known that colleges and universities consider voluntary service as a major criterion in admissions. https://www.volunteerglobal.com/users/broader-view-volunteers-corp

AVSO - Association of Voluntary Service Organisations ...

https://www.facebook.com/AVSO.org s...

1.VolunteerMatch - Where Volunteering Begins

www.volunteermatch.org/

VolunteerMatch provides volunteer information and listings in your local community. Find local ... What do you care about in San Francisco, CA? ... Let us start connecting you with passionate volunteers ... 99,615. Participating Organizations ...

2.VA Voluntary Service Home

www.va.gov/volunteer/

United States Department of Veterans Affairs

Jan 26, 2015 - VAVS Home; Volunteer or Donate Now; Directory of Local VAVS ... Over 140,000 volunteers gave more than 11 million hours in service to ...

3.Catholic Volunteer Network

https://catholicvolunteernetwork.org/

Catholic Volunteer Network, established in 1963, is a non-profit membership organization of 215 domestic and international volunteer and lay mission programs. ... options, Response 2015 is the most comprehensive guide for faith-based service opportunities. Order your copy of Response or search the directory online!

4. ChristianVolunteering.org: Search over 10,000 Christian ...

www.christianvolunteering.org/

Search over 10000 Christian mission trips and volunteer opportunities: ... Volunteers ... Kevin Maples never expected to help organizations rescue children from ... TechMission's Executive Director, Andrew Sears, explains in Christianity ...

5. Volunteer Guide

www.volunteerguide.org/

Opportunities and community service projects to make a difference right ... Volunteer Guide has a directory of virtual volunteering opportunities that you ... is a free service of Charity Guide, which is a 501(c)(3) nonprofit organization ...

6. Volunteer Abroad - GoAbroad.com

www.goabroad.com/volunteer-abroad

GoAbroad.com is a comprehensive Volunteer Abroad directory of 5475 Volunteers provide rewarding experiences in developing countries. ... With program fees starting from just USD 10 per day, IVHQ is the volunteer organization.

7. Volunteer, work, intern, organize, hire and connect.

www.idealist.org/

Action Without Borders

Directory of nonprofit web resources: 16000 organizations in 130 countries; resources for nonprofit managers; computing and the Internet, fundraising and ...

672 http://www.afsc.org/where-we-work

673 (Elgin: Brethren Press, 2001)

674 http://mcc.org/learn/what/relief has become

CPSIA information can be obtained
at www.ICGtesting.com
Printed in the USA
BVHW07054504082l
613438BV00002B/305